RHETORICAL SCOPE AND PERFORMANCE: THE EXAMPLE OF TECHNICAL COMMUNICATION

ATTW Contemporary Studies in Technical Communication

M. Jimmie Killingsworth, Series Editor
Published in Cooperation with the Association of
Teachers of Technical Writing

To Dee, Stephen, Mark, and Elizabeth

RHETORICAL SCOPE AND PERFORMANCE: THE EXAMPLE OF TECHNICAL COMMUNICATION

by
Merrill D. Whitburn
Rensselaer Polytechnic Institute

Ablex Publishing Corporation
Stamford, Connecticut

Printed in the United States of America

Library of Congress Cataloging-in-Publication Data

Whitburn, Merrill D.
    Rhetorical scope and performance : the example of technical communication / by Merrill D. Whitburn.
        p. cm. — (ATTW contemporary studies in technical communication ; v. 13)
    Includes bibliographical references and index.
    ISBN 1-56750-514-7 (cloth)—ISBN 1-56750-515-5 (pbk.)
    1. Communication   of   technical   information. 2. Rhetoric.
I. Title. II. Series.
  T10.5. W48   2000
  601′.4—dc21   00-021219
                                            CIP

Ablex Publishing Corporation
100 Prospect Street
P.O. Box 811
Stamford, CT 06904-0811

Contents

Acknowledgments

This project began with funding from the Mina Shaughnessy Scholars Program of the Fund for the Improvement of Postsecondary Education (FIPSE), with partial funding from the Carnegie Corporation. I am particularly indebted to Richard Hendrix, then a FIPSE program officer, for his encouragement, support, and early critical help.

I could not have completed this book without the generous assistance of my university, Rensselaer Polytechnic Institute, especially in the form of a series of sabbaticals that gave me time.

A number of scholars have helped me with responses to parts or all of various manuscript versions of this book: Richard Leo Enos, James J. Murphy, Debra Journet, Charles H. Sides, M. Jimmie Killingsworth, and Mark S. Whitburn.

My wife, Diane, helped considerably with a close reading and numerous suggestions for revision. To her; my sons, Stephen and Mark; and my daughter, Elizabeth, I owe special thanks not just for editorial help but also for support.

In the course of working on this book, I have introduced parts of it and various ideas to my graduate students, especially those in "Rhetorical Theory." I thank them for all their helpful reactions.

Finally, I want to thank all of the rare and used booksellers—too numerous to list here—who found me publications that were exceedingly hard to track down.

Foreword

M. Jimmie Killingsworth
Series Editor, ATTW Contemporary Studies
in Technical Communication

Reading the provocative work of Merrill Whitburn made me remember two student comments on technical communication, both of which were very disturbing when I first heard them and which continue to haunt me today. I heard the first one in the early 1980s when I was an assistant professor in a pioneering undergraduate program in technical communication at New Mexico Tech. A quiet but very talented student came to my office toward the end of an introductory course on the profession of technical communication, which had included readings and visits by practicing technical writers as well as site visits. He told me he would not be continuing in the program. When I asked why, he said he wanted a more intellectually stimulating and personally challenging career. He had come to think of technical writers as "a bunch of bootlickers," meeting the needs of subject matter specialists who couldn't do their own writing, users who had trouble with their machines, and corporate managers trying desperately to bring experts and users together. My student had no objection to work in the "service sector," but he felt that most technical communicators were serving not in the capacity of free and independent citizens, but had been reduced to the role of corporate slaves. He left my office and my college and went off to study history at the state university.

The enduring memory of this student's remark contributed strongly to my commitment to study technical communication in its broadest possible contexts—to scholarship on the rhetoric, history, ethics, and politics of information, as well as more obviously practical matters like the mechanics of English language and style, techniques for graphical display, and the analysis of tasks and audiences. I have made that commitment clear in all my scholarly work as well as in my text-book *Information in Action: A Guide to Technical Communication* (1996; second edition with Jacqueline S. Palmer, 1999).

My textbook was the object of the second comment. It came in a letter from a student at a regional state college who had used the text in a required course. He complained that my instructions on writing were not very helpful and that I spent far too much time "pontificating on matters of ethics and politics," matters that, in his view, had nothing to do with good writing.

Both of these students had come to accept a severely restricted and specialized view of technical writing. Without knowing it, they were participating in the long and damaging tradition that Merrill Whitburn exposes and critiques in this new book. The idea is that the teaching and practice of writing can be narrowly chan-neled into a stream of skills and actions cut off from the great ocean of human deci-sion-making and the principles of good thinking and responsible action in the wide world. Professor Whitburn has spent a long and distinguished career observing and documenting this phenomenon. He traces it to its sources, which he locates in the contempt for rhetoric and the preference for an abstract form of ideal knowledge among the early Greek philosophers, Plato and Aristotle, who thought that rhetoric (the theory of communication in the ancient world) was at best a feeble companion to philosophy and at worst a form of pandering to the ignorant masses. Whitburn follows the course of this contempt for practical communication down through his-tory to discover it again in attempts to "purify" science of its connection (and responsibility) to the world of human action and parallel attempts to make English departments into havens for the study of imaginative literature, free from the "con-tamination" of relevance to the world of practical arts like technical writing. In his own work in industry, his scholarship, and his teaching, Whitburn has striven to develop an alternative view, building upon the early rhetoric of Isocrates, Cicero, and Quintilian, and finding help in the educational philosophy of John Dewey's pragmatism. This book is the culmination of that work. Whitburn began to write it as a Shaughnessy scholar about the time that my student came to tell me he was quitting technical communication. The book is 17 years in the making, the product of serious observation, scholarship, and deep reflection.

We don't have many books like this in technical communication. One of the rea-sons is that none of us have time to reflect at length upon our practice. Tied to the grinding demands of teaching, consulting, or working in fast-paced, rapidly changing, and understaffed jobs (the pace is similar in industry or academe), reflection with its demand that we look at our work in the largest possible context is easily victimized. Another reason is that, consciously or unconsciously, we accept the limited scope that the world seems to have offered us. The challenge of this book is to step back and take the time to see the big picture. Whitburn has done us the great service of summarizing years of research into a sketch of intellectual history that is as readable as it is provocative. If you are tempted to think that the history of philosophy, science, and even religion that you are asked to ponder in these pages has little relevance to your daily work, I urge you to wonder if you have defined your work too narrowly and thus fallen prey to the very things Whitburn criticizes.

Very few people in the field of technical communication could have written this book. It is the product of habitual reflection over many years, condensed into a single volume. Technical communication is still relatively young, an "emerging discipline," as Katherine Staples and Cezar Ornatowski suggest in the first volume of this series. It is a sign of our advancing maturity that we now have senior scholars like Merrill Whitburn with the experience and knowledge to write books like this one. It will be a further sign of maturity if we can follow his lead and begin to reflect seriously on our place in intellectual history and apply these reflections to our current teaching, research, and practice.

1

Introduction

Two colleagues and I recently visited Microsoft Corporation to explore the problems of developing technical communication for international audiences. In meeting after meeting, Microsoft employees emphasized that American high tech corporations had to export abroad to be successful, but in far too many instances lacked the scope in their approaches to communicate well with audiences in other cultures. Narrowness in goals, corporate structures, and methodologies militated against the development of information that was appropriate for these audiences. We were encouraged to join the few educators who were helping to address these problems.

I was not surprised to discover that yet another problem confronting technical communication was associated with insufficient scope. In engaging a whole host of problems in technical communication over the course of my career, I discovered that many of them were associated with insufficient scope in one way or another. In attempting to understand and alleviate these problems, I fully expected to confine my attention to the second half of the 20th century, but instead found myself driven back into history, first to the scientific revolution of the late 17th century, then to classical antiquity, then to the religious philosophers of the Middle Ages. What I discovered was that many of the problems that I was addressing had at least part of their origin in the struggle between rhetoric and philosophy in the history of Western civilization. My set of problems were part of a larger set of problems having to do with the decline of rhetoric and the triumph of philosophy beginning in classical antiquity and continuing throughout the 20th century.

At the heart of these problems was a narrowing of attention in human deliberation. Since classical antiquity, a growing division of attention has compromised performance by limiting the scope of human goals, social structures, and methodologies. What has become clear is that improving our lives in many respects is contingent on reversing a trend that received its greatest impetus from a struggle between Isocrates, on the one hand, and Plato and Aristotle, on the other, some 24 centuries ago. In the very cradle of civilization, Western history began going awry and has continued on that path ever since.

This book is an effort to convey part of what I have discovered. For three reasons, I intend to focus primarily on problems in the history of technical communication ranging from the 1950s through the 1980s. First, problems associated with insufficient scope seemed particularly acute during this period. Second, we have experienced so many changes in our profession since then that we are already able to view this period from some historical distance. Third, we are able to see the extent to which we have responded or failed to respond to problems of scope that arose in this period.

I understand that my effort to engage problems in technical communication through an exploration of the history of rhetoric flies in the face of a growing skepticism among some about the value of rhetoric in my field. The skepticism in the work of Saul Carliner exemplifies this trend. Carliner (1995) doubts that anything at all can be gained from the study of rhetoric: "Faculty talk about rhetorical theories, ancient people like Aristotle...concerns that seem to have nothing to do with anything useful" (p. 552).

Carliner refers to Aristotle and seems unaware that the dominant rhetorician in ancient Greece is Isocrates and that Isocratean rhetoric—with adjustments—has sufficient scope to be exceedingly useful in engaging many contemporary problems in technical communication. Among its uses, it can help expose the narrowness of goals in governments, industries, and universities. It can also expose the problems caused by overly narrow social structures in modern society, helping us understand the necessity of working toward a seamless society that avoids divisions of attention that militate against the full range of matters critical to deliberation about a problem. Lastly, it can expose the all-too-frequent methodological ineptitude of the 20th century, particularly the tendency to use preset methodological approaches to problems without using the full particularity of problem situations to generate the unique methodologies appropriate to them.

As we move into a new millennium, the unique rhetorics generated by the engagement of problems in technical communication must be compared to the unique rhetorics generated by the engagement of other kinds of problems in modern society. The resulting art of comparative rhetoric could help the 21st and following centuries—if humanity lasts that long—attain the flexibility of deliberation essential to enable humans to approach problems with the scope they require. The revolution that would follow would maximize ethical deliberation in human affairs, transform much of the specialization in modern society into interlocking collaborative networks, and dramatically improve the approaches to problems.

2

The Conflict between Rhetoric and Philosophy in Ancient Greece

When, at the beginning of courses, I ask students to name the educator who attracts the greatest respect in ancient Athens, most name Plato and the rest Aristotle. Powerful forces such as Roman Catholicism (which incorporated the ideas of these philosophers) and science (which used their ideas as foundations) have supported the inherent strengths of Plato and Aristotle until their philosophies dominated intellectual life in America in the 20th century. One result of this dominance is a tendency among far too many to assume that the ideas of Plato and Aristotle must have dominated the educational life of ancient Athens as well. In truth, however, the crown of education in ancient Athens was rhetoric, and the most respected educator of the day was the rhetorician Isocrates.

The 21st century confronts us with new problems that are not unlike some of the problems confronted by Isocrates in ancient Athens. While governments and industries are increasingly forced to consider global issues, Isocrates felt the need to encourage his contemporaries to consider the welfare of all the city-states of ancient Greece instead of confining their interests to the city-state of Athens. While we increasingly feel ourselves compelled to break through previous boundaries and expand the scope of our deliberations, Isocrates, at his best, warned

5

against narrowness in deliberation and encouraged the scope necessary to bring all the required issues to bear on a problem. As these affinities have inclined us to devote greater attention to Isocrates and his relationship to contemporaries, we have discovered that many of the boundaries that we are having to break through have origins in his own work and the work of his academic competitors, Plato and Aristotle.

An academic competition between Isocrates, on the one hand, and Plato and Aristotle, on the other, gave impetus to a conflict between rhetoric and philosophy at the time that furthered a narrowing of deliberation in Western civilization. On one side of the competition, Isocrates tried to attract students to *his* area of specialization—the art of choice in human affairs, especially politics—while, on the other, Plato and Aristotle tried to attract students to *their* primary area of focus—the identification of truths in such areas as theology, science, and mathematics. The divisions resulting from this competition set the stage for historical processes that limited the scope of human goals, social structures, and methodologies.

ISOCRATES

Isocrates (436–338 B.C.E.) and Plato (about 428–347 B.C.E.) were academic competitors in Athens when it was the intellectual capital of the world (Edwards, 1967/1972, Vol. 6; Isocrates, trans. 1928/1954, Vol. 1). Both called their ideals "philosophy," and, as Werner Jaeger (1939–1944) suggested, "in the opposing claims made by both sides to ownership of the title 'philosophy', and in the widely different meanings given to the word by the opponents, there is symbolized the rivalry of rhetoric and science for leadership in the realm of education and culture" (Vol. 3, p. 49). Granting Plato's claim to the word *philosophy* and associating Isocrates with the word *rhetoric* (a common practice in the 20th century), Jaeger called the opposition between Plato and Isocrates "the first battle in the centuries of war between philosophy and rhetoric" (Vol. 3, p. 46). As Jerrold E. Seigel (1968) suggested, the stakes of this conflict were high: "Rhetoric and philosophy emerge as the bases for contrasting perspectives on the whole of man's intellectual and moral life" (p. xii).

Even a scholar as admittedly unsympathetic to Isocrates as H. I. Marrou (1956) confirmed that the victor of this conflict in classical antiquity was Isocrates:

> On the level of history Plato had been defeated: posterity had not accepted his educational ideals. The victor, generally speaking, was Isocrates, and Isocrates became the educator first of Greece and then of the whole ancient world. His success had already been evident when the two were alive, and it became more and more marked as the generations wore on. Rhetoric is the specific object of Greek education and the highest Greek culture. (p. 194)

Marrou stated: "On the whole it was Isocrates, not Plato, who educated fourth-century Greece and subsequently the Hellenistic and Roman worlds" (p. 79).

Isocrates opened his school in Athens—the date usually given is 392 B.C.E.—after a decade (about 403–393 B.C.E.) of writing speeches for others to deliver in the law courts. Russell H. Wagner (1965) called it "the first real school of rhetoric" (p. 181) and perhaps "the most successful school of rhetoric ever known" (p. 170). Marrou conveyed the success of the school by imagining Isocrates as an old man thinking back on his many star pupils from such fields as politics, literature, history, and oratory. Toward the end of his career, in *Antidosis*, Isocrates boasted that he had taught more students than all the other teachers of philosophy combined. He presented to his students a rhetoric that, at its best, contained ideas about goals, social structures, and methodologies sufficiently broad that they could serve as alternatives to various kinds of 20th-century narrowness and, at its worst, promoted divisions that gave impetus to narrowness in Western culture.

The best critics have long acknowledged that the most important goal of Isocrates's philosophy was ethical conduct. For instance, Norlin wrote: "Isocrates prides himself more upon the sound moral influence of his work and teaching than upon any other thing. The primary object of his instruction is right conduct in the man and the citizen" (Isocrates, Vol. 1, p. xxv). The evidence can be found in Isocrates's moral treatise *To Demonicus*, where he called virtue "that possession which is the grandest and the most enduring in the world" (5–6). He also wrote in *To Nicocles*: "the noblest sacrifice and the greatest devotion is to show yourself in the highest degree a good and just man" (20). Surveying his work in *Antidosis* at the end of his career, he claimed that all his writings "tend toward justice and virtue" (67).

Some critics have made the mistake of restricting Isocrates's goals too narrowly to oratory. Bruce A. Kimball (1986), in his *Orators & Philosophers*, found a tendency in Isocrates "to equate philosophy with oratory" (p. 28). But Isocrates explicitly distinguished his goal of ethical conduct from oratorical skill. In *To Demonicus*, he argued:

> Those...who point out to the young, not by what means they may cultivate skill in oratory, but how they may win repute as men of sound character, are rendering a greater service to their hearers in that, while the former exhort them to proficiency in speech, the latter improve their moral conduct. (3–4)

Isocrates made the same distinction in *Panathenaicus*: "I take more pleasure in those of my disciples who are distinguished for the character of their lives and deeds than in those who are reputed to be able speakers" (87). Teaching students proficiency in speech, then, is inferior to teaching them a broad concern for ethical conduct in all activities.

Isocrates included within his philosophy not just the preparation and delivery of speeches, but also deliberation about private affairs and other activities not ending in oratory. In his *Antidosis*, for instance, he seems concerned about actions in addition to vocal utterance. He wants to enable us to make wise choices not just about "what we should say," but also about "what we should do" (271). He would have us choose the best course not just "in our speech," but also "in our actions" (266). Isocrates encourages us to excel not just "in oratory," but also "in managing affairs or in any line of work" (187). He would enable us to govern wisely not just "the commonwealth," which might involve considerable oratory, but also "our own households," which might involve little or none (285). He focuses, then, on governance, management, or administration in the widest sense of those terms— sometimes involving oratory, sometimes not. Clearly, then, later educators who limited rhetoric to oratory and defined it so as to exclude ethics were describing an endeavor far narrower than that of Isocrates.

The scope of Isocratean philosophy, then, is noteworthy. In *Nicocles or the Cyprians*, Isocrates wrote: "if there is need to speak in brief summary of this power, we shall find that none of the things which are done with intelligence take place without the help of speech, but that in all our actions as well as in all our thoughts speech is our guide, and is most employed by those who have the most wisdom" (8–9). In suggesting that speech guides us in all of our actions and all of our thoughts, that it helps us with all of the things done with intelligence, and, as he indicated in *Antidosis*, that "the teachers of philosophy impart all the forms of discourse in which the mind expresses itself" (183–184), Isocrates ascribed a scope to his performance so encompassing that, if we take him at his word, it is hard to see him excluding any form of human endeavor.

As Norlin suggested, Isocrates, in his *Panathenaicus*, attacked those teachers who specialized in particular areas (29). Norlin understood that the culture that Isocrates professed to impart was "more broad than the disciplines of other teachers" (Vol. 1, p. xxv). He elaborated: "it was more broad in that he thought of it as embracing all of the relations of human existence. He criticizes the professors of the sciences and of the arts in general because they do not envisage the whole of life in their culture" (p. xxv). Norlin appreciated the all-encompassing nature of Isocrates's statements about the scope of his ethical performance: "The art of discourse may, therefore, be as broad as the whole life of civilized man; and this is just what Isocrates insisted that it should be" (pp. xxiii–xxiv).

If Isocrates, in the very cradle of Western civilization, gave his philosophy a scope as broad as the whole life of civilized man, however, he included much in his works that compromised that scope, limiting both goals and social structures. For instance, he so favored political deliberation as a focus for philosophy that he sometimes seemed to lose sight of the art of deliberation in private affairs, which he so stressed on occasion. Furthermore, even though he wrote speeches for the law courts early in his career, he contemptuously discredited this major area of rhetorical activity (forensic rhetoric) in ancient Athens and excluded it from his purview (*Antidosis*, 47–49).

Isocratean scope was also compromised by positions taken as a result of academic competition. One of the most useful books for understanding this competition is Christoph Eucken's (1983) *Isokrates: Seine Positionen in der Auseinandersetzung mit den zeitgenoessischen Philosophen* [*Isocrates: His Positions in the Conflict with Contemporary Philosophers*]. Isocrates's most important competition was with Plato. His struggle with Plato over the value of their educational programs turned out to be the major battle for academic supremacy in Western civilization, a battle that Isocrates eventually lost after victories in ancient Greece and ancient Rome. If you open *The Encyclopedia of Philosophy* (Edwards, 1967/1972), you will discover no entry for Isocrates and a 19-page entry for Plato, a clear sign who won the struggle for the term "philosophy" in the 20th century. The adulation for Plato in the 20th century was encapsulized in Alfred North Whitehead's celebrated oral remark that the safest general characterization of the European philosophical tradition was that it consisted in a series of footnotes to Plato. Among the results of Plato's victory, modern scholars have associated Plato with the term "philosophy" and Isocrates with the term "rhetoric"—a term that Isocrates did not usually use for himself.

Isocrates, however, often seemed more concerned about his object of attention than the word or words he used to designate it. Although he tended to use the term "philosophy" for his ideal, he also used this term to refer to the ideals of his competitors. In addition, he not infrequently used other words for his ideal, including "art of discourse," "eloquence," "wisdom," "liberal education," and even "rhetoric." For instance, in his letter *To Alexander*, probably written when Alexander was a boy of 14 and had just begun studying under Plato's student Aristotle, Isocrates suggested that Alexander wants "the training which rhetoric gives, which is of use in the practical affairs of everyday life and aids us when we deliberate concerning public affairs" (4). Scholars, then, have not been unjustified in using a term such as "rhetoric" for the ideal that Isocrates proposed in his competition with Plato.

In his *Euthydemus*, Plato presented a portrait of Isocrates as an academic competitor. According to Plato's (trans. 1961/1973) portrait, Isocrates and his followers considered Socrates and his followers as their only serious rivals, and they attacked their rivals to gain undisputed academic supremacy (305 c–d). Although Isocrates was not identified by name, the prestige ascribed to this competitor by Plato was one of the characteristics pointing to Isocrates. Among others, Plato had Socrates refer to Isocrates and his followers as "frontiersmen between philosophy and politics" (*Euthydemus*, 305c), a clear reference to the Isocratean emphasis on both philosophy and political discourse as ideals. Plato also has Socrates describe this competitor as writing speeches for the courts but not delivering them himself. As has been already indicated, Isocrates did begin his career by writing speeches for the courts. Furthermore, throughout his career, he distributed his speeches in writing rather than deliver them himself because of a want of nerve and weakness in voice (*Panathenaicus*, 10). As Eucken indicated, Isocrates is the only person we know from his time to whom these characteristics could apply. Eucken cited a long list of scholars who agreed that the portrait refers to Isocrates (p. 48).

Plato (trans. 1961/1973) also had his Isocrates level an argument against dialectic (Plato's ideal) that was in line with Isocrates's own arguments. Plato's Isocrates discounts the dialectitions as "people talking nonsense and making an unworthy fuss about matters worth nothing at all" (*Euthydemus*, 304e). The emphasis on usefulness was one of the key distinctions Isocrates made in preferring his philosophy to Plato's. When Isocrates advised the monarch Nicocles, he wrote: "you ought...to judge what things are worthy or what men are wise...in the light of conduct that is useful" (*To Nicocles*, 50–51). In *Antidosis*, he chose the goal of usefulness as the basis for disparaging Plato and his like, whom he referred to as "teachers who are skilled in disputation and those who are occupied with astronomy and geometry and studies of that sort." He suggested that most men reject such studies as useless, and he agreed with this majority: "those who hold that this training is of no use in practical life are right" (262–263).

Still, Isocrates allowed that these subjects were not entirely without merit: "while we are occupied with the subtlety and exactness of astronomy and geometry...,we gain the power, after being exercised and sharpened on these disciplines, of grasping and learning more easily and more quickly those subjects which are of more importance and of greater value" (264–265). Some cautious attention, then, should be paid to such subjects in youth (268), but adults need pay them no attention whatever (*Panathenaicus*, 27–28). As might be expected, then, Isocrates excluded such training from his philosophy: "I do not...think it proper to apply the term 'philosophy' to a training which is no help to us in the present either in our speech or in our actions, but rather I would call it a...preparation for philosophy" (*Antidosis*, 266).

Isocrates elaborated on the differences between himself and these competitors by making a distinction between his focus on conjecture and their focus on exact knowledge. He wrote: "likely conjecture about useful things is far preferable to exact knowledge of the useless, and that to be a little superior in important things is of greater worth than to be pre-eminent in petty things that are without value for living" (*Helen*, 5). He indicated that only conjecture or judgment—not exact knowledge—is possible in the practice of his philosophy: "since it is not in the nature of man to attain a science by the possession of which we can know positively what we should do or what we should say, in the next resort I hold that man to be wise who is able by his powers of conjecture to arrive generally at the best course" (*Antidosis*, 271).

If, then, Isocrates's philosophy included all human actions and thoughts, everything done with intelligence, he nevertheless promoted exclusions, either implicitly or explicitly, that limited its scope and too narrowly restricted attention. For instance, he focused too narrowly on political deliberation and conjecture (judgment), left private deliberation in the shadows, and excluded forensic rhetoric and various kinds of exact knowledge, such as astronomy and geometry. In explicitly excluding science and mathematics from adult concern, he failed to see their potential value in both furthering civilization and providing pleasure. Such a position would inevitably be exposed as untenable—even by followers. For instance, if science and mathematics seemed useless to Isocrates, that was not the case with Quintilian, writing in ancient Rome more than four centuries later.

Isocrates's exclusion of subjects such as science and mathematics from the goals of his philosophy profoundly affected the structures of education in ancient Athens. It enabled less successful competitors such as Plato and his followers to seize on these subjects as their own and to establish a competitive philosophy that distinguished itself from and excluded Isocratean philosophy. In *Antidosis*, Isocrates indicated his awareness of these competitive philosophers and their desire to refuse him the term "philosophy" (285). What this mutual exclusion helped promote were divisions of attention in Western culture, highlighted by such terms as "disciplinarity" and "specialization." These divisions affected both goals and social structures and militated against the scope necessary to engage many problems.

Among the methodologies that Isocrates praised in approaching the subjects that he did include within his philosophy was imitation. He believed that students of philosophy could improve themselves substantially by imitating excellence. For instance, in *Against the Sophists*, he stated that the teacher "must in himself set such an example of oratory that the students who have taken form under his instruction and are able to pattern after him will, from the outset, show in their speaking a degree of grace and charm which is not found in others" (18). It is noteworthy that the poets are among those whom Isocrates specifically singled out for students to imitate (*To Nicocles*, 12–13). As Jaeger (1939–1944) suggested, Isocrates believed "that he is continuing the poets' work, and taking over the function which until a short time before him they had fulfilled in the life of his nation" (Vol. 3, p. 62). The high value that Isocrates placed on the poets contrasts sharply with Plato's exclusion of the poets from his republic.

Another methodology helpful in Isocratean philosophy is history. In *To Demonicus*, Isocrates wrote: "In your deliberations, let the past be an exemplar for the future; for the unknown may be soonest discerned by reference to the known" (34). In *Panegyricus*, he used history to address a range of serious problems confronting the city-states of ancient Greece and argued that the ability to make proper use of history at the appropriate time is the peculiar gift of the wise (8–10). As Eucken (1983) suggested, Isocrates differed from Plato in founding his ideal state on what can be learned from history rather than some form of ideal knowledge.

Since, in engaging human affairs, one situation is rarely like another, humans cannot devise rules or universals that hold for all situations. In *Against the Sophists*, Isocrates complained about those teachers who "undertake to transmit the science of discourse as simply as they would teach the letters of the alphabet, not having taken trouble to examine into the nature of each kind of knowledge" (10). He wrote:

> I marvel when I observe these men setting themselves up as instructors of youth who cannot see that they are applying the analogy of an art with hard and fast rules to a creative process. For, excepting these teachers, who does not know that the art of using letters remains fixed and unchanged, so that we continually and invariably use the same letters for the same purposes, while exactly the reverse is true of the art of discourse? For what has been said by one speaker is not equally useful for the speaker who comes after him. (12)

As Isocrates indicated in his attacks on the Platonic philosophers, he believed that only judgment or conjecture and not exact knowledge is possible in deliberation about human affairs.

Much more research is essential before we will gain the fullest appreciation of Isocrates's philosophy or rhetoric. Although Isocrates has been called the leading educator of ancient Greece, the father of humanistic culture and eloquence, and the true fountainhead of humanistic rhetoric, he received surprisingly little attention from 20th-century scholars until recently. Wagner (1965) wrote: "Perhaps no one of the great rhetoricians of the past has exerted so great an influence upon the succeeding ages of oratory; and perhaps none has been so much underestimated" (p. 169). John C. Briggs (1984) noted "the lack of modern interest in Isocrates's orations as important documents about rhetorical theory" (p. 98). Takis Poulakos (1997), who tried to help rectify this situation with *Speaking for the Polis: Isocrates' Rhetorical Education*, wrote: "From scholars of rhetoric he did not receive a great deal of attention....Aristotle drew all scholarly interest" (p. 2). As one of the goals of my book, I hope to provide a better understanding of the reasons why so important a historical figure has received so little attention and why events are now forcing him on our attention.

Even the little that is known, however, is sufficient to expose some of the misreadings of Isocrates. These misreadings have tended to proliferate among critics who sympathized with Isocrates's academic competitors—Plato and Aristotle—and viewed the work of Isocrates through the conceptual frameworks of these competitors and their successors. George Kennedy's (1963) approach to Isocrates in his *Art of Persuasion in Greece* can serve as an example. Among the problems with Kennedy's approach, he accepted Aristotle's distinction between politics and rhetoric and attempted to focus on Isocratean oratory and exclude Isocratean politics even though Isocrates himself considered ethical performance in political deliberation to be at the very heart of his rhetoric (p. 174). To mention just one additional problem, Kennedy placed Isocrates's speeches in a category called "epideictic rhetoric," which tends to be a catch-all for speeches that usually honor or attack someone and often served in antiquity as a means of displaying oratorical excellence in such forms as funeral orations and satires; while

Isocrates did write some discourses that could be considered epideictic, he explicitly stated that he was concerned with political discourse and even—in *Panathenaicus* as elsewhere—distinguished his own political discourse from epideictic and forensic rhetoric (271). A sympathetic reading of Isocrates is only possible if he is approached on his own terms.

To try to take some specialized or local view of Isocrates is to rob him of the very strength that makes him so important as we move into the 21st century—his breadth in addressing human well-being. We are looking back at one of the most appalling centuries in history, and well-intentioned humans—those with at least some hope of improving our lot—are attempting to discover whether the art of governance can be strengthened in any way. Among their realizations has been a growing awareness of a disjunction between narrow specialization in Western civilization and the scope of human interrelations. Although decisions can have the widest-ranging impacts on other humans, deliberations are often so bounded that these impacts are never fully considered, and the results can be disastrous. In such an environment, Isocratean scope can be salutary. Poulakos (1997) called Isocrates's writings "perhaps the last successful deployment of rhetoric against the forces of fragmentation and the pressures of difference" (p. 106). It is true that Isocrates has left us with no more than a scattering of statements about an art of governance. We search in vain for the kind of articulation of theory found in Aristotle or Quintilian. But the seeds we find in Isocrates, if properly planted, could yield a rich harvest in future centuries.

If Isocrates's works contain the seeds of improvement, however, his scope at its broadest—encompassing the whole life of civilized man—is compromised by positions taken in academic debate. Ancient Athens was clearly a hotbed of academic competition with feverish posturing for competitive edge, and the leading educator of the time, although theoretically inclined toward inclusion and seemingly strong enough to have stood above the fray, attacked his competitors in ways that created implicit and explicit exclusions from his philosophy or rhetoric. Among the results was conflict and division rather than collaboration and inclusion. In this way, Isocrates limited the scope of rhetoric and contributed to its decline—a decline that was furthered by Plato and Aristotle.

PLATO

Scholars have long detailed—and relished—the difficulties of determining Plato's intent in his dialogues. Since the ideas in the dialogues are expressed not by Plato but by others, Plato himself was not necessarily committed to any of them. Since the tone in the dialogues is not infrequently ironical and since it is sometimes debatable whether irony is present or not, varying interpretations are inevitable. And attitudes in some dialogues are contradicted by attitudes in other dialogues; for instance, Plato's Socrates in many of the earlier dialogues directs attention *away from* human affairs, but Plato's Athenian in the later dialogue *Laws* directs attention *toward* human affairs—perhaps an indication of a change in Plato's thinking over time. The very presence of rich and complex puzzles in Plato's work has no doubt been a source of some of his attraction to modern scholars.

I have no interest here in determining Plato's intent or representing his ideas in all their richness and complexity. This section will tend to focus on those ideas in Plato's works that have narrowed attention in human deliberation and limited the scope of human goals, social structures, and methodologies. These ideas, which are highly influential, have been responsible for the most profound division of attention in Western civilization. As is the case with Isocrates, Plato's work contains ideas that reduce the range of actions that constitute the good. In numerous passages, while accepting some of Isocrates's divisions, Plato elaborates on them, adds others, and reverses preference. He reduces the stature and scope of rhetoric, using definitional exclusion to make it no more than an instrument of persuasion. What results is the sharp contrast between Plato and Isocrates noted by scholars. It should not escape notice how close the resulting complex of ideas corresponds to what so many commentators throughout history have considered central to his work and have called "Platonism."

While Isocrates focused his attention on human affairs, Plato—in numerous passages—directed attention away from the world of human affairs to a supposedly divine or spiritual world arranged hierarchically above it. In *Theaetetus*, for instance, Socrates argues: "we should make all speed to take flight from this world to the other, and that means becoming like the divine so far as we can" (trans. 1961/1973, 176b). In *Phaedrus*, Socrates describes the ideal human as one who "stands apart from the common objects of human ambition and applies himself to the divine" (trans. 1973/1985, 249d). He "fixes his gaze on the heights to the neglect of things below" (249d). Such humans are also described by Socrates in *Republic*: "those who have attained to this height are not willing to occupy themselves with the affairs of men, but their souls ever feel the upward urge and the yearning for that sojourn above" (trans. 1961/1973, 517d). A sharp opposition between this-worldliness and otherworldliness is established with ultimate value associated with the latter.

In *Republic*, Socrates describes the otherworldly as an eternal and changeless reality that the ideal human must strive to imitate or assimilate: "the man whose mind is truly fixed on eternal realities has no leisure to turn his eyes downward upon the petty affairs of men...,but he fixes his gaze upon the things of the eternal and unchanging order, and...he will endeavor to imitate them and, as far as may be, to fashion himself in their likeness and assimilate himself to them" (500b,c). These ideal humans who contemplate the eternal and changeless reality of the otherworldly are called "philosophers," while "those who are incapable of this, but lose themselves and wander amid the multiplicities of multifarious things, are not philosophers" (484b). Since Isocrates was concerned about the art of choice to enable the best lives possible in this world, a focus on what Socrates calls the "petty affairs of men," he is denied the title of "philosopher."

Philosophers find little of value or interest in human affairs. In *Republic*, Socrates and Glaucon agree "that a mind habituated to thoughts of grandeur and the contemplation of all time and all existence" cannot "deem this life of man a thing of great concern" (486a). This sentiment is echoed later in the same dialogue: "nothing in mortal life is worthy of great concern" (604c). To the extent that "humanist," "humanism," and "humanities" are cognates that carry as part of their meaning a deep concern for human welfare between birth and death, they are inappropriately ascribed to these philosophers and appropriately ascribed to Isocrates—a fact little appreciated by many 20th century "humanists."

A sharp contrast is drawn between those who focus on human affairs and those who direct attention away from human affairs, the philosophers. In *Gorgias*, Socrates establishes a sharp disjunction between "all those manly pursuits of speaking in Assembly and practicing rhetoric and going in for politics" and "the life of philosophy" (trans. 1925/1953, 500c). In *Republic*, Socrates again distinguishes between this-worldly activities and philosophy:

> This, then,...is my division. I set apart and distinguish those of whom you were just speaking, the lovers of spectacles and the arts, and men of action, and separate from them again those with whom our argument is concerned and who alone deserve the appellation of philosophers or lovers of wisdom. (476a,b)

In these passages, Socrates has identified particular activities that Isocrates associated with philosophy and excluded them from association with the term.

As Socrates and Glaucon agree in *Republic*, the changing multiplicities of this world are called "becoming," while the unchanging and eternal reality of the otherworldly toward which philosophers should direct their attention is called "being." Humans consist of two parts, one part associated with this-worldliness or becoming called "body" and another part associated with otherworldliness or being called "soul." As the Stranger in *Sophist* represents Theaetetus's argument, body engages our changing world of becoming through sense, while soul engages the unchanging world of being through reflection: "we have intercourse with becoming by means of the body through sense, whereas we have intercourse with real being by means of the soul through reflection. And real being...is always in the same unchanging state, whereas becoming is variable" (trans. 1961/1973, 248a).

In line with those ideas that direct attention from this-worldliness to otherworldliness, a substantial complex of ideas directs attention away from body and toward soul. In *Phaedo*, Socrates and Simmias agree that the philosopher "is not concerned with the body, but keeps his attention directed as much as he can away from it and toward the soul" (trans, 1961/1973, 64e). Socrates argues that the philosopher should cut "himself off as much as possible from his eyes and ears and virtually all the rest of his body, as an impediment which by its presence prevents the soul from attaining to truth and clear thinking" (66a). Both the physical senses and the emotions are an obstruction to the acquisition of knowledge (65c, 66c). Socrates and Simmias agree that the philosopher should not concern himself with the pleasures of food, drink, and sex (64d).

While one complex of ideas in Plato's dialogues rejects experiences associated with body, another complex of ideas embraces experiences associated with soul. In this complex of ideas, soul is drawn toward manifestations of the otherworldly, primary among them a purported creator or god. Timaeus, in the dialogue that carries his name, states that the creator of this world, the world of generation, "desired that all things should be like himself as they could be" (trans. 1961/1973, 29d,e; 30a). In *Laws*, the Athenian states: "it is God who is...of a truth 'the measure of all things'....So he who would be loved by such a being must himself become such to the utmost of his might, and so, by this argument, he that is temperate among us is loved by God, for he is like God" (716c,d). The philosopher, then, imitates or approximates this god by attempting to share certain ideal characteristics with him.

These ideal characteristics are called "forms;" in *Parmenides*, for instance, Socrates and Parmenides agree that there is "a form of rightness or of beauty or of goodness, and of all such things" (trans. 1961/1973, 130b). In *Symposium*, Diotoma describes to Socrates how the philosopher must move from an appreciation of earthly manifestations of a form such as beauty to an appreciation of the form itself:

> Starting from individual beauties, the quest for the universal beauty must find him ever mounting the heavenly ladder, stepping from rung to rung—that is, from one to two, and from two to *every* lovely body, from bodily beauty to the beauty of institutions, from institutions to learning, and from learning in general to the special lore that pertains to nothing but the beautiful itself—until at last he comes to know what beauty is. (211c)

An appreciation of a form is an awareness of what something is, a kind of identification.

Such an identification is called a "truth." As Socrates states in *Cratylus*, "a true proposition says that which is" (trans. 1961/1973, 385b). Consequently, in attempting to identify the nature or essence of virtue in *Protagoras*, Socrates equates that task with the discovery of the truth about virtue or what it is (360c; 361a). This identification of the truth about something, the discovery of what it is, is called "knowledge" (*Theaetetus*, 186c; *Republic*, 477a), and this knowledge is called "science" (*Republic*, 478a). The identification of a form, then, is an effort to determine what it is, to capture the truth about it, and such truths constitute knowledge and science. The philosopher's goal is equated with the effort to capture truth for the sake of knowledge (*Republic*, 499a). In *Laws*, the Athenian claims, "of all things good, truth holds the first place among gods and men alike" (730c). While Isocratean philosophers deliberate about what choices to make, about what to do, these philosophers focus on questions of identification, on truths about what is.

In attempting to determine what each form is, to discover its truth or essence, the philosopher uses a methodology or process called "dialectic." In *Republic*, Socrates and Glaucon agree that dialectic is the only "way of inquiry that attempts systematically and in all cases to determine what each thing really is" (533b). In addition to the name "philosopher," they "give the name dialectician to the man who is able to exact an account of the essence of each thing" (534b). In *Phaedrus*, Socrates states that dialectic consists of the two processes of "perceiving and bringing together in one idea the scattered particulars" (265d) and "dividing things again by classes, where the natural joints are" (265e)—processes that we might call "synthesis" and "analysis." Socrates calls himself "a lover of these processes of division and bringing together" and calls those who can perform them "dialecticians" (266b,c).

Humans can be inclined toward dialectic or philosophy in various ways. In *Republic*, Socrates claims that he is one of the few humans or perhaps the only human to be drawn to philosophy by a "divine sign" (496c) In *Socrates' Defense (Apology)*, he elaborates: "I am subject to a divine or supernatural experience....It began in my early childhood—a sort of voice which comes to me, and...debars me from entering public life" (trans. 1961/1973, 31d). Humans can also be inclined toward philosophy by appropriate studies. In *Republic*, Socrates and Glaucon inquire into the studies that have the power to "draw the soul away from the world of becoming to the world of being" and ascend to "true philosophy" (521c,d). They include mathematics (522e; 525d; 526b), geometry (527b), and astronomy (529a). These studies are called "indispensable preparation for dialectic" (536d). It should be remembered that two of these studies, geometry and astronomy, were rejected by Isocrates as useless in practical life and excluded from his philosophy.

Turning away from this-worldliness to otherworldliness leads to happiness both in this life and in some purported life after death. Timaeus, in the dialogue that carries his name, describes the prospects of the philosopher in this life:

> he who has been earnest in the love of knowledge and of true wisdom, and has exercised his intellect more than any other part of him, must have thoughts immortal and divine, if he attain truth, and in so far as human nature is capable of sharing in immortality, he must altogether be immortal, and since he is ever cherishing the divine power and has the divinity within him in perfect order, he will be singularly happy. (90c)

After death, the immortal soul confronts a judge, who rewards the human who has practiced philosophy: "when he discerns another soul that has lived a holy life in company with truth...—a philosopher's who has minded his own business and not been a busybody in his lifetime—he is struck with admiration and sends it off to the Isles of the Blessed" (*Gorgias*, 526c).

As Socrates indicates in *Republic*, only a few humans can become perfect philosophers (491a,b), and the masses tend to attack philosophy (494a). He states that "philosophers are not honored in our cities" (489b) and that philosophy "is undeservedly reviled" (536c). He speaks of the "injustice of the calumniation of philosophy" (497a) and "her present low estate" (495d). Among those responsible for the low reputation of philosophy are the rhetoricians, who are attacking their only serious rivals in education to gain undisputed academic supremacy (305 c,d). The Isocrates portrayed by Plato in *Euthydemus* could hardly speak more severely about dialectic: "the whole system and the men engaged in the system are contemptible and ridiculous" (305a).

Gorgias contains another sharp attack on philosophy from the standpoint of the rhetoricians. In this dialogue, Callicles—like Isocrates—favors the pursuits of speaking in Assembly and practicing rhetoric and going in for politics. Also like Isocrates, he suggests that philosophy is appropriate for boys but not for men (484c). Philosophers so direct attention to the otherworldly that they remain ignorant and ineffective in human affairs:

> such people are shown to be ignorant of the laws of their city, and of the terms which have to be used in negotiating agreements with their fellows in private or public affairs, and of human pleasures and desires; and, in short, to be utterly inexperienced in men's characters. So when they enter upon any private or public business they make themselves ridiculous. (484d,e)

Plato gives Callicles's argument force, but it is weakened not only by Callicles's overbearing character, but also by the ease with which so many of his positions are proven untenable by Socrates.

Although some make distinctions between sophists and rhetoricians, Socrates—in *Gorgias*—equates them: "Sophist and orator, my estimable friend, are the same thing, or very much of a piece...; but you in your ignorance think the one thing, rhetoric, a very fine affair, and despise the other" (520a,b). The equation of "rhetorician" and "sophist" is justified by usage elsewhere in the dialogues. For instance, in the dialogue that carries his name, Protagoras is called a Sophist and describes what his student learns in terms that Isocrates used to describe his philosophy or rhetoric: "The proper care of his personal affairs, so that he may best manage his own household, and also of the state's affairs, so as to become a real power in the city, both as speaker and man of action" (318e; 319a). Like Isocrates, Protagoras emphasizes "the art of politics" (319a).

Another attack on philosophy found in the works of Isocrates—that likely conjecture about useful things is preferable to exact knowledge of the useless—has responses in the dialogues. Plato's Socrates agrees with Isocrates that a distinction should be made between conjecture about changing matters and certainty about stable matters, but, as is made clear in *Republic*, he disparages the former as mere opinion and values the latter as knowledge or science (476d; 477b; 478a). The "real lover of knowledge" strives "emulously for true being" and "would not linger over the many particulars that are opined to be real" (490a,b). He is the exact opposite of the rhetorician, "who has gone hunting after opinions instead of learning the truth" and attains "a pretty ridiculous sort of art, in fact no art at all" (*Phaedrus*, 262c).

Yet another attack on philosophy found in the works of Isocrates—that philosophy is useless—has a response in Plato's dialogues that constitutes one of the most surprising reversals in the history of thought. In *Republic*, Socrates agrees that philosophers are of no use to the multitude at the moment, but he suggests that the multitude could make use of them (489b). Astonishingly, the multitude should use philosophers as rulers: "neither city nor polity nor man either will ever be perfected until some chance compels this uncorrupted remnant of philosophers, who now bear the stigma of uselessness, to take charge of the state whether they wish it or not, and constrains the citizens to obey them" (499b). In effect, the goal of the Socratean and Isocratean philosophers becomes the same—to improve society by governing it.

Although the whole thrust of philosophy is to direct attention away from human interests toward the divine, away from becoming and toward being, and away from change and toward the unchanging, although the whole happiness of philosophers in this life and the next is dependent on this orientation, and although this polarization is intensified by attacks on rhetoricians for being associated with this-worldliness and a glorification of philosophers for being associated with otherworldliness, Plato's dialogues contain the grandest "Never mind!" in the history of philosophy: side by side with the extensive complex of ideas promoting otherworldliness we find another extensive complex of ideas directing attention to this-worldliness and suggesting approaches to governance.

This latter complex of ideas, while conflicting in various ways with ideas promoting otherworldliness, nevertheless continues to further the educational ideal of philosophy. The portrait of this-worldliness that emerges affords some fruitful comparisons and contrasts with that provided by Isocrates. Participants in Plato's dialogues create their ideal society in ways that both implicitly and explicitly degrade all rhetoric that does not in some way approximate philosophy, both reducing its stature and limiting its scope. Plato's this-worldliness, then, constitutes support for his educational program and serves, at least in most respects, to undermine the programs of Isocrates and other rhetoricians and sophists.

When humans are born, their natures are already such that they are fitted for specific occupations in this life. As a result, according to *Republic*, they "must be sent to the task for which their natures were fitted, one man to one work" (423d). Such specialization creates the most productive society: "more things are produced, and better and more easily when one man performs one task according to his nature, at the right moment, and at leisure from other occupations" (370c). As an example of specialization, a few humans are born philosophers (494b), and these better natures must "attain the knowledge which we pronounce the greatest" (519c) and then "take charge of the other citizens and be their guardians" (520a). Only through this conjunction of politics and philosophy can human troubles be alleviated:

> Unless...either philosophers become kings in our states or those whom we now call our kings or rulers take to the pursuit of philosophy seriously and adequately, and there is a conjunction of these two things, political power and philosophical intelligence,...there can be no cessation of troubles...for our states, nor...for the human race either. (473c,d,e)

In *Statesman* (trans. 1961/1973), governance is viewed with the kind of breadth that we find in the works of Isocrates. Governance includes the activities of "the statesman, the king, the slavemaster, and the master of a household" (258e), and the same science covers all these activities and can be called "royal science, political science, or science of household management" (259c). The Stranger ascribes to governance the same extraordinary scope as Isocrates: "It weaves all into its unified fabric with perfect skill. It is a universal art and so we call it by a name of universal scope. That name is one which I believe to belong to this art and to this alone, the name of 'statesmanship'" (305e). Importantly, the Stranger calls "statesmanship" what Isocrates called "philosophy" or 'rhetoric."

Ideally, humans and not laws should govern (297c); the use of laws is only a second best alternative (297e). Humans are preferable to laws because human situations are too variable for hard and fast rules: "The differences of human personality, the variety of men's activities, and the inevitable unsettlement attending all human experience make it impossible for any art whatsoever to issue unqualified rules holding good on all questions at all times" (294b). The Stranger comes to the same conclusion as Isocrates: "It is impossible...for something invariable and unqualified to deal satisfactorily with what is never uniform and constant" (294c). This impossibility, however, is the goal of the philosopher-kings in *Republic*—to "fix their eyes on absolute truth, and always with reference to that ideal and in the exactest possible contemplation of it establish in this world also the laws of the beautiful, the just, and the good" (484c,d).

In different Platonic dialogues, the role of rhetoric in society varies, but it never becomes equivalent to governance, as it does in the works of Isocrates. In *Gorgias* and *Phaedrus*, Socrates seems willing to entertain a positive notion of rhetoric that approximates in some way his philosophy. In *Gorgias*, for instance, Socrates distinguishes between the life to which Callicles invites him—speaking in Assembly, practicing rhetoric, and going in for politics—and the life of otherworldly philosophy, which includes striving for the just. At the end of the dialogue, Socrates encourages Callicles to turn his back on this-worldly governance, an Isocratean concept of rhetoric, and to pursue a "rhetoric...to be used for this one purpose always, of pointing to what is just" (527c). He states: "This way of life is best—to live and die in the practice alike of justice and of all other virtue. This then let us follow, and to this invite everyone else; not that to which you trust yourself and invite me, for it is nothing worth, Callicles" (527e). In *Paideia*, Jaeger (1939–1944) concluded that Plato "believed philosophy to be the only true rhetoric" (Vol. 3, p. 71).

However, this notion of rhetoric, is not pursued in other dialogues. The most common approach to rhetoric is to equate it with persuasion and place it under the control of the politician or statesman. In *Statesman*, rhetoric "persuades men to do what is right and therefore takes its share in controlling what goes on in a true community" (304a). But it is the statesman who must decide "whether in any particular situation we must proceed by persuasion, or by coercive measures against a group of men, or whether it is right to take no action at all" (304d). The art of choice, then, is in the hands of the statesman and not the rhetorician: "The art which can teach us how to decide that will be the art which controls rhetoric and the art of public speaking" (304d). While Isocrates included the art of choice in governance within his philosophy or rhetoric, then, Plato severed this art from rhetoric and reduced the scope and stature of rhetoric to no more than a tool of politics and an instrument of persuasion.

The rhetorician, then, surrenders the art of ethical choice to the statesman and does not need to know what is good, just, or true. In the dialogue that carries his name, Phaedrus states that the orator "does not need to know what is really just, but what would seem just to the multitude who are to pass judgment, and not what is really good or noble, but what will seem to be so; for they say that persuasion comes from what seems to be true, not from the truth" (260a). In *Gorgias*, Socrates agrees with this view of the rhetorician: "he does not know what is really good or bad, noble or base, just or unjust, but he has devised a persuasion to deal with these matters so as to appear to those who, like himself, do not know to know better than he who knows" (459d,e). According to Socrates, then, "rhetoric...is a producer of persuasion for belief, not for instruction in the matter of right and wrong" (455a); while the most important goal of Isocrates's philosophy or rhetoric was ethical conduct, then, Plato's notion of rhetoric as persuasion did not include ethical choice.

If rhetoric is persuasion devoid of ethical choice, it can be used for unethical ends. In fact, in *Gorgias*, Socrates and Callicles agree that none of the orators of the day speak "always with a view to what is best, with the single aim of making the citizens as good as possible by their speeches." On the contrary, they are "set on gratifying the citizens" and "sacrificing the common weal to their own personal interest" (502e). Since the rhetoric of Socrates's day is all unethical, Socrates unleashes a bitter attack on his contemporary rhetoricians and sophists. In *Euthydemus*, Socrates discusses those rhetoricians who, like Isocrates, make speeches and do not deliver them, and he attacks this art: "it is a portion of the art of enchanters, but falls short a little. For the enchanter's art is the charming of adders and tarantulas and scorpions and other vermin and pests, but this is really the charming and persuasion of juries and parliaments and any sort of crowds" (289d,e; 290a). In *Gorgias*, he calls rhetoric "base" (463d), "a part of a certain business which has nothing fine about it" (463a), a "branch of flattery" (463b), a pursuit that "is not an art but a habitude or knack" (463b). Socrates clusters orators with despots and overlords (479a).

The attacks on sophists in the dialogues are also harsh. In *Sophist*, the Stranger savages the sophistic art as the "art of contradiction making, descended from an insincere kind of conceited mimicry" (trans. 1961/1973, 268c). In *Statesman*, the Stranger calls Sophists "the chief pundits of the deceiver's art" (291c) and "supreme imitators and tricksters" (303c). In *Meno*, Anytus states that the Sophists are "the manifest ruin and corruption of anyone who comes into contact with them" (trans. 1961/1973, 91c). The attacks on rhetoricians and sophists correlate well with the action in many of the dialogues. In these dialogues, Socrates easily overcomes rhetoricians and sophists, some of whom have been identified as Isocrates's teachers and some of whom voice Isocratean positions. The attacks also correlate well with the omission of rhetoric from the studies recommended in the *Republic* and Menexenus's statement, in the dialogue that carries his name, that Socrates is "always making fun of the rhetoricians" (235c).

While a number of the dialogues contain the use of dialectic or definition to separate rhetoric from the art of ethical choice in governance, *Gorgias* contains ideas that further narrow the scope of rhetoric and reduce its stature. Among these ideas, Socrates and Gorgias limit rhetoric to speech (449d) and, as a result, exclude from rhetoric those activities whose "object may be achieved actually in silence, as with painting, sculpture, and many other arts" (450c,d). They also agree that some kinds of speech are excluded from rhetoric, for example, medicine, "which shows sick people by what regimen they could get well" (449e). They even agree that some kinds of persuasion, such as enumeration, are excluded from rhetoric (450c) and that "rhetoric is not the only producer of persuasion" (454a). Socrates and Gorgias, then, further diminish the scope of rhetoric through definitional exclusion.

The dialogues treat poetry almost as harshly as they do rhetoric. In *Gorgias*, Socrates and Callicles agree that poetry is a kind of "rhetorical public speaking" and therefore, as with rhetoric generally, is "an art that we do not quite approve of, since we call it a flattering one" (502d). In *Republic*, Socrates and Glaucon agree that poetry "waters and fosters...feelings when what we ought to do is to dry them up" (606d). They also agree that God produces the forms of things, that humans make copies of these forms, and that artists such as painters and poets imitate these copies—at a third remove from truth; consequently, poetry and other arts of imitation should be disparaged (603b). They consider themselves justified in not admitting poets into a well-ordered state (605b). Somehow it does not surprise us to hear Socrates report: "there is from of old a quarrel between philosophy and poetry" (607b).

Ideas in Plato's dialogues, then, further the process of division in human goals, social structures, and methodologies begun in the works of Isocrates. While accepting Isocrates's divisions between changing human affairs and more stable areas of study, such as mathematics and science, and between judgment and exact knowledge, participants in Plato's dialogues—in one complex of related ideas— elaborate on the division and reverse the preference. Like Isocrates, some participants are willing to equate philosophy and rhetoric, but the ideas associated with this philosophy/rhetoric stand in stark opposition to the philosophy/rhetoric of Isocrates. They direct attention away from this world of becoming to a supposedly divine world of being arranged hierarchically above it, from questions of choice (efforts to determine what to do) to questions of identification (efforts to determine what is). Attention is directed away from the full range of human actions toward a partial set.

This preference carries with it corresponding attitudes toward the characteristics associated with these areas of attention. Humans have this dualism within them— a body associated with this world and something called a soul associated with the otherworldly. They are encouraged to turn away from experience associated with body—for instance, sensations resulting from hearing and sight or emotions such as love and fear—and turn toward experiences associated with soul—for instance, thinking, reasoning, and knowing. They are inclined to disparage the use of judgment to make decisions about what is particular, concrete, changing, and temporary and to praise the effort to acquire certainty about what is universal, abstract, unchanging, and permanent. They turn away from action in human affairs toward contemplation of divinity and the forms, which results in truth, knowledge, and science. They disparage politics and admire mathematics, geometry, and astronomy.

If Isocratean philosophy/rhetoric dominated ancient Greece and Rome, Platonic otherworldliness—as A. O. Lovejoy suggested in *The Great Chain of Being* (1936/1960)—became "the dominant official philosophy of the larger part of civilized mankind through most of its history" (p. 26). This focus on otherworldliness would not have had such a profound impact on Western civilization without inherent appeals. Among them, we are born into a world of overwhelming human suffering, and many cannot bear the presence of that pain and seek escape. Others become disillusioned by the fickleness of fortune, the awful baseness of humanity, and the sheer complexity of choice; they, too, seek a place of peace and rest from the boiling cauldron of human society. Still others, working to change human society, are forced to flee to the safety of withdrawal by an entrenched force of power and privilege with an interest in preserving the status quo. All of these inherent appeals and others incline countless humans to find the truly good in what is antithetic to human affairs.

The success of Platonic otherworldliness carries implications for Isocratean educational ideals. The battle for the term "philosophy" is lost, and these ideals are called "rhetoric." Activities associated with them are ascribed little or no value. If you fix your gaze on the heights to the neglect of things below, you are not, like Isocrates, inclined to do some good in the world—found cities and make laws and invent arts. On the contrary, you are inclined to stand apart from the common objects of human ambition. You turn away from the hurly-burly of practical, everyday life and its associated characteristics and embrace the life of ascetic or monastic withdrawal, favoring those characteristics associated with otherworldliness.

If, as Lovejoy suggested, otherworldliness became the dominant "official" ideal of much of civilized mankind, however, he was quick to suggest the limitations of this victory:

> I have said 'official philosophy' because nothing, I suppose, is more evident than that most men...have never quite believed it, since they have never been able to deny to those things disclosed by the senses a genuine and imposing and highly important kind of realness, and have never really truly desired for themselves the end which otherworldliness held out to them. (pp. 26–27)

Lovejoy added: "the plain man...has manifestly continued to find something very solid and engrossing in the world in which his own constitution was so deeply rooted and with which it was so intimately interwoven" (p. 27). In short, "Nature in the main has been too potent" (p. 27). Indeed, Plato's dialogues themselves contain the suggestion that few are born with the natural qualities to become philosophers.

Whether Plato himself felt the potency of this-worldliness, whether he wished to show his superiority to the rhetoricians and sophists at their own game, or whether the interests of potential students forced him to broaden his educational program, he included in his dialogues—despite a complex of ideas promoting an ideal of otherworldliness—a substantial complex of ideas that addressed human affairs. In engaging human affairs, however, participants in the dialogues tend to focus on the same goals and methodologies highlighted in the practice of other-worldly philosophy. Among the results, we encounter a heavy emphasis on the goal of truth, on dialectically shaped social organization, such as specialization, and on the use of synthesis and analysis—approaches to human affairs that are, at best, insufficient.

As an example of insufficiency, philosophers, who have kept their attention away from human affairs, are made rulers without any effort to suggest how they will receive the contextual and experiential awareness to perform well. Given such insufficiencies, it is not surprising that Plato's students proved less successful in human affairs than Isocrates's students. Jaeger, in *Paideia*, contrasted their respective levels of success in this way: "the long line of statesmen and great public figures who had gone through Isocrates' school...were a living witness to the force which had flowed from his teaching all through the life of his native city" (Vol. 3, p. 137). Many of Plato's students, however, "had a brief and violent life as political experimentalists and revolutionaries" (p. 137). Jaeger attributed this fact "to their extreme interest in theoretical problems, which led them so often to become thoughtful recluses" (p. 137). He added: "from the standpoint of the real state of their day, most of them were characterized by their inability to do any real service to it and exert any real influence upon it" (p. 137).

The ideas in the dialogues associated with this-worldliness also further the attack on rhetoric contained in the ideas associated with otherworldliness, as contrasts with the works of Isocrates suggest. While the most important goal of Isocrates's rhetoric is ethical choice in governance, Plato's dialogues sever that responsibility from rhetoric, divorcing it from ethics altogether, and making it nothing more than an instrument of persuasion that can be used for either ethical or unethical ends. Since the rhetoric of the times is being used for unethical ends, rhetoricians, sophists, and the related poets are attacked in the dialogues. Within the context of ideas on this-worldliness in the dialogues, then, the stature and scope of rhetoric are severely diminished by definitional exclusion—an attack that serves Plato's educational program.

ARISTOTLE

Like Plato, Aristotle (384–322 B.C.E.) was in academic competition with Isocrates. E. M. Cope (1867), in *An Introduction to Aristotle's Rhetoric*, cited "a crowd of ancient witnesses" who testified to "an overt antagonism and rivalry" between Isocrates and Aristotle. Among Cope's witnesses, Dionysius "quotes a sneer of Aristotle at the loads of Isocrates' forensic speeches which were hawked about by the booksellers, and adds that Aristotle wanted to 'befoul' him,...to bespatter him with calumny and abuse" (p. 39). Cope cited Quintilian's claim "that Aristotle set up a rival school of rhetoric in *the old age* of Isocrates" (p. 40). As George Kennedy suggested in *The Art of Persuasion in Greece* (1963): "the success of Isocrates' school was probably a challenge first to Plato and later to Aristotle to take a position on the nature of rhetoric and the importance of rhetorical education" (pp. 83–84). Aristotle, however, had as little success as Plato in educating students who would become notable orators. Richard Jebb (1909), in *The Rhetoric of Aristotle*, wrote: "the school of Aristotle...produced not a single orator of note except Demetrius Phalereus; the school of Isocrates produced a host" (p. xx).

Aristotle supported his teacher, Plato, in the academic struggle between their philosophy and the philosophy or rhetoric of Isocrates. Like Plato, Aristotle established a hierarchy of human activities in which philosophy is distinguished from and valued above rhetoric. Aristotle's distinctions and values affected goals, social structures, and methodologies, which furthered the narrowing of attention in human deliberation already explored in the works of Isocrates and Plato. In his process of defining rhetoric, Aristotle excluded so much included by Isocrates that the decline of rhetoric—if this definition is accepted—was inevitable. As was the case with Plato, then, Aristotle reduced the stature and scope of rhetoric through definitional exclusion. He excluded the art of ethical choice, the selection of subject matter, and the multiplicity of human goals beyond persuasion. Although a scholar such as George Kennedy (1963) called the influence of Aristotle's *Rhetoric* "largely salutary" (p. 123), Aristotle was one of the two forces—Plato was the other—who contributed most to the decline of rhetoric in Western civilization.

In establishing his hierarchy of human activities, Aristotle followed Plato in his emphasis on definition, specialization, and the celebration of the expert. According to Aristotle, human activity should be divided into specializations, and every specialization "marks off a certain class of things for itself and busies itself about this" (*Metaphysics,* trans. 1941, XI,7). Specialists confine themselves to questions in a particular field: "There is a limit, then, to the questions which we may put to each man of science; nor is each man of science bound to answer all inquiries on each several subject, but only such as fall within the defined field of his own science" (*Posterior Analytics,* I,12). The exchange of information within specializations should be limited to experts: "One should therefore not discuss geometry among those who are not geometers, for in such a company an unsound argument will pass unnoticed. This is correspondingly true in the other sciences" (*Posterior Analytics,* I,12). It should be noted that Aristotle hardly practiced what he preaches here.

Among his efforts at definition, Aristotle divided the areas of human activity into practical sciences, theoretical sciences, and productive sciences. Aristotle included within the practical sciences those areas of human activity that Isocrates considered most important; among these areas is that "concerned with a man himself—with the individual; and this is known by the general name 'practical wisdom'; of the other kinds one is called household management, another legislation, the third politics, and of the latter one part is called deliberative and the other judicial" (*Nicomachean Ethics,* trans. 1941, VI,8).

While Isocrates placed greatest value on the practical sciences, Aristotle followed Plato in placing greater value on attentions directed elsewhere. The affairs of human beings are simply not as important as other matters: "it would be strange to think that the art of politics, or practical wisdom, is the best knowledge, since man is not the best thing in the world" (*Nicomachean Ethics,* VI,7). After all, "there are other things much more divine in their nature even than man, e.g., most conspicuously, the bodies of which the heavens are framed" (VI,7). Aristotle ranked the theoretical sciences highest and divided them into three kinds—theology, mathematics, and physics—with theology being the most important (*Metaphysics,* XI,7). Aristotle closely resembled Plato, then, in the value placed on theology, mathematics, and science.

The theoretical sciences focus on questions of identification—efforts to determine what is—while the practical sciences focus on questions of choice—efforts to determine what to do (*Nicomachean Ethics,* II,2). In another way of expressing this distinction, Aristotle suggested that the goal of theoretical sciences is "understanding" or "the grasping of scientific truth," while the goal of practical sciences or practical wisdom is directive, leading to decisions about what "ought to be done or not to be done" (VI,10). Like Plato, Aristotle associated philosophy with the theoretical sciences and pursuit of the truth: "It is right also that philosophy should be called knowledge of the truth. For the end of theoretical knowledge is truth" (*Metaphysics*, II,1).

The philosophical pursuit of the truth in the theoretical sciences is called "contemplation," while the pursuit of choice in the practical sciences is called "action." In line with the elevation of the theoretical sciences above the practical sciences, the life of action leads to less happiness than the life of contemplation: "So if among virtuous actions political and military actions are distinguished by nobility and greatness,...the activity of reason, which is contemplative, seems...to be superior in serious worth" (*Nicomachean Ethics*, X,7). In turning away from action and production and embracing contemplation, humans are participating in the same kind of activity as God and will therefore achieve their highest happiness (X,8).

The theoretical sciences attempt to grasp scientific knowledge of the eternal and universal, while the practical sciences seek opinion about the variable and a combination of the universal and particular. According to Aristotle, "philosophic wisdom is scientific knowledge" (*Nicomachean Ethics*, VI,7), and scientific knowledge focuses on the eternal (VI,3) and universal (VI,6). Aristotle suggested how a practitioner of the theoretical sciences, such as a mathematician, moves from the particular toward the universal: "the mathematician investigates abstractions (for before beginning his investigation he strips off all the sensible qualities, e.g., weight and lightness, hardness and its contrary, and also heat and cold and the other sensible contrarieties, and leaves only the quantitative and continuous)" (*Metaphysics*, XI,3).

In the practical sciences, on the other hand, "men do not study the eternal, but what is relative and in the present" (*Metaphysics*, II,1). The focus is on what is variable (*Nicomachean Ethics*, VI,7), and humans engage the variable with opinion or practical wisdom (VI,5). Opinion or practical wisdom focuses not only on the variable or temporary, but also on a combination of universals and particulars: "Nor is practical wisdom concerned with universals only—it must also recognize the particulars; for it is practical, and practice is concerned with particulars" (VI,7). Since the theoretical sciences are valued more than the practical sciences, the attempt to grasp scientific knowledge of the eternal and universal is valued more than the use of opinion to engage the variable and a combination of the universal and particular.

While the practical sciences attempt to respond to the needs of humans, the theoretical sciences or philosophy are motivated by curiosity or wonder alone: "it is owing to their wonder that men both now begin and at first began to philosophize" (*Metaphysics*, I,2). Philosophers have not been motivated by utilitarian goals: "since they philosophized in order to escape from ignorance, evidently they were pursuing science in order to know, and not for any utilitarian end" (I,2). Some past philosophers can serve as examples:

> This is why we say Anaxagoras, Thales, and men like them have philosophic but not practical wisdom, when we see them ignorant of what is to their own advantage, and why we say that they know things that are remarkable, admirable, difficult, and divine, but useless; viz. because it is not human goods that they seek. (*Nicomachean Ethics*, VI,7)

Aristotle makes a virtue of the uselessness that Isocrates condemned. The pursuit of the truth for its own sake is preferable to action with utilitarian ends: "that which is desirable on its own account and for the sake of knowing it is more of the nature of Wisdom than that which is desirable on account of its results" (*Metaphysics*, I,2).

Clearly, then, Aristotle reversed the values that we find in Isocratean philosophy or rhetoric. Not Isocratean philosophy or rhetoric, a study focusing on choices about what to do or say, but Aristotelian philosophy, a study to determine truths about what exists, became the ultimate in education. The Isocratean glorification of the utilitarian and rejection of mathematics and science as useless was turned on its head; Aristotle rejected utilitarian goals and glorified the very studies disparaged by Isocrates—mathematics and science—because they are prompted by wonder alone. The Isocratean studies of action, for instance, efforts to derive policy recommendations from deliberations of state, were classed as practical sciences and subsumed beneath studies—theology, mathematics, and physics—classed as theoretical sciences and associated with contemplation. The value Isocrates placed on the use of judgment to make decisions about human activity that is unique, variable, and temporary was replaced by an apotheosis of the effort to acquire certainty about what is away from humanity, about what is universal, unchanging, and eternal. Isocratean breadth, the concern for all of the forms of discourse in which the mind expresses itself, the devotion to the full range of choices that lead to speech and action, was exchanged for a highly classified system of specialization, in which experts pursue knowledge within the narrow boundaries of a discipline.

Aristotle, then, furthered the competition between an Isocratean philosophy or rhetoric and a philosophy associated with himself and Plato. He reinforced the dualism initiated partially by Isocrates and furthered by Plato. He sought to take the crown of education from rhetoric and give it to philosophy. The fact that Plato and Aristotle find themselves on the same side in promoting philosophy over rhetoric should not be allowed to obscure differences in their works. Among these differences, Aristotle—in, for example, *Nicomachean Ethics*—rejected Plato's notion of the Forms. In the area of rhetoric, Plato is willing to entertain the notion of a true rhetoric identical with philosophy, but we find no such idea in Aristotle. Nor did Aristotle ever savage rhetoric in the way that Plato did in *Gorgias*. But Aristotle's disparaging attitudes toward rhetoric were closer to Plato's than many commentators have been willing to admit.

Aristotle agreed with Isocrates and Plato that there is an area of human activity concerned with ethical choice in governance. While Isocrates associated this area with the terms "philosophy" and "rhetoric," however, Aristotle followed Plato in disassociating these terms from this area. Aristotle did not follow Plato in calling this area "statesmanship," preferring the name "politics," an area he included in his practical sciences. As was the case with Isocrates's philosophy or rhetoric, Aristotle's politics "legislates as to what we are to do and what we are to abstain from" (*Nicomachean Ethics*, I,2). As was the case with Isocrates's philosopher or rhetorician, Aristotle's "true student of politics...is thought to have studied virtue above all things" (I,13). Aristotle was at least willing to suppose that virtue was "the end of political life" (I,5). He was even willing to view ethical studies and politics as identical (*Rhetoric*, I,2,7; *On Rhetoric,* trans. 1991).

However, Aristotle specifically repudiated those such as Isocrates who equated politics and rhetoric. In what is clearly a direct attack on a passage in Isocrates's *Antidosis* (80–84), Aristotle wrote: "those of the sophists who profess the art [of politics] seem to be very far from teaching it. For, to put the matter generally, they do not even know what kind of thing it is nor what kinds of things it is about, otherwise they would not have classed it as identical with rhetoric or even inferior to it" (*Nicomachean Ethics*, X,9). In his *Rhetoric*, Aristotle allowed some venom to creep into his repudiation: "rhetoric dresses itself up in the form of politics, as do those who pretend to a knowledge of it, sometimes through lack of education, sometimes through boastfulness and other human causes" (I,2,7). In contrast to Isocrates, Aristotle subsumed rhetoric beneath politics: "we see even the most highly esteemed of capacities to fall under this [politics], e.g., strategy, economics, rhetoric" (*Nicomachean Ethics*, I,2).

Political science deals with subject matter, but its offshoot—rhetoric—does not. Aristotle viewed political science as including a rather narrow list of important subjects: "finances, war and peace, national defense, imports and exports, and the framing of laws" (*Rhetoric*, I,4,7). By definition, however, he excluded these subjects from rhetoric: "all these subjects belong to politics, not to rhetoric" (I,4,12). He reinforced this notion elsewhere: "the more [speakers] fasten upon [the subject matter] in its proper sense, [the more] they depart from rhetoric" (I,2,20). He criticized sophists such as Isocrates who included such subject matter: "much more than its proper area of consideration has currently been assigned to rhetoric" (I,4,4). Aristotle's acknowledgement here that he is narrowing the definition of rhetoric cannot be more explicitly stated.

Rhetoric resembles dialectic in its separation from subject matter: "Rhetoric is partly...dialectic and resembles it...; for neither of them is identifiable with knowledge of any specific subject, but they are distinct abilities of supplying words" (*Rhetoric*, I,2,7). Aristotle's discussion of rhetoric seems to plunge him into elaborate discussions of the subject matter of political science, but his distinction is one of degree. He is analyzing political science only to the degree that he must; fuller discussion of the subject belongs elsewhere:

In so far as someone tries to make dialectic or rhetoric not just mental faculties but sciences, he unwittingly obscures their nature by the change, reconstructing them as forms of knowledge of certain underlying facts, rather than *only* of speech. Nevertheless, let us now say what it is worthwhile to analyze, while leaving the full examination to political science. (emphasis added, I,4,6)

In his *Rhetoric*, then, Aristotle had no need to delve thoroughly into subjects:

It is not necessary at the present moment to enumerate these subjects accurately, particular by particular, and to divide them into species on the basis of what is customary in deliberation or to say what would be a true definition of them, since that is not a matter for the rhetorical art, but for a more profound and true [discipline]. (I,4,4)

Aristotle could hardly be more disdainful of rhetoric here; rhetoric is not as profound or true as other studies such as politics.

Aristotle further limited rhetoric in his formal definition of the area: "Let rhetoric be [defined as] an ability, in each [particular] case, to see the available means of persuasion" (*Rhetoric*, I,2,1). His restriction of the goal of rhetoric to persuasion was in accord with a similar restriction that we find in Plato's works. This restriction is understandable, given Aristotle's tendency to limit rhetoric to three kinds of persuasive speeches delivered to groups of people—judicial, deliberative, and demonstrative or epideictic (I,3,1-3).

In judicial rhetoric, prosecutors often try to evoke assent to the truth of a statement such as the following: "John killed Mary." That is, prosecutors try to "persuade" their audiences to agree with their representations of reality. Some form of resistance to their arguments is implicit in their situations because opposing arguments are expected from the defense. Aristotle emphasized the notion of dispute or debate inherent in judicial rhetoric: "In the law court there is either accusation or defense; for it is necessary for the disputants to offer one or the other of these" (*Rhetoric*, I,3,3). This sense of the word *persuasion* is among its more common senses.

Aristotle directed attention to another sense of the word by including deliberative rhetoric as one of his three kinds of persuasive speeches. To suggest a modern example of deliberative rhetoric, Republicans in the 1980s would no doubt have supported a proposition such as the following: "We ought to increase the allocation for national defense." As is the case with the previous notion of "persuasion," Republicans would have set out to evoke assent or agreement, and they would have expected resistance in the form of opposing arguments, this time from the Democrats. In this case, however, the proposition is not a statement about the past, the truth of which has the possibility of being verified. It is a proposal for a future action that, however supported by truths, cannot be construed as an effort to represent or mirror reality in and of itself. Aristotle emphasized the notion of dispute or debate in this sense of "persuasion" as well: "someone urging something advises it as the better course and one dissuading dissuades on the ground that it is worse" (*Rhetoric*, I,3,5).

Aristotle directed attention to yet another sense of the word by including demonstrative or epideictic rhetoric as one of his three kinds of persuasive speeches. In this kind of speech, as Aristotle suggested, "there is either praise or blame" (*Rhetoric*, I,3,3). Among modern examples of epideictic rhetoric would be memorial speeches at funerals to honor the dead. Although epideictic rhetoric might include disputes or debates about someone's character, opposition or resistance is often absent in epideictic situations. In funeral orations down through history, for instance, speeches were often more designed to impress audiences with the capabilities of the speaker, to display oratorical excellence, than to convince an audience about a view of someone's character.

If focusing attention on the persuasive dimensions of language can prove fruitful, that focus can also direct attention away from other important concerns. In Aristotle's works, rhetoric usually becomes limited to persuasion designed to overcome resistance and prompt one of two or more choices: "Its function is concerned with the sort of things we debate....And we debate about things that seem to be capable of admitting two possibilities; for no one debates things incapable of being different either in past or future or present, at least not if they suppose that to be the case; for there is nothing more [to say]" (*Rhetoric*, I,2,12). Much discourse, however, is not of this kind. A computer corporation's statement to "push the F9 key" may be persuasive in focusing attention in one place as opposed to other places, but it is not intended to overcome resistance or prompt one of two or more choices. To the extent that the word *rhetoric* comes to be associated with resistance and choices, then, this kind of discourse is excluded.

Too sharp a focus on persuasion in rhetoric can also be misleading. As Lloyd F. Bitzer (1978) has suggested in "Rhetoric and Public Knowledge," rhetoric must be broad enough in scope to enable humans to cooperate in making choices in response to problems and threats: "The central goal of rhetorical practice...is the Isocratic goal—to fashion means and provide impetus toward civilization, with regard to all humanity. An art of discourse—a knowledge and method—sufficient to this achievement is the practical rhetoric we seek" (p. 91). Isocrates's philosophy or rhetoric, which includes all of the choices that lead to speech and action, was broad enough to include the goals of Bitzer's rhetoric, but Aristotelian rhetoric, with its focus on persuasion, was not. Furthermore, when a modern scholar such as George Kennedy wrote a history of Greek rhetoric and called it *The Art of Persuasion in Greece* (1963), clearly following the lead of Plato and Aristotle, the title was not broad enough to encompass the educational program of Isocrates, the dominating teacher of rhetoric at the time.

The limitations of Aristotle's definition of rhetoric do not end with his focus on persuasion. Aristotle was even more exclusive in his focus on means; to repeat his definition, rhetoric is the ability in each particular case to see the available *means* of persuasion. When Aristotle discusses deliberative rhetoric, he indicates that "the objective of the deliberative speaker is the advantageous" and that the speaker does "not deliberate about this objective but about means that contribute to it" (*Rhetoric*, I,6,1). Aristotle believed that there are three means of producing persuasion, that is, three proofs: "All people are persuaded either because as judges they themselves are affected in some way or because they suppose the speakers have certain qualities or because something has been logically demonstrated" (III,1,1). We now call these three proofs the emotional argument, the ethical argument, and the logical argument.

Aristotle's subjection of rhetoric to politics, his exclusion of subject matter from rhetoric, and his limitation of rhetoric to the discovery of the available means of persuasion in a given case shed light on the relationship of rhetoric to the act of ethical choice. In at least three passages in his *Rhetoric*, he broached the subject of ethics. Early in *Rhetoric*, he wrote: "one should be able to argue persuasively on either side of a question...,not that we may actually do both (for one should not persuade what is debased) but in order that it may not escape our notice what the real state of the case is" (I,1,12). Elsewhere in *Rhetoric*, he added: "it is wrong to warp the jury by leading them into anger or envy or pity: that is the same as if someone made a straightedge rule crooked before using it" (I,1,12). He also argued that justice has a natural advantage if all of the available means of persuasion are brought to bear: "rhetoric is useful [first] because the true and the just are by nature stronger than their opposites, so that if judgments are not made in the right way [the true and the just] are necessarily defeated [by their opposites]. And this is worthy of censure" (I,1,12). These passages might be cited as support for the view that Aristotle included the act of ethical choice within the compass of rhetoric.

But much in his work militates against such a view. If rhetoric legislates what we are to do or abstain from, it is identical with politics, and Aristotle clearly repudiated such an equation. In any event, he excluded subject matter from rhetoric, and it is hard to see how the act of ethical choice could be performed in the absence of total command of a subject. Furthermore, his limitation of rhetoric to the discovery of the available means of persuasion in a given case, whether those means are ethical or not, suggests that the unethical can be as much a part of rhetoric as the ethical; one of Aristotle's most telling statements was a reaction to a declaration of Protagoras: "it is a lie and not true but a fallacious probability and a part of no art except rhetoric and eristic" (*Rhetoric*, II,24,11). Clearly, in developing the available means of persuasion, it is not part of the rhetorical art to exclude unprincipled acts. The rhetorical art is limited to the development of all of the available means of persuasion on both sides of a case, and the principled selection of what to use lies outside rhetoric.

Perhaps the strongest argument for the exclusion of the act of ethical choice from rhetoric, however, can be found in Aristotle's distinction between the virtues and arts. According to Aristotle, while politicians pursue virtue, rhetoricians pursue "the activity of an art" (*Rhetoric*, I,1,2). Aristotle drew a sharp distinction between the arts and virtues: "the case of the arts and that of the virtues are not similar" (*Nicomachean Ethics*, II,4). The politician pursuing virtues "must be in a certain condition when he does them; in the first place he must have knowledge, secondly he must choose the acts,...and thirdly his action must proceed from a firm and unchangeable character. These are not reckoned in as conditions of the possessions of the arts, except the bare knowledge" (II,4). Rhetoricians pursuing their art, then, resemble Plato's rhetoricians in *Statesman* in their exclusion from the act of ethical choice. In the same way that Aristotle both excluded and discussed subject matter in *Rhetoric*, he also seemed to both exclude and discuss the act of ethical choice.

Aristotle grouped the means of persuasion or proofs with style and organization as the three major provinces of study that concern the making of a speech: "there are three matters that need to be treated in discussion of speech—first, what will be the sources of the *pisteis* [proofs], second concerning the *lexis* [style], and third how the parts of a speech must be arranged" (*Rhetoric*, III,1,1). Within the area of style, Aristotle included delivery—the effort to attain the appropriate "volume, change of pitch, and rhythm" (III,1,4). This division of the study of rhetoric was accepted with some modifications by later writers in antiquity, such as Cicero. Cicero (trans. 1942/1949) added memory in dividing rhetoric into five parts: invention, organization, style, memory, and delivery (*De Oratore* I,xxxi, 142–143).

With his discussion of deliberative, judicial, and epideictic speeches in his treatment of persuasion and with his discussion of the provinces of study that concern the making of a speech, Aristotle tended to limit rhetoric to oratory—despite his occasional use of examples from other areas. This focus on oratory necessitated other exclusions from rhetoric. Among them, rhetoricians are precluded from using materials that are overly difficult to understand. Since oratory in ancient Greece is directed to general audiences, it must avoid the abstruse, all intricate reasoning beyond the grasp of the majority (*Rhetoric*, I,2,12). This limitation would tend to exclude any kind of discourse beyond the average comprehension. Not only science and mathematics, then, but any abstruse subject would be excluded. Such an exclusion provides opportunities for the emergence of a rival area of study called "philosophy" to define these areas as its domain and to promote their apotheosis over rhetoric.

The need to avoid the abstruse also carries implications for the kinds of proofs that orators can use. For instance, Aristotle, in *Posterior Analytics*, makes a sharp distinction between the proofs possible for the select few of superior understanding and those possible in rhetoric. For the former, his methodology begins with some basic premises established through induction, through a determination of a single universal truth from a large range of particulars (II,19). Our intuition is the faculty we use in this process (II,19). Once we have our primary premises, we can demonstrate new truths by building syllogisms (I,2). For instance, if we have as our primary premises that all men are mortal and that Plato is a man, we can, through syllogism, deduce that Plato is mortal. Aristotle's methodology, then, consists of processes of induction and deduction—processes that have been strongly emphasized in logic ever since. In rhetoric, however, because general audiences cannot follow long trains of reasoning, premises in inductions and deductions likely to be intuitively understood by audiences are left unexpressed, an approach that results in shorter trains of reasoning, called "paradigms" and "enthymemes" (*Rhetoric*, I,2,8–14).

Like Plato, then, Aristotle not only reduced the stature of rhetoric by placing it in the hierarchy of human activities beneath philosophy. He also reduced the scope of rhetorical invention by definitional exclusion. In defining rhetoric, he excluded full treatment of a subject and the choice of what is good and bad for humans. He limited invention to persuasion, excluding the multiplicity of goals besides persuasion. Far from interpreting persuasion in its broadest senses, he excluded all implications of the term beyond the effort to overcome resistance and prompt one of two or more choices. He further delimited his focus on persuasion by directing attention to the means of accomplishing this motive, to the forms of argument or proofs, an exclusion from rhetoric of a consideration of the ends of human activity. Finally, he focused on oratory directed to crowds, which excluded the abstruse and complicated trains of reasoning. The emphasis on clear division in Aristotle that led to these severe limitations on invention later led others to cut away invention altogether and—with it—organization and memory as well. In the hands of Aristotle, rhetoric became so limited that it is little wonder that he considered it not as instructive or real as other subjects, that he disdained it.

It is more of a wonder why so many 20th-century rhetoricians well-disposed toward rhetoric have been so favorably inclined toward Aristotle. For instance, Aristotle has been favorably cited more in 20th-century scholarship about rhetoric than any other rhetorician. Perhaps the greatest tribute to the *Rhetoric* has been acceptance. One of the most notable scholars of rhetoric in the 20th century, Kenneth Burke (1950), acknowledged his total acceptance of Aristotle's definition of rhetoric by using it as his own: "Rhetoric is the art of persuasion, or a study of the means of persuasion available for any given situation" (p. 46). Lane Cooper (1932), in his introduction to *The Rhetoric of Aristotle*, wrote: "the Rhetoric not only of Cicero and Quintilian, but of the Middle Ages, of the Renaissance, and of modern times, is, in its best elements, essentially Aristotelian" (p. xvii). George Kennedy's (1963) high praise is also notable: "If one looks back over the first hundred and fifty years of rhetorical theory, Aristotle's *Rhetoric* seems to tower above all the remains....Its influence has been enormous and still continues" (p. 123).

The value that Cooper, Kennedy, and other 20th-century commentators found in Aristotle's *Rhetoric* has some credence. For instance, Friedrich Solmsen (1974) gave Aristotle credit for a number of innovations, among them, the rejection of an artificial means of organizing speeches; new approaches to deduction and induction using enthymemes and examples; new analysis of emotional, ethical, and logical arguments; the division of oratory into three kinds—forensic (judicial), deliberative (political), and epideictic (demonstrative); and new insights into style. Such innovations proved valuable in classical antiquity and continue to help us today.

But if Aristotle's *Rhetoric* contributed much of value, if it stands as a contribution of originality and articulation, Aristotle's works and Plato's works were the documents most responsible for the decline of rhetoric in history. They lowered rhetoric in the scale of values and narrowed the concept of rhetoric so sharply that this art became inadequate to the tasks that confronted it. Isocrates's works, while containing ideas that could have countered such narrowing influences, took positions in academic debate that reduced the scope of rhetoric as well.

As works such as Richard Leo Enos's *Greek Rhetoric Before Aristotle* (1993) suggested, a substantial number of contemporaries and predecessors of Isocrates, Plato, and Aristotle took positions on rhetoric. But it is Plato and Aristotle in classical antiquity who have had the greatest adverse impact on the emergence and development of technical communication in the 20th century. They not only have been directly cited as important influences in certain contexts for technical communication. They have also been influential through such forces as Roman Catholicism and experimental science, which incorporated and built on their ideas and also had an adverse impact on technical communication.

To the extent that the ideas of Plato and Aristotle gained strength in Western civilization, humans were inclined by wonder to acquire certain truths about unchanging matters that result in knowledge rather than prompted by utilitarian goals to make judgments about choices in changing human affairs. Furthermore, the area of endeavor associated with the latter activity was called "rhetoric," and its scope and stature were diminished by definitional exclusion. The art of ethical choice, the selection of subject matter, and the multiplicity of human goals beyond persuasion were stripped from the purview of rhetoric so that it became nothing more than an instrument of persuasion, largely in oral discourse, that could be used for either ethical or unethical ends—a pursuit that was likely to evoke a condescension that echoes that found in Plato and Aristotle.

The academic competition between the rhetorician Isocrates and the philosophers Plato and Aristotle, together with the emphasis in the works of the philosophers on definition, specialization, and the celebration of the expert, supported an ever-growing division and subdivision of social structures in Western civilization until fragmentation almost seemed to be the rule in the second half of the 20th century. Within the resulting narrow social structures, humans found themselves confronted by overly narrow goals in confined environments that did not enable them to access everything they needed to address their problems.

Methodologies associated with philosophy and science gained stature, while methodologies associated with the art of choice in human affairs remained undeveloped and underappreciated. Little effort was devoted to the development of an art of choice that could adequately support ethical deliberation in any area of endeavor and insure that all relevant issues could be brought to bear in the engagement of problems. Instead, methodologies developed to determine truths about unchanging phenomena gained such stature that they were inappropriately used to address problems in changing human affairs.

Although rhetoric continued to win its conflict with philosophy in ancient Rome, the narrowing of rhetoric that gained such impetus from the competition between the rhetorician Isocrates and the philosophers Plato and Aristotle progressed to the point that the two major rhetoricians—Cicero and Quintilian—both felt impelled to engage this problem.

3

The Attack in Ancient Rome on the Narrowing of Rhetoric

Overly sharp contrasts between ancient Greece and ancient Rome were far too common in twentieth-century histories of classical antiquity. As Richard Leo Enos suggested in *Roman Rhetoric: Revolution and the Greek Influence* (1995), scholars "enjoyed making bold and distinctive generalizations about the 'glory that was Greece' and the 'grandeur that was Rome'" (p. 115). Another way of making the same contrast was to refer to the "golden age of Greece" and "the silver age of Rome." In the process of making such sharp contrasts, scholars too often lost sight of the unbroken centrality of rhetoric in the two cultures and the extent to which Greek rhetoric influenced Roman rhetoric, which, in turn, helped shape Roman culture.

While historians of rhetoric largely avoided this tendency, too many were prone to an error in the opposite direction—an overemphasis on similarities in classical rhetoric. Far too many rhetoric scholars have suggested that rhetoric in various cultural periods in classical antiquity was relatively monolithic; they have lost sight of sharp differences. Similarly, rhetoric scholars have been precipitous about suggesting broad similarities between specific ancient rhetoricians while ignoring fundamental differences separating them. As Enos (1995) indicated, contexts were crucial in shaping the individuality of both cultural periods and specific rhetoricians in classical antiquity.

Both the stature and scope of rhetoric were affected by the contexts of Cicero's Republic and Quintilian's Empire in ancient Rome. In Cicero's Republic, the stature of rhetoric was as great as it was in Isocrates's Athens. Cicero himself demonstrated the extent to which rhetoric could be a major source of power; as Enos (1995) indicated, although Cicero lacked patrician birth, military talent, and wealth, he achieved such success through rhetoric in the courts that he was able to secure the political post of consul. In many respects, Cicero can be perceived as an exemplar of Isocratean philosophy/rhetoric. If the stature of rhetoric remained intact, however, the narrowing of rhetoric that gained such impetus from the conflict between Isocrates, Plato, and Aristotle progressed so far that Cicero felt compelled to call for a resurrection of a rhetoric of Isocratean scope. Since his own rhetorical efforts were so focused on forensic and deliberative oratory, however, he compromised his own call for rhetorical scope.

By the time of the Empire, Augustus completely controlled Rome, and rhetoric was not so much a source of political power as a force in the courtroom and an emphasis in education (Enos, 1995). Rhetoric, then, had a somewhat diminished stature, and the educator Quintilian, no doubt influenced by his own experience as a pleader in the courts, tended to focus narrowly on forensic rhetoric. Like Cicero, he reaffirmed the stature of rhetoric and called for the resurrection of a rhetoric of Isocratean scope, but, also like Cicero, his own rhetorical efforts were so focused on forensic oratory that he compromised his call for scope. With the failures of both Cicero and Quintilian to resurrect the scope of rhetoric, the decline of rhetoric and triumph of philosophy in Western civilization became inevitable.

CICERO

In 55 B.C.E. Cicero responded to the narrowing of rhetoric with *De Oratore*. Many commentators about *De Oratore* strike me as more confident in their ability to determine a consistent line of Ciceronian thinking than they should be. The most reliable of the speakers in the work is the narrator "I," or Cicero himself, who is informing his brother Quintus about a three-part dialogue concerning rhetoric involving the Roman orators Crassus and Antonius. While Cicero's narrative self does establish some reliable insights into Cicero's thinking, he appears only briefly at the beginning of each of the three parts of the work and therefore provides only a limited number of insights. Furthermore, he is not presenting a dialogue that he himself experiences as a participant, but is rather attempting to reconstruct a report heard from someone else. Despite hearing only "general lines of argument and opinions," the narrator provides detailed statements of the participants (trans. 1942/1949, III.iv.16).

The high praise directed toward the two major contributors to the dialogue—Crassus and Antonius—certainly encourages the reader to give some weight to their statements; as an example of this praise, according to the narrator, "each of them...not only exceeded everybody else in devotion to oratory, in natural talent and also in learning, but also was an absolute master in his own class" (III.iv.16). Furthermore, while noting some opposition between Crassus and Antonius, Vickers (1988/1990) found that the two agree so often as to enable the following conclusion: "Antonius and Crassus are not fully-formed independent characters, then, but complementary, both expressing many of Cicero's own convictions about rhetoric. Much of *De Oratore* only seems like a debate, it is in fact an exposition split up between two personae" (p. 33).

Crassus appears to be the most reliable speaker after the narrator. The narrator tends to reserve his highest praise for Crassus, referring, for instance, to "his genius" (III.iv.14). With regard to the major theme, the views of the narrator and Crassus coincide, the narrator's reliability therefore strengthening that of Crassus. Still, Crassus's views about rhetoric are neither complete nor unquestioned. Crassus leaves some of the areas of rhetoric for Antonius to explore and does not react to them. Furthermore, after the first part of the dialogue, he raises questions about his own statements: "I personally have never been so dissatisfied with myself as I was yesterday" (II.iv.15). Oppositions to Crassus's opinions by Antonius and others are not totally without force. And, most importantly of all, Crassus not infrequently contradicts himself.

Antonius is even less reliable than Crassus. It is true that some of his views receive force from their acceptance without comment by other participants and the high praise that he receives. It is also true that some of his views receive force from their agreement with those of the narrator and Crassus; in fact, Sulpicius says to Crassus: "from the lips of Antonius we shall be learning your own views also" (I.xlvii.206). But doubt is cast on many of Antonius's statements by his assumption of the role of devil's advocate. At the end of one set of Antonius's statements, Crassus questions whether Antonius really believes what he is saying: "I rather suspect you are really of a different opinion, and are gratifying that singular liking for contradiction" (I.lxii.263). Later, Antonius himself admits: "Yesterday it was my design, if I should have succeeded in refuting your arguments, to steal these pupils from you, but to-day, with Catulus and Caesar among my hearers, I think it my duty not so much to fight with you as to enunciate my own personal views" (II.x.40–41).

A work such as Cicero's *De Oratore*, then, confronts readers with many interpretive problems. Readers not infrequently find themselves in doubt about the reliability of statements, whether that doubt is created by the secondhand nature of the report, differing views that carry weight, self-contradiction, self-criticism, or an assumption of the role of devil's advocate. Far from presenting ideas in coherent relation within a system, Cicero tested at least his major ideas in combat with their opposites, and it is not always clear where victory lies. What we find, then, is at least a measure of indecision that clusters well with the love of debate, suppleness of intellect, and skepticism.

Much of Cicero's *De Oratore* focuses on precisely the issue that is central to my analyses of Isocrates, Plato, and Aristotle—the scope of rhetoric. Despite doubts raised about some statements in *De Oratore*, critics have tended to agree with the view expressed by J. W. H. Atkins in *Literary Criticism in Antiquity* (1934/1952): "Cicero was protesting against the narrowing of the province of rhetoric, attempting also to restore something of its earlier scope and vitality....And in this aim he was following in the steps of Isocrates" (Vol. 2, p. 23). A major cluster of ideas presents the picture of a rhetoric that has declined through history to the point that the bounds of this art are considered too constraining to achieve excellence. Fired by the spirit of Isocrates, speakers try to suggest the scope of a more encompassing rhetoric. This cluster of ideas is not presented without opposition, however. Another cluster of ideas suggests the extent to which minds alert to the narrowing of rhetoric can perpetuate and even further that narrowness.

Cicero associated Isocrates with that ideal scope that has been lost in the course of history. For instance, in *Brutus*, another of Cicero's (trans. 1939/1971) works on oratory, the narrator—again representing Cicero—suggests that Isocrates is superior to his predecessors and credits him with a fullness or scope superior to that of anyone since (viii,32). In *De Oratore*, the narrator calls Isocrates "that eminent father of eloquence" (II.iii.10), and Antonius, in a list of orators to be imitated, emphasizes Isocrates more than anyone else: "Then behold! there arose Isocrates, the Master of all rhetoricians, from whose school, as from the Horse of Troy, none but leaders emerged" (II.xxii.94).

Crassus, in *De Oratore*, attributes the blame for the narrowing of rhetoric to Plato and Socrates, whom he only knows through Plato's dialogues. He longs for the kind of reunification of rhetoric and ethics and politics that constitutes Isocratean education and attacks Socrates and his followers for the split between rhetoric and philosophy:

> The older masters down to Socrates used to combine with their theory of rhetoric the whole of the study and the science of everything that concerns morals and conduct and ethics and politics; it was subsequently...that the two groups of students were separated from one another, by Socrates and then similarly by all the Socratic schools. (III.xix.72–73)

Crassus does not, as I do, attribute some share of the blame for the split between rhetoric and philosophy to Isocrates.

Crassus suggests that what remains for the rhetoricians after the split is something trifling and diminished: "we have been ousted from our own estate and left in occupation of a trifling little property, and that contested" (III.xxvii.108). Crassus perceives the ouster as forcible, stemming from Plato, and seems to find the restriction of rhetoric to judicial and deliberative matters too confining:

> There were many others besides, of distinguished fame as philosophers, by all of whom, with one voice as it were, I perceived that the orator was driven from the helm of State, shut out from all learning and knowledge of more important things, and thrust down and locked up exclusively in law-courts and petty little assemblies....But I was neither in agreement with these men, nor with the author and originator of such discussions, who spoke with far more weight and eloquence than all of them—I mean Plato—whose *Gorgias* I read with close attention. (I.x.46–47)

This statement reflects a clear awareness of Plato's efforts to diminish rhetoric through definitional exclusion.

Crassus claims that the province of rhetoricians should include "pronouncements on the subjects of justice and duty and the constitutional government of states, in short, the entire field of practical philosophy" (Cicero, trans. 1942/1949, III.xxxi.122-23). He characterizes the split between rhetoric and philosophy as a separation of speaking from thinking. Although initially the whole study and practice of the liberal sciences is entitled "philosophy," according to Crassus, "Socrates robbed them of this general designation, and in his discussions separated the science of wise thinking from that of elegant speaking, though in reality they are closely linked together" (III.xvi.60). Socrates is inclined toward this separation by his low opinion of rhetoric (III.xvi.59–60). Crassus perceives the division between philosophy and rhetoric as a change for the worse and promotes a reunification that once again, as in the work of Isocrates, makes philosophy and rhetoric synonymous: "At this stage I give full leave to anybody who wishes, to apply the title of orator to a philosopher who imparts to us an abundant command of facts and of language, or alternatively I shall raise no obstacle if he prefers to designate as a philosopher the orator whom I on my side am now describing as possessing wisdom combined with eloquence" (III.xxxv.142).

If Plato's Socrates has a low opinion of rhetoric, speakers in *De Oratore* follow Isocrates in proclaiming rhetoric the crown of education. The narrator remarks about Rome: "in this city of our own assuredly no studies have ever had a more vigorous life than those having to do with the art of speaking" (I.iii.13). Antonius calls eloquence the "governing force in every tranquil and free community" (II.viii.33). Crassus makes equally strong claims for the art of discourse: "In every free nation, and most of all in communities which have attained the enjoyment of peace and tranquillity, this one art has always flourished above the rest and ever reigned supreme." For Crassus, as for Isocrates, the art of discourse has played the chief role in advancing civilization (I.iii.30–34).

At times Crassus calls for a rhetoric with a scope that echoes Isocrates at his best. Like Isocrates, he attacks contemporaries who belittle rhetoric through inadequate treatment. He considers them exceedingly foolish persons, as they only write about the classification of cases and the elementary rules and the methods of stating the facts; whereas eloquence is so potent a force that it embraces the origin and operation and developments of all things, all the virtues and duties, all the natural principles governing the morals and minds and life of mankind, and also determines their customs and laws and rights, and controls the government of the state. (III.xx.75–76)

Crassus uses the word *eloquence* for rhetoric and clearly tries to extend its scope. Orators must be familiar with a wide range of studies: poetry, history, the common law, the ways of the Senate, political philosophy, the rights of allies, treaties and conventions, and the policy of empire (I.xxxiv.158–159). Cicero's narrator agrees with Crassus about the scope of the studies essential to the ideal orator: "no man has ever succeeded in achieving splendour and excellence in oratory...without taking all knowledge for his province" (II.i.5).

In expressing the importance of the scope of the studies essential to the ideal orator, Crassus attacks divisions that would separate the orator from any of his needs. He not only criticizes divisions such as those between rhetoric and philosophy or rhetoric and ethics, but also warns against the separation of content from form. He argues that we cannot separate "the topics of oratory" from "the proper method of embellishing them." To do so is to separate "from one another things that cannot really stand apart." Crassus argues against separation, division, and specialization generally: "nowadays we are deluged not only with the notions of the vulgar but also with the opinions of the half-educated, who find it easier to deal with matters that they cannot grasp in their entirety if they split them up and take them piecemeal, and who separate words from thoughts as one might sever body from mind—and neither process can take place without disaster" (III.vi.24). He later elaborates by speaking of the losses "that have been inflicted on the wide domain of science by its being split up into separate departments" (III.xxxiii.132–133). Such an attack on specialization stands in stark contrast to Aristotle's support for intellectual partitioning.

Crassus attempts to capture that fullness of vision—that all-encompassing scope for rhetoric—that is essential to its success:

In my own view the great men of the past, having a wider mental grasp, had also a far deeper insight than our mind's eye can achieve, when they asserted that all this universe above us and below is one single whole, and is held together by a single force and harmony of nature; for there exists no class of things which can stand by itself, severed from the rest, or which the rest can dispense with and yet be able to preserve their own force and everlasting existence. (III.v.20)

This emphasis on an all-inclusive vision is shared by Cicero's narrator, who claims that rhetoric has no delimited territory within whose borders it is enclosed (II.i.5).

Other ideas in *De Oratore* and elsewhere in Cicero's works, however, have the potential to perpetuate and even further the narrowness of the ideas that I have highlighted from Plato and Aristotle. In fact, early in his career, Cicero may have regarded Aristotle more highly than Isocrates. In *De Inventione*, a work from Cicero's (trans. 1949/1976) youth, we catch a glimpse of how profoundly the young Cicero was influenced by Aristotle:

> Aristotle collected the early books on rhetoric...and wrote them out in plain language....And he so surpassed the original authorities in charm and beauty that... everyone who wishes to know what their doctrines are, turns to Aristotle. (II.ii.6–7)

That strong influence is borne out by a comparison of the theories in Aristotle's *Rhetoric* and Cicero's *De Inventione*.

Isocrates is given his due, however, as the second major influence on the youthful Cicero: "From another fountain head has come a stream of teachers of rhetoric who have also done much to improve oratory....For in Aristotle's day there was a great and famous teacher of oratory named Isocrates,...I have...found many treatises on the art by his pupils and by those who carried on his doctrines." Even the youthful Cicero understood the differences between Aristotle and Isocrates; he saw them as belonging to opposing sects: "These two opposing sects (as we may call them), one busy with philosophy, but devoting some attention to the art of rhetoric as well, the other entirely devoted to the study and teaching of oratory, were fused into one group by later teachers who took into their own books from both sources what they thought was correct" (II.ii.7–9). Cicero saw no problem with an eclecticism that combined opposing sects; he worked the same way himself.

The older Cicero was far more wary about both philosophy and Aristotle. In *De Oratore*, we find ambivalent attitudes about philosophy. Crassus calls philosophy "mighty and arrogant" (I.xliii.193). He prefers the authority and usefulness of the Twelve Tables, the earliest code of Roman laws, to the entire corpus of ancient philosophy (I.xliii.195). He notes that philosophers have a tendency "to despise and look down on" orators (III.xxi.80). Still, as has been suggested, one set of ideas in *De Oratore* acknowledges the orator's need for knowledge developed by philosophy and calls for the reunification of philosophy and rhetoric.

Attitudes toward Aristotle in *De Oratore* are also ambivalent. On the one hand, Aristotle is not excepted from Crassus's general criticisms of philosophy and philosophers. On the other hand, Scaevola argues: "Aristotle and Theophrastus wrote not only better but also much more [on the subject of rhetoric] than all the teachers of rhetoric put together" (I.x.43). While Antonius admits Aristotle's scorn for rhetoric, he praises his ideas about the art: "he surveyed these concerns of the art of rhetoric, which he disdained, with that same keen insight, by which he had discerned the essential nature of all things"

(II.xxxviii.160). If the views of Scaevola and Antonius do not carry the same weight as those of Crassus, Crassus, while criticizing philosophy and philosophers, reflects his own high opinion of Aristotle by incorporating many of Aristotle's ideas in his theory of rhetoric.

If, at times, the rhetoric described in *De Oratore* seems unlimited, participants in the dialogue are quick to hedge. Both Scaevola and Antonius offer reservations about Crassus's view of rhetoric as unlimited. Scaevola states: "as for the claim you made...that whatever the topic under discussion, the orator could deal with it in complete fullness—this...I would not have borne with, and I should be at the head of a multitude who would...fight you by injunction...for so wantonly making forcible entry upon other people's possessions" (I.x.41). Antonius agrees: "the orator, since it is he whom we are studying, I myself do not picture as Crassus did, who I thought included, under the single vocation and title of orator, omniscience in every topic and every art" (I.xlix.213). In later addressing Crassus, he reinforces this point: "all else that you have brought together from various and dissimilar pursuits and arts, though you yourself have attained everything, I nevertheless regard as lying outside the strict business and function of an orator" (I.lxi.262). Antonius asserts that the orator needs to focus on the essential: "the essential needs of an orator are many and weighty and hard to come by, so that I would not dissipate his energy over too wide a field of study" (I.lix.250).

Antonius criticizes Crassus for equating rhetoric with statesmanship, and, in contrast with Isocrates and in line with Plato and Aristotle, attempts to separate these activities. He claims that the statesman Marcus Scaurus relies on "his knowledge of higher politics" rather than the "art of oratory," a distinction that excludes such knowledge from oratory. He adds:

> If a man is capable in both ways, such as the originator of national policy who is also a good senator, he is not just for that reason an orator; nor did the accomplished orator, who happens also to be outstanding in public administration, attain that special knowledge through his fluency in speaking. There is a vast difference between these gifts, and far apart are they sundered. (I.xlix.214–215)

Antonius distinguishes between statesmanship and oratory by associating statesmanship with knowledge and oratory with fluency in speaking.

Also limiting the scope of rhetoric in *De Oratore* is a large complex of ideas focusing on forensic and deliberative oratory, on speeches delivered by lawyers and statesmen. Exceptions to this focus can easily be found, of course. Crassus calls Plato a "consummate orator" (I.xi.47). And Antonius, noting the focus on forensic and deliberative rhetoric in Rome, claims that historians dominated the field of eloquence in Greece (II.xiii.55). Antonius mentions two students of Isocrates as examples: "from what I may call that most famous factory of rhetoricians, there issued a pair of outstanding talent in Theopompus and Ephorus, who betook themselves to history at the instance of their teacher Isocrates" (II.xiii.57).

Still, as indicated, Antonius does suggest a focus on forensic and deliberative rhetoric in Rome. And Crassus does not appear to question the Aristotelian division of rhetoric into forensic, deliberative, and epideictic categories (I.xxi,141). In fact, for all that Crassus concludes that rhetoricians need philosophy to perform well, in some passages he draws sharp lines between the performance of some philosophers and the ideal orator who is the focus of his attention:

> But from among the systems still surviving, the philosophy that has undertaken the championship of pleasure, although some may accept it as true, is nevertheless quite remote from the man whom we are seeking and whom we wish to be the political leader of the nation, guiding the government and pre-eminent for wisdom and eloquence in the Senate, in the assembly of the people and in public causes. (III.xvii.63)

Clearly, Crassus is not examining all of the forms of discourse in which the mind expresses itself; he is not helping us with all of the things done with intelligence; he is not enabling us to make wise choices about everything we do or say; he is not advising us on the best course in all of our speech and actions. On the contrary, he sees the philosophies of pleasure as remote from his concern. Implicit in this passage is an acceptance of the Platonic opposition of the life of philosophy to activities such as speaking in the courtroom or otherwise engaging in public affairs. Crassus' ideal orator might be able to use the ideas of philosophers, but he is primarily concerned about their use in judicial and political oratory and not in philosophy.

This focus helps us to improve our understanding of Crassus's complaints about the division of philosophy from rhetoric, of wise thinking from elegant speaking. Crassus is not concerned about philosophy and wise thinking in and of themselves; he is only concerned about them to the extent that they are useful in oratory. He is concerned about being shut up in courtrooms and assemblies without access to those areas of philosophy relevant to oratory. Such a focus enables him to exclude—at least in large part—some of the provinces of thought from oratory:

> Since philosophy is divided into three branches, which respectively deal with the mysteries of nature, with the subtleties of dialectic, and with human life and conduct, let us quit claim to the first two, by way of concession to our indolence, but unless we keep our hold on the third, which has ever been the orator's province, we shall leave the orator no sphere wherein to attain greatness. For which reason this division of philosophy, concerned with human life and manners, must all of it be mastered by the orator; as for the other matters, even though he has not studied them, he will still be able, whenever the necessity arises, to beautify them by his eloquence, if only they are brought to his notice and described to him. (I.xv.68–69)

Little wonder that Crassus finds no fault with Isocrates's exclusion of mathematics and science from rhetoric. Crassus himself rejects science and dialectic. Furthermore, since Crassus focuses so narrowly on oratory, his compass is not as broad as that of Isocrates, which includes governing households, managing affairs generally, and making decisions in any line of work. Finally, the end of the above quote should not escape our notice. Here, oratory has begun to turn into a process of beautifying something that already exists. Such a stance moves rhetoric toward a concern for presentation and distances it from the development of thought.

The focus on judicial and political oratory in *De Oratore* is sharpened by a concern for the audiences of such oratory. This concern leads to other exclusions. For instance, Antonius expresses reluctance about the appropriateness of definitions for these audiences: "some lay down a rule that each side shall concisely define the debatable term, a proposition which I myself always think thoroughly childish" (II.xxv.108). The reason is clear: "the definition cannot reach the understanding and reason of the arbitrator, as it slips by him before he has taken it in" (II.xxv.109). Antonius seems to be making the same distinction in excluding formal argument from oratory. He states that the orator must speak "in the same way as the founders of rules of law, statutes and civil communities spoke, frankly and lucidly, with no formal train of argument or barren verbal controversy" (II.xvi.68). Antonius's concern for the audiences of judicial and political oratory is shared by Crassus, who claims that all of the language used in public speaking must be "adapted to the general understanding of the crowd" (I.xxiii.108–109). Implicit in the recommendations of both Antonius and Crassus, then, is an agreement with Aristotle that orators should avoid the abstruse, all intricate reasoning beyond the grasp of the majority. Excluded from oratory is any kind of discourse beyond the average comprehension.

If the emphasis on judicial and political oratory in *De Oratore* is strengthened by a focus on the audiences for such oratory, it is further strengthened by a concern for procedures peculiar to these kinds of rhetoric. For instance, Antonius describes his approach to courtroom oratory:

> When I am launched on a case and have to the best of my ability passed all the facts under consideration, having discerned and ascertained the arguments that belong to the case and also the topics calculated to win the favor of the court and those adapted to arouse its emotions, I then decide what are the good and what the bad points in the case of each of the parties...my own method in a speech usually is to take the good points of my case and elaborate these...,while any bad part or weakness in my case I leave on one side. (II.lxxii.291–292)

Like Aristotle, then, Antonius's goal in his rhetoric is that kind of persuasion designed to overcome resistance and prompt a choice. Furthermore, Antonius is not after the best decision in a case; he is not concerned about ultimate justice. On the contrary, in line with Aristotelian thinking, he finds himself on a particular side in a case—an attorney for the prosecution or defense—and his focus is on the means to support that side. We are not surprised to see Antonius use Aristotle's classification of means. Aristotle classifies the means of persuasion into logical, ethical, and emotional arguments, and Antonius does the same (II.xxvii.115–116). What Antonius excludes with his focus, then, are all of the goals other than persuasion that I have explored as well as a consideration of the impact of the ends of discourse on humanity.

Crassus shares this approach to courtroom oratory, and his association of this view with Aristotle is telling:

> If there has really ever been a person who was able in Aristotelian fashion to speak on both sides about every subject and by means of knowing Aristotle's rules to reel off two speeches on opposite sides on every case...,and who to that method adds the experience and practice in speaking indicated, he would be the one and only true and perfect orator. (III.xxi.80)

Such an approach, however, has ethical implications. If the orator's goal is limited to winning for his client and himself, then the orator can conceivably assume positions that can be detrimental to ultimate justice and the good of humanity—subject to the charges of immorality made by Plato. Eloquent men are capable of damage because of their absence of scope. Their positions are determined by their own interests and not necessarily the broader interests of humanity. Ethics is excluded from the notion of rhetorical excellence.

Since both Antonius and Crassus view the orator through the realistic lens of an attorney, their view of rhetoric is limited by the actual practice of attorneys. The studies of attorneys tend to be prompted by the cases they confront. Experts conduct original research in a particular field, and attorneys avail themselves of this research if they need it for a case, adapting it for their purposes. Unlike the philosopher of Isocrates, who determines what to say or do, the orator of Antonius takes what is already said and weaves it skillfully into his discourse. Antonius states:

> I hold that all things relating to the intercourse of fellow-citizens and the ways of mankind, or concerned with everyday life, the political system, our own corporate society, the common sentiments of humanity, natural inclinations and morals must be mastered by the orator; if not in the sense that he is to advise on these matters one by one, as the philosophers do, yet so far at least as to enable him to weave them skilfully into his discourse. (II.xvi.68)

Obtaining content is not that difficult for an attorney: "anything in the law that is of use for a particular case, may be fetched, as hurriedly as you please, from experts or text-books!" (I.lix.252).

Such a stance assumes a content-form split, and we might expect Crassus to oppose it. After all, as already indicated, Crassus claims that everything in the universe is interrelated; he attacks separation, division, and specialization in general. According to him, eloquence has no delimited territory and embraces all creation, operation, and development. He condemns the split between rhetoric and philosophy, between speaking and thinking, between content and style. But Crassus is not always against division: "Therefore whatever the theme, from whatever art or whatever branch of knowledge it be taken, the orator, just as if he had got up the case for a client, will state it better and more gracefully than the actual discoverer and the specialist" (I.xi.51–52). Crassus actually elaborates on this sharp distinction between discovery and presentation:

> The speaker will not be able to achieve what he wants by his words, unless he has gained profound insight into the characters of men, and the whole range of human nature, and those motives whereby our souls are spurred on or turned back. All this is considered to be the special province of philosophers, nor will the orator, if he take my advice, resist their claim; but when he has granted their knowledge of these things, since they have devoted all their labour to that alone, still he will assert his own claim to the oratorical treament of them, which without that knowledge of theirs is nothing at all. (I.xii.53–54)

Crassus concludes his elaboration with a significant emphasis on style: "For this is the essential concern of the orator, as I have often said before,—a style that is dignified and graceful and in conformity with the general modes of thought and judgement" (I.xii.54).

In addition to style, Crassus places great emphasis on delivery. In fact, he considers it dominant:

> Delivery, I assert, is the dominant factor in oratory; without delivery the best speaker cannot be of any account at all, and a moderate speaker with a trained delivery can often outdo the best of them. The story goes that when Demosthenes was asked what is the first thing in speaking, he assigned the first role to delivery, and also the second, and also the third. (III.lvi.213)

According to Crassus, style and delivery are among five tasks confronting the orator; the others are invention, organization, and memory (I.xxxi.142). Crassus, then, has added memory to the four tasks described by Aristotle.

One reason that Antonius gives for the emphasis of orators on style is that the development of stylistic excellence is far more difficult than the determination of content:

> While in our cases we have these two objectives, first what to say, and secondly how to say it, the former, which seems to be art pure and simple, cannot indeed dispense with art, though it needs but ordinary skill to discover what ought to be said; but it is in the latter that the orator's godlike power and excellence are discerned, that is, his delivery of what he has to say in a style elegant, copious and diversified. (II.xxvii.120)

This sharp distinction between "what to say" and "how to say it" also reinforces or promotes a content-form split, a discovery-presentation split. Style is conceived as the embellishment of something that already exists. We find no awareness in Cicero of the possibility of stylistic techniques serving as a powerful source of invention, of discovering content.

If discovery or invention can be relatively ignored because it is so easy, that is a happiness for the orator because he has so little time. According to Antonius, the demands of oratory limit the breadth of learning possible. A statesman is simply too busy to emulate philosophers in the scope of their studies:

> The copiousness of their learning and the wide range of their art I am so far from despising that in fact I ardently admire these: yet for ourselves, busied in the public life of this community, it is enough to know and give expression to such things concerning human characters as are not alien to human character. (1.11.219)

Like Crassus, then, Antonius limits the scope of the orator to learning important to oratory. Arguments such as these by Antonius have provided the foundation for the success of Aristotle in promoting specialization in Western civilization.

Cicero, then, seems fired by the spirit of Isocrates, yet imprisoned by the intellect of Aristotle. We find contradictory impulses in a work like *De Oratore*. No scholar would disagree with George Kennedy's (1972) assertion, in *The Art of Rhetoric in the Roman World*, that "the central question of *De oratore*" is "the extent to which the orator needs a wide general knowledge" (p. 217). That Cicero did indeed challenge specialization, division, and narrowness seems undeniable. Cicero's narrator, while contributing only a few passages to the dialogue, and Cicero's spokesman Crassus, while often ambivalent in his statements, both promote a wider scope for rhetoric. Furthermore, much of Crassus's eloquence against narrowness and in behalf of scope is placed emphatically in Book III—toward the end of *De Oratore*. Scholars have been correct in drawing parallels between the arguments for scope in *De Oratore* and what we find in the works of Isocrates. H.I. Marrou (1956), in *A History of Education in Antiquity*, described Cicero's appeal to the youth of his day as follows: "Cicero...tried hard to enlarge their conception of the ideal orator, harking back to Isocrates' original ideal in all its noble simplicity. He wanted the orator's training to be based on the widest possible culture" (p. 285). Lester Thonssen and A. Craig Baird (1965) agreed: "Cicero tried...to restore rhetoric to something of its earlier scope and vitality." He was "'protesting against the narrowing of the province' of the speaking art....In this effort Cicero was influenced and guided by the doctrines of Isocrates" (p. 142). What we find in *De Oratore*, then, is the notion of historical regress or primitivism; that is, Cicero recognized that there had been a change, that the change had been negative in its impact, and that the ideal lay somewhere in the past. Cicero can be credited with a major contribution to the history of ideas—a recognition of the confinements of definition and the dangers of their institutionalization in society.

Twentieth-century readers, however, have tended to underestimate the importance of this issue. For instance, M. L. Clarke in his *Rhetoric at Rome* (1953) agreed that the controversies concerning Cicero centered on this point: "whether the general questions of a philosophical or quasi-philosophical nature which the orator might often have occasion to handle belonged to the province of rhetoric or were rather the property of philosophy" (p. 55). But Clarke showed no awareness whatsoever of the importance of these controversies: "the controversies of the first century B.C., important though they no doubt seemed at the time, are of minor interest today" (p. 55). What Clarke did not realize was that Cicero, in challenging the specialization, the division, the narrowing that had their origin in Plato and Aristotle, was raising one of the most serious issues confronting the 20th century—that humans working in defined communities do not have sufficient breadth, range, or scope to address their problems.

For all the calls to breadth in *De Oratore*, however, the work also has the potential to reinforce and even further the thrusts toward specialization, division, and narrowness that have their origin largely in Plato and Aristotle. These thrusts are often supported by the expressed views of participants in the dialogue other than Crassus and the narrator, especially Antonius. It might be argued that these views are only expressed as a foil to enable Crassus to promote greater scope in approaching oratory. Certainly, this argument has some validity; but many of these views are allowed to stand unanswered, and, as we have seen, Crassus himself uses language that strengthens specialization, division, and narrowness. Crassus himself draws lines between philosophers and rhetoricians. Crassus himself allows science and dialectic to lie outside the realm of rhetoric. Crassus himself associates oratory with presentation and distinguishes it from discovery. Crassus himself focuses on judicial and political oratory—with a concomitant rejection of the abstruse based on audience. Crassus himself emphasizes adeptness in using the means of persuasion to argue both sides of questions. And Crassus himself associates oratory with style and delivery and assigns the topics of discourse to philosophy and other disciplines. Crassus's own statements, then, sometimes give added weight to those of Antonius and other participants—even though they are contradicted elsewhere.

To some degree, then, Cicero can be charged with ambivalence in *De Oratore*. While much of the thrust of the work does indeed promote scope, that thrust is weakened by another thrust in the direction of specialization, division, and narrowness. The extent to which that ambivalence was intentional is unclear. Certainly, Cicero's love of debate, suppleness of intellect, and skepticism played some role. But it also seems likely that Cicero—at least in part—was limited both by his focus on judicial and deliberative oratory and his unwitting acceptance of categories of thought originating in Plato and Aristotle. George Kennedy (1972), in *The Art of Rhetoric in the Roman World*, has expressed a similar sentiment: "Cicero...had difficulty escaping from the rigid categories of the ancient mind" (p. 227).

Whatever Cicero's intention, he did not succeed—beyond influencing Quintilian, some Italian humanists, and a few others—in promoting greater scope in the approach to rhetoric. Marrou (1956), in discussing the success of Cicero's drive to base the orator's training on the widest possible culture, wrote: "Cicero convinced neither his young contemporaries nor succeeding generations. Nor was Quintilian listened to either, when, a century later, he taught practically the same doctrine" (p. 285).

QUINTILIAN

Cicero's *De Oratore* was not the only Roman work in classical antiquity to raise the issue of the scope of rhetoric. About 150 years later, Quintilian (trans. 1920/1980) completed his *Institutio Oratoria* (94 or 95 C.E.)—a work that imitates *De Oratore* in many ways and also raises the issue. In contrast to *De Oratore*, however, the *Institutio Oratoria* is not a dialogue, an example of dialectic with ideas in combat and the author's point of view not always clear. Rather, the *Institutio Oratoria* is a sustained argument. Quintilian presented ideas in coherent relation within a system and always tried to let the reader know where he stood. Still, the *Institutio Oratoria* does not escape ambivalence. While it resembles *De Oratore* in containing some ideas that call for the broadening of rhetoric, it also resembles *De Oratore* in containing other ideas that limit the scope of rhetoric. Quintilian was strongly influenced by Cicero and—like him—limited by ideas expressed in works by Plato and Aristotle. He was also limited by developments in the Roman Empire of his time.

With the advent of the Empire, political or deliberative rhetoric found little encouragement—one of the forces inclining Quintilian to focus narrowly on forensic or judicial rhetoric. Quintilian's own experience as a pleader in the courts no doubt reinforced this focus. As a result, as Vickers (1988/1990) suggested, "Quintilian goes into more detail about specific courtroom techniques than any other classical rhetorician, and his work is an invaluable guide to Roman legal practices" (p. 38). In his presentation of legal rhetoric, Quintilian was also influenced by the extensive development of the technical side of Roman law. Marrou (1956) wrote:

> The tremendous development of the technical side of Roman law had made it a matter for specialists, and there had developed a kind of division of labour between the jurist and the advocate. The advocate had technical advisors...who...supplied him with a file of the legal arguments. His own particular task was to present these effectively. (p. 289)

Such a division tended to direct Quintilian's attention away from the development of technical arguments and toward techniques of presenting such arguments.

The tension between ideas that promote scope and those that limit scope has not prevented Quintilian's *Institutio Oratoria* from evoking some extraordinary praise down through the centuries. In 1759, John Ward, in his *System of Oratory*, wrote: Quintilian's "*Institutions* are so comprehensive, and writen with that great exactness and judgement; that they are generally allowed to be the most perfect work of this kind" (Vol. 1, pp. 14–15). In 1783, Hugh Blair, in his *Lectures on Rhetoric and Belles-Lettres*, wrote: "of all the Antient Writers on the subject of oratory, the most instructive, and most useful, is Quinctilian" (Vol. 2, p. 244). And a current writer such as George Kennedy (1972), in *The Art of Rhetoric in the Roman World*, could be equally generous in his praise: "The twelve books *De institutio oratoria* are the finest statement of ancient rhetorical theory" (p. 496).

Quintilian echoed Isocrates and Cicero in the high stature that he accorded rhetoric. He gave oratory credit for the development of cities and the institution of law (II.xvi.8–10). According to him, oratory was "the queen of all the world" (I.xii.18), "the fairest gift of god to man" (XII.xi.30), and "the noblest and most sublime of tasks" (II.xvii.3). Unlike Aristotle, he did not consider rhetoric less real than other subjects; he did not subsume rhetoric beneath politics and then subsume politics beneath theoretical science. For Quintilian, as for Isocrates and Cicero's Crassus, rhetoric was the crown of education.

Quintilian praised both Isocrates and Cicero. He called Isocrates "the prince of instructors, whose works proclaim his eloquence no less than his pupils testify to his excellence as a teacher" (II,viii.11). The breadth of Isocrates was reflected in the achievements of his students: "The pupils of Isocrates were eminent in every branch of study" (III.i.14). In oratory, they dominated: "it is to the school of Isocrates that we owe the greatest orators" (XII.x.22). But Quintilian reserved his highest praise for Cicero: "it was Cicero who shed the greatest light not only on the practice but on the theory of oratory; for he stands alone among Romans as combining the gift of actual eloquence with that of teaching the art" (III.i.20–22). He asserted that "the name of Cicero has come to be regarded...as the name of eloquence itself." He encouraged us to imitate Cicero: "Let us, therefore, fix our eyes on him, take him as our pattern, and let the student realize that he has made real progress if he is a passionate admirer of Cicero" (X.i.112).

Certainly Quintilian echoed Cicero's call for a more encompassing rhetoric. Like Cicero, Quintilian recalled a time when oratory and philosophy were one subject and the orator and philosopher one person:

> These two branches of knowledge were, as Cicero has clearly shown, so closely united, not merely in theory but in practice, that the same men were regarded as uniting the qualifications of orator and philosopher. Subsequently this single branch of study split up into its component parts, and thanks to the indolence of its professors was regarded as consisting of several distinct subjects. (trans. 1920/1980, I.Pr.13)

Quintilian rejected specialization, fragmentation, division. He ascribed the cause of this fragmentation to the laziness of professors.

Quintilian's desire for the reunification of oratory and philosophy becomes a plaintive and longing cry at one point:

> O that the day may dawn when the perfect orator of our heart's desire shall claim for his own possession that science that has lost the affection of mankind through the arrogance of its claims and the vices of some that have brought disgrace upon its virtues, and shall restore it to its place in the domain of eloquence, as though he had been victorious in a trial for the restoration of stolen goods! (XII.ii.9–10)

Quintilian's judgment about contemporary attitudes toward philosophy here should not be ignored. He claimed that some philosophers had not been virtuous, that philosophy generally had made arrogant claims, and that these developments had diminished the attractiveness of the subject. It was time once again for the orator to assume the title of "philosopher": "Let our ideal orator then be such as to have a genuine title to the name of philosopher" (I.Pr.18).

Orators need philosophy in order to achieve excellence in their oratory: "those fields of knowledge, which were annexed by philosophy on their abandonment by oratory, once were ours and without the knowledge of all such things there can be no perfect eloquence" (I.x.11). Quintilian devoted special attention to that part of philosophy called ethics. Like Cicero's Crassus, he recalled a time in the past when ethics was subsumed under rhetoric. He blamed orators for abandoning ethics and criticized philosophers for usurping the subject (I.Pr.13–14). He paralleled Cicero's Crassus in urging orators to include the study of human conduct in their education once again. He indicated the importance of an awareness of ethics in epideictic, deliberative, and forensic rhetoric, calling oratory "a virtue" (II.xx.8–9). In calling oratory a virtue, that is, in including ethics in the very notion of rhetorical excellence, Quintilian went beyond Cicero and Aristotle and gave ethics an importance in rhetoric not unlike what we discover in Isocrates.

Quintilian's very definition of rhetoric made oratory a virtue. He understood that "the common definition of rhetoric" was "the power of persuading" (II.xiv.3). Quintilian cited many authorities, Aristotle among them, as evidence: Cicero in more than one passage defines "the duty of an orator as 'speaking in a persuasive manner'"; Apollodorus asserts "that the first and all-important task of forensic oratory is *to persuade the judge and lead his mind to the conclusions desired by the speaker*"; Aristotle "says '*rhetoric is the power of discovering all means of persuading by speech*'"; and Cornelius Celsus "defines the end of rhetoric as *to speak persuasively on any doubtful subject within the field of politics*" (II.xv.5–22). Quintilian explicitly rejected such definitions and made persuasion secondary to virtue; rhetoric, for him, was "*the science of speaking well*" (II.xv.34). For him, "the first and greatest of the aims we set before us" was not persuasion, but rather "that we shall be good men" (XII.xi.11). In the final paragraph of *Institutio Oratoria*, in the climactic concluding position of the book, Quintilian stated that his primary goal was to produce in students "the will to do well" (XII.xi.31).

Quintilian noted that those who make persuasion the orator's primary goal include bad men within the ranks of oratory: "some think that even bad men may be called orators....These persons have as a rule held that the task of oratory lies in persuasion or speaking in a persuasive manner: for this is within the power of a bad man no less than a good" (II.xiv.2–3). Quintilian excepted himself from this position: "others, of whom I am one, restrict the name of orator and the art itself to those who are good" (II.xiv.1–2).

Clearly, winning was less important to Quintilian than virtue: "our orator and his art, as we define it, are independent of results. The speaker aims at victory, it is true, but if he speaks well, he has lived up to the ideals of his art, even if he is defeated" (II.xvii.23–24). Quintilian cited the example of Socrates as someone who rightfully chose to preserve the integrity of his character rather than save his life through compromise (XI.i.9–10). Since Quintilian saw most arguments as having a good and bad side, virtue prevents a good man from being able to argue on both sides of a question: "it can scarcely happen even under the most exceptional circumstances that an orator, that is to say, a good man, will speak indifferently on either side" (II.xvii.31–32). Given that Aristotle often suggested how to argue both sides in a case and Cicero's Crassus associates this ability with his ideal orator, Quintilian was directly repudiating them here.

In making rhetoric a virtue, Quintilian was attempting to respond to Plato's charge that rhetoric is immoral. He claimed that Plato's charge was an attack not on rhetoric as an ideal, but only on rhetoric as it was practiced in his day:

> It is only rhetoric as practised in...[his] own day that is condemned by Plato...: rhetoric in itself he regards as a genuine and honourable thing....It is clear therefore that Plato does not regard rhetoric as an evil, but holds that true rhetoric is impossible for any save a just and good man. (II.xv.27–29)

We are not surprised to see him call Plato the best of the philosophers: "Plato is supreme whether in acuteness of perception or in virtue of his divine gift of style" (X.i.81). Unlike Cicero, Quintilian did not censure Plato for initiating the division between philosophy and rhetoric. Nor did he appear to see the fundamental differences between Platonic rhetorics and the rhetoric of the *Institutio Oratoria*. Vickers (1988/1990) tried to absolve Quintilian of ignorance here: "Quintilian can reach this position only by knowingly distorting the sense of what Plato writes, at such length, and with such reiteration. Perhaps Quintilian thought that by claiming Plato as a friend of rhetoric he would enhance its stature and credibility" (p. 169).

Like Cicero's Crassus, Quintilian suggested the scope of an adequate rhetoric by detailing the studies essential to the ideal orator. For instance, he echoed Isocrates in emphasizing the value of history. Quintilian noted "the advantage derived from the knowledge of historical facts and precedents, with which it is most desirable that our orator should be acquainted; for such knowledge will save him from having to acquire all his evidence from his client and will enable him to draw much that is germane to his case from the careful study of antiquity" (X.i.34). He also echoed Isocrates in perceiving the poets as helpful: "Theophrastus says that the reading of poets is of great service to the orator, and has rightly been followed in this view by many. For the poets will give us inspiration as regards the matter, sublimity of language, the power to excite every kind of emotion, and the appropriate treatment of character" (X.i.27). Even geometry and music should not be ignored (I.x.6).

Some subjects such as literature, geometry, and music should be taught before boys are handed over to the teacher of rhetoric, while other subjects—such as ethics—are the province of the teacher of rhetoric himself. Together, these subjects cover considerable ground: "The orator's task covers a large ground, is extremely varied and develops some new aspect almost every day, so that the last word on the subject will never have been said" (II.xiii.17). The ground is so considerable that the rhetor can countenance no distractions: "if the intelligence is to be concentrated on such a vast subject as eloquence it must be free from all other distractions, among which must be included even those preoccupations which are free from blame" (XII.i.5). His effort must be extraordinary: "He must burn the midnight oil, persevere to the end and grow pale with study" (VII.x.14).

In fact, the rhetor must work so hard and study so many subjects that Quintilian feared he may have frightened potential rhetors away:

> I fear, however, that I may be regarded as setting too lofty an ideal for the orator by insisting that he should be a good man skilled in speaking, or as imposing too many subjects of study on the learner. For in addition to the many branches of knowledge which have to be studied in boyhood and the traditional rules of eloquence, I have enjoined the study of morals and of civil law, so that I am afraid that even those who have regarded these things as essential to my theme, may be appalled at the delay which they impose and abandon all hope of achievement before they have put my precepts to the test. (XII.xi.9)

The education required by the orator is clearly of formidable scope, and the *Institutio Oratoria* articulates more fully than any other book in classical antiquity the details of that scope. The very scope of the book buttresses the scope of rhetoric. As Thomas M. Conley suggested in *Rhetoric in the European Tradition* (1990), the *Institutio Oratoria* "is one of the fullest records of rhetorical lore in the Isocratean-Ciceronian tradition ever written, as it covers in 12 books a program of education from the cradle to the grave" (p. 38).

If the *Institutio Oratoria*, like Cicero's *De Oratore*, contains much that promotes breadth in the approach to rhetoric, however, it also parallels *De Oratore* in containing ideas related to those in Plato and Aristotle that narrow the scope of rhetoric. Quintilian certainly praised Plato and Aristotle considerably. As already indicated, he considered Plato supreme among philosophers and praised Plato's perception and style. He criticized Aristotle's definition of rhetoric, yet his praise of Aristotle was lavish:

> I hesitate whether to praise him more for his knowledge, for the multitude of his writings, the sweetness of his style, the penetration revealed by his discoveries or the variety of the tasks which he essayed. (X.i.83)

Quintilian was apparently open to the ideas of Plato and Aristotle.

Quintilian accepted Aristotle's division of human activities into theoretical, practical, and productive—although Quintilian called them arts, whereas Aristotle called them sciences. Quintilian first described the theoretical arts:

> Some arts...are based on examination, that is to say on the knowledge and proper appreciation of things, as for instance, astronomy, which demands no action, but is content to understand the subject of its study; such arts are called *theoretical*. (II.xviii.1)

Quintilian associated the theoretical arts with examination, knowledge, and understanding; like Aristotle, he placed sciences such as astronomy in this category. Unlike Plato and Aristotle, Quintilian did not value the theoretical and contemplative over other kinds of activities.

Quintilian next described the practical arts: "Others again are concerned with action: this is their end, which is realised in action, so that, the action once performed, nothing more remains to do: these are arts we style *practical*" (II.xviii.1–2). For the most part, Quintilian saw rhetoric as belonging in this category (II.xviii.2–3). Quintilian followed Cicero in distinguishing the kinds of questions associated with action and those associated with knowledge: "Cicero distinguishes two kinds, the one concerned with *knowledge*, the other with *action*. Thus `Is the world governed by providence?' is a question of knowledge, while `Should we enter politics?' is a question of action" (III.v.6). One kind of question asks what is, while the other explores what to do. Quintilian called rhetoric, which is associated with action and questions about what to do, an "active or administrative art" (II.xviii.5). Quintilian's association of rhetoric with administration is not unlike Isocrates's association of philosophy or rhetoric with management.

Quintilian concluded his classification with the productive arts:

> Thirdly there are others which consist in producing a certain result and achieve their purpose in the completion of a visible task: such we style *productive*, and *painting* may be quoted as an illustration. (II.xviii.2)

While rhetoric is largely an active art, it can also be theoretical and productive. Orators sometimes withdraw from action into their private studies and enjoy the delights of literature, and they develop products when they write speeches and historical narratives (II.xviii.3–5).

Quintilian's suggestion that rhetoric could be associated with private affairs is strengthened by a passage about one of Socrates's arguments in Plato's *Phaedrus*:

> in the *Phaedrus* he clearly proves that rhetoric is concerned not merely with law-courts and public assemblies, but with private and domestic affairs as well: from which it is obvious that this was the view of Plato himself. (II.xxi.4–5)

If Quintilian paid lip service to the association of rhetoric with private affairs, however, he followed Isocrates and Cicero in emphasizing the association of rhetoric with public life. This emphasis became clear in his contrast of the activities of the ideal orator with the withdrawal of the philosopher. Quintilian perceived his ideal orator as "one who reveals himself as a true statesman, not in the discussions of the study, but in the actual practice and experience of life" (XII.ii.7–8). In stark contrast, philosophy "no longer moves in its true sphere of action and in the broad daylight of the forum, but has retired first to porches and gymnasia and finally to the gatherings of the schools" (XII.ii.8).

Indeed, Quintilian so focused on public address—that is, orations—that private deliberations were effectively, if not nominally, excluded from his consideration. He wrote: "the material of rhetoric is composed of everything that may be placed before it as a subject for speech" (II.xxi.4). If an orator does not need to speak about a subject, he need not concern himself about it (II.xxi.19). This focus on public address was intensified by Quintilian's acceptance of Aristotle's classification of the kinds of rhetoric into forensic, deliberative, and epideictic speeches. Unlike Isocrates, then, Quintilian was not examining all of the forms of discourse in which the mind expresses itself, not helping with all of the things done with intelligence, not making wise choices about everything we do or say, not advising us on the best course in all of our speech and actions. On the contrary, he was in Cicero's camp looking almost exclusively at public address.

Such a limited focus enabled Quintilian to contrast his ideal orator with experts in various kinds of subject matter:

> if the orator receive instruction from the builder or the musician, he will put forward what he has thus learned better than either, just as he will plead a case better than his client, once he has been instructed in it. The builder and the musician will, however, speak on the subject of their respective arts, if there should be any technical point which requires to be established. (II.xxi.16–17)

Quintilian was not concerned about advancing architecture and music in themselves; he was only concerned about them to the extent that they were useful in oratory. He followed Plato's Socrates, Aristotle, and Cicero's Crassus in so limiting the scope of the orator. He may have been influenced here by the division of labor in the courts of law between specialists in legal technicalities and forensic orators.

Not only did Quintilian focus on public address; he also favored a particular kind of public address. He favored what was impressive, praising Pericles for his ability "to thunder and lighten" (II.xvi.19), and such oratory requires large audiences (I.ii.29,31). Large audiences include many who are unable to grasp the abstruse, so Quintilian agreed with Aristotle and Cicero's Antonius and Crassus that language must be adapted to the general understanding of the crowd (III.viii,2). Such a stance accords well with Quintilian's view that technical points should be discussed by specialists, such as builders and musicians, and not orators.

Quintilian also followed Aristotle and Cicero's Antonius and Crassus in his emphasis on that kind of persuasion designed to overcome resistance and prompt a choice. It must be granted, as has already been suggested, that Quintilian explicitly rejected the equation of rhetoric with persuasion found in the works of Aristotle and Cicero. The scope of the ideal orator must extend beyond the desire to win an argument, regardless of the impact of that argument on others. The ideal orator does not position himself indifferently on either side of an argument; rather, he must position himself only on that side that enables him to be a good man. It is better for the ideal orator to fail to be persuasive rather than to assume an unjust or unbecoming cause. The will to do well is more important than the will to persuade. Still, according to Quintilian, the desire to be expedient or persuasive does not often conflict with the desire to be becoming or of good character: "the expedient and the becoming will, as a rule, be identical in every kind of case" (XI.i.14). Although Quintilian's argument or position here could hardly be weaker, it enabled him to focus on persuasion in much the same way as Aristotle and Cicero—in fact, in even greater detail in many places.

Quintilian's emphasis on resistance in his notion of persuasion is strengthened by his extensive discussion of bases. According to Quintilian, "every question has its *basis*, since every question is based on assertion by one party and denial by another" (III.vi.7). A basis is a point around which an argument revolves, and an oration can have one or more bases. The ideal orator will choose that basis or those bases that will enable him to overcome his opponent. If Quintilian suggested that we should have goals other than persuasion, that virtuous behavior should take precedence, he did not pursue in any detail the ways in which we achieve good character, but rather focused his attention almost exclusively on the techniques of overcoming an opponent such as the discovery of bases. The incorporation of ethics is nominal rather than substantive—a response to Platonic attack rather than a careful broadening of the scope of rhetoric.

Quintilian's ideal orator acts like the attorney described by Cicero's Antonius and Crassus. His attention is directed by the cases he confronts. He studies those subjects "concerning which he has to speak, as occasion may demand, and will speak on those which he has studied" (II.xxi.15). Quintilian distinguished his position from one he attributed to Cicero. He cited Cicero as calling for the ideal orator to know all important subjects and arts—a position, as we have discovered, that is more nominal than substantive—and then stated his own contrasting position: "I however regard it as sufficient that an orator should not be actually ignorant of the subject on which he has to speak" (II.xxi.14–15). Although Quintilian contrasted his position with Cicero's, it is actually very similar to views expressed by Cicero's Antonius and Crassus, which have already been explored.

Quintilian's ideas about invention, then, are highly limited. Invention is restricted to the art of choosing what to do or say largely in the area of speaking publicly to large audiences. It embraces the pursuit of virtue as at least nominally primary, but it nevertheless focuses on forensic, deliberative, and epideictic speeches and the kind of persuasion designed to overcome resistance and prompt a choice. It is the invention of an orator on a particular side in a case—for instance, the invention of an attorney for the prosecution or defense—and, like Aristotle and Cicero's Antonius, that attorney tends to focus his attention on the discovery of the available means of persuasion in a given case. Admittedly, the coverage of invention in the *Institutio Oratoria* is quite extensive; both Books V and VI explore logical, emotional, and ethical appeals. But invention hardly has much status.

This absence of status is reflected in passages that celebrate the mastery of style as more difficult and more important than the mastery of invention and arrangement. Quintilian wrote: "I have now to discuss the theory of style, a subject which, as all orators agree, presents the greatest difficulty" (VIII.Pr.13). In contrast, invention and arrangement are not as demanding: "Even the untrained often possess the gift of invention, and no great learning need be assumed for the satisfactory arrangement of our matter" (VIII.iii.2). He cited Cicero as support (VIII.Pr.14–16). As soon as Quintilian had diminished invention, however, his good judgment checked him: "I would have the orator, while careful in his choice of words, be even more concerned about his subject matter" (VIII.Pr.20–21). The emphasis in the *Institutio Oratoria*, however, focuses attention on style rather than invention, on presentation rather than discovery.

Like Cicero's Crassus, Quintilian also emphasized the importance of delivery. He appealed to the authority of Demosthenes in words similar to those used by Cicero:

Demosthenes, when asked what was the most important thing in oratory, gave the palm to delivery and assigned it second and third place as well, until his questioner ceased to trouble him. We are therefore almost justified in concluding that he regarded it not merely as the first, but as the only virtue of oratory. (XI.iii.6–7)

Quintilian rightfully suggested that Cicero agreed with Demosthenes: "Cicero likewise regards *action* [delivery] as the supreme element of oratory" (XI.iii.7–8). If Quintilian valued delivery highly, however, he did not devote much attention to it. He disposed of delivery in a single chapter of Book XI.

Like Isocrates, Quintilian emphasized the importance of imitation in the development of oratory, but he added the concept of avoidance as well. He stressed both concepts in his description of the origin of rhetorical education:

> It was, then, nature that created speech, and observation that originated the art of speaking. Just as men discovered the art of medicine by observing that some things were healthy and some the reverse, so they observed that some things were useful and some useless in speaking, and noted them for imitation or avoidance, while they added certain other precepts according as their nature suggested. These observations were confirmed by experience and each man proceeded to teach what he knew. (III.ii.3–4)

The art of oratory, then, develops through the observation of positive and negative characteristics of actual speeches and judgments about what to imitate and avoid in future speech occasions. Although Quintilian placed greatest emphasis on imitation in *Institutio Oratoria*, he at least mentioned the concept of avoidance.

Quintilian so favored imitation in education that he preferred examples to rules: "For in everything which we teach examples are more effective even than the rules which are taught in the schools" (X.i.15). Quintilian's skepticism about rules stemmed from his criticism of the use of universals in the development of oratory. He wrote: "Let no one however demand from me a rigid code of rules such as most authors of textbooks have laid down, or ask me to impose on students of rhetoric a system of laws immutable as fate." He complained that some speakers follow such rules "as though they had no choice but to regard them as orders and as if it were a crime to take any other line." But, he argued, "most rules are liable to be altered by the nature of the case, circumstances of time and place, and by hard necessity itself" (II.xiii.1–2). He went even further: "there is hardly a single commonplace of such universal application that it will fit any actual case" (II.iv.30). The consequences for Quintilian's own practice are clear: "It has always, therefore, been my custom not to tie myself down to *universal* or *general* rules....For rules are rarely of such a kind that their validity cannot be shaken and overthrown in some particular or other" (II.xiii.14–15). What is important for an orator "is a wise adaptability since he is called upon to meet the most varied emergencies" (II.xiii.2). Little wonder, then, that Quintilian considered the best of student exercises to be declamations, which are much like our modern case studies—examples of actual or imagined situations that a student must analyze in an effort to create discourse (II.ix.1–2).

Quintilian's attitude toward rules is amplified in the following statement: "rules are helpful...so long as they indicate the direct road and do not restrict us absolutely to the ruts made by others" (II.xiii.16). Judgment must be the ultimate arbitrator: "the art of speaking can only be attained by hard work and assiduity of study, by a variety of exercises and repeated trial, the highest prudence and unfailing quickness of judgment" (II.xiii.15–16). In Book XII.i.42–44, Quintilian provided an example of the balancing that he perceives as important to a good judgment. In his emphasis on judgment, he followed Isocrates.

Although Quintilian had suggested how much hard work it takes to become an ideal orator, he was quick to downplay the amount of time it takes. He indicated that we cannot take as long as Cinna and Isocrates on some of their projects:

> the fact that Cinna took nine years to write his Smyrna, and that Isocrates required ten years, at the lowest estimate, to complete his Panegyric does not concern the orator, whose assistance will be of no use, if it is so long delayed. (X.iv.4)

Nor need we take so long. To learn how to be a virtuous man takes only a few years' study (XII.xi.11–12). The rest of the knowledge we need can also be obtained within a reasonable length of time (XII.xi.16). Quintilian followed Cicero's Antonius in quieting fears about the amount of time required to become an ideal orator.

Quintilian's *Instituto Oratoria*, then, contains a mix of broadening and narrowing approaches to rhetoric. Among broadening approaches, Quintilian followed Cicero's Crassus in calling for a reunification of rhetoric and philosophy; he urged orators to add the study of ethics to their education once again. Quintilian differed from Cicero's Crassus, however, by insisting that choices that contribute to one's being a good man have priority over choices that help one win an argument, should any conflict between these sets of choices ever result. Cicero's Crassus, viewing rhetoric through the realistic lens of an attorney, does not consider situations where the goal of winning a case might conflict with some sense of ultimate justice. Rather, like Aristotle, he limits his focus to the development of the means of persuasion—an awareness of ethics among them—that might be effective in winning any side of a case; in *De Oratore*, the study of ethics is a means of enhancing persuasiveness. Quintilian, on the other hand, explicitly rejected persuasiveness as some ultimately controlling goal and gave ethics primacy. In doing so, he followed Isocrates and responded to the charges of immorality leveled at rhetoric in Plato's dialogues.

While this distinction between Cicero's Crassus and Quintilian is substantive, Quintilian minimized it. He claimed that the desire to be expedient and persuasive does not often conflict with the desire to be of good character—a claim so counter to personal experience and history that one has difficulty accepting that the usually judicious Quintilian wrote it. Such a claim has the effect of dismissing the necessity of considering ethics to any great degree—much as Aristotle did with his statement that the ethical position on an issue is likely to be the inherently most persuasive. Furthermore, while Quintilian did devote some space to the primacy of ethics, he did not go beyond mere statement to explore implications, and the material on the primacy of ethics is dwarfed by the far greater space devoted to the development of the means of persuasion in a given oratorical situation—an emphasis that Quintilian shared with Cicero's Crassus and Aristotle.

Quintilian's claim about the primacy of ethics, while a response to the charges of immorality leveled at rhetoric in Plato's dialogues, should not be used to draw undue conclusions about similarities between Quintilian and Plato. In *The Art of Rhetoric in the Roman World*, George Kennedy (1972) made this mistake: "In broad outline Quintilian's perfect orator does not differ from the ideal of the latter part of Plato's *Phaedrus*" (p. 509). The portraits of the rhetorician in Plato's rhetorics and Quintilian's rhetoric, however, differ considerably. For instance, Cicero's Crassus is correct in indicating that Plato—in at least one complex of ideas—inclined us away from the full range of motivations that give rise to discourse and restricted our attention narrowly to truth, which—in Quintilian's rhetoric—is only a means to an end. Plato inclined us away from the forensic and deliberative centers—the law courts and governmental assemblies—and celebrated a life of contemplation, an identification of what is permanent and unchanging in areas such as mathematics and science; Quintilian, on the other hand, reaffirmed the central importance of action in the courts and assemblies, focused our attention on the temporary and forever changing morass of everyday life, and was interested in mathematics and science not in themselves, as was the case with Plato, but only to the degree that they were useful in oratory. Both are narrowing in their own ways. Plato's otherworldliness is narrowing by inclining attention away from human ambition, away from sense impressions, away from body, and away from emotion. Quintilian's thisworldliness is narrowing in its exclusive focus on oratory, an activity not broad enough to include the full practice of professionals such as scientists and mathematicians.

In Plato's other complex of ideas, which explores the functioning of the state, Plato's suggestions about the rhetorician also diverge from those suggested by Quintilian. While Plato denied the rhetorician any responsibility for ethical choice and made him a statesman's instrument of persuasion, Quintilian explicitly rejected a definition of the rhetorician as limited to a focus on persuasion and at least nominally assigned him ethical responsibility. Furthermore, Plato's bitter attacks on rhetoric, including his suggestions that all rhetoricians are unethical, differed substantially from Quintilian's glorification of rhetoric as the crown of education, a necessity in the progress of civilization, and queen of all the world. In both scope and stature, then, Quintilian's and Plato's ideas about the rhetorician in the state diverged sharply.

As is the case with Quintilian and Plato, similarities between Quintilian and Isocrates should not be allowed to obscure differences. George Kennedy (1972) went too far here as well: "In broad outline Quintilian's perfect orator does not differ from the ideal of...Isocrates' *Antidosis*" (p. 509). It is true that Quintilian's *Institutio Oratoria* and Cicero's *De Oratore* cluster more closely with Isocrates's *Antidosis* than with Plato's *Gorgias* and *Phaedrus* and Aristotle's *Rhetoric*; they share a favorable view of rhetoric, an awareness of the need for scope in engaging rhetorical problems, a predisposition to focus their attention on human activity and to value that focus, and a concern for the appropriate use of judgment to make choices in variable or even unique situations.

But the differences between Quintilian and Isocrates are not negligible. While Quintilian devoted most of his attention to forensic oratory, Isocrates distanced himself from this area and focused on political deliberation. Quintilian focused on the use of impressive public speeches to persuade large, general audiences, while Isocrates was broader, including not only such public speaking but all situations in which humans choose what to do or what to say—with the exception of the practice of science and mathematics. With his focus on public speaking, Quintilian tended to limit his attention to the adaptation of materials already developed by experts to particular oratorical situations, while Isocrates' rhetoric embraces the world of choice in professional contexts.

In much the way that commentators have overstated similarities between Quintilian and Plato and Isocrates, they have pushed comparisons between Quintilian and Aristotle too far as well. I have already expressed my fundamental disagreement with Lane Cooper's (1932) statement that Quintilian's rhetoric is, in its best elements, essentially Aristotelian. Quintilian shared the Isocratean and Ciceronian view that rhetoric is the crown of education, while Aristotle subsumed rhetoric under politics, which, as a practical science, is not valued as highly as the theoretical sciences. While Quintilian did not share Cicero's sense of urgency about the need for scope in developing speeches, he called for the reunification of oratory and philosophy, emphasized the need for the orator to study ethics, and considered it more important for the orator to be a good man than to win his case; such positions run counter to Aristotle's emphasis on specialization and his limitation of the field of rhetoric to questions about persuasion. Quintilian considered the world of human affairs—the very embodiment of volatile change—to be of central importance, while the worlds of science, mathematics, and theology—those more marked by stability and permanence—were more favored by Aristotle. Quintilian did not follow Aristotle in elevating contemplation motivated by curiosity or wonder as the ultimate human activity. He was not as interested as Aristotle in questions of identification or questions about what is; he was far more interested in questions of choice or questions about what humans ought to say or do.

For all the fundamental differences between Quintilian and Aristotle, however, similarities do abound. Quintilian may have explicitly distinguished his rhetoric from Aristotle's, especially in his insistence that it is more important for the orator to be a good man than to persuade others, but, relatively speaking, so little space is devoted to exploring this distinction and so much space is devoted to ideas shared by Quintilian and Aristotle that similarities seem to dwarf differences.

Both focused on persuasion designed to encourage humans to agree or disagree with particular positions in courts of law. Both focused on the development of the means of persuasion, that is, on the analysis of proofs. As a result, both distinguished between rhetoricians and subject matter specialists; subject matter specialists determine what to say in a specific field, and orators take such specialist statements and adapt them for speeches, simplifying them for relatively uninformed audiences. All serious analysis of subject matter, anything at all abstruse, is beyond the field of rhetoric.

Clearly, Quintilian—like Isocrates, Plato, Aristotle, and Cicero—has his individuality. This individuality necessitates a restriction in the meaning of the term "classical rhetoric." It is perfectly appropriate to use the term to refer to a time period ranging from the beginnings of rhetoric, often associated with Corax and Tisias in Syracuse in the 5th century B.C.E., to someone such as Cassius Longinus in Athens and Syria in the 3rd century C.E. But it is inappropriate to use the term to suggest that the views of rhetoric held during this period are similar. Unfortunately, too many commentators use the term "classical rhetoric" in ways that suggest that thought about rhetoric in antiquity is relatively monolithic, that sharp differences do not exist. For instance, Patricia Bizzell and Bruce Herzberg (1990), in *The Rhetorical Tradition: Readings from Classical Times to the Present*, wrote: "To speak of classical rhetoric is...to speak of Aristotle's system and its elaboration by Cicero and Quintilian" (p. 3). They later added: "In the classical view, rhetoric manages knowledge, conveying but not creating it; the rhetorician's activities are subordinate to the truth-seeking of the scientist and the philosopher" (p. 5). Such statements, which clearly reflect the strength of Aristotle in the 20th century, suggest a lack of awareness of the dominance of Isocrates in ancient Greece, the strong influence of the Isocratean tradition on Cicero and Quintilian, and the conflict between rhetoric and philosophy in classical antiquity.

Even Edward P. J. Corbett (1965), who acknowledged that Isocrates "was the most influential Greek rhetorician among his contemporaries" (p. 527), used "classical rhetoric" in the title of his most notable textbook—*Classical Rhetoric for the Modern Student*—yet admitted that his textbook was essentially Aristotelian: "this textbook is so much indebted to Aristotle's theory that it can be regarded as a mere restatement, with some modifications and extensions, of the *Rhetoric*" (p. 540). Corbett compounded the problem by blurring distinctions: "From its beginnings and throughout its history, classical rhetoric was thought of as the art of persuasive speech" (p. 21). Clearly, however, a narrow focus on persuasion as the end of rhetoric was implicitly rejected by the breadth of Isocrates and explicitly rejected in Quintilian's *Institutio Oratoria*. Too many commentators have ignored fundamental differences separating Isocrates, Plato, Aristotle, Cicero, and Quintilian.

Views about the scope of rhetoric have been equally problematic. Bizzell and Herzberg (1990) wrote: "After the classical period, the bounds of rhetoric expanded, until today virtually all forms of discourse and symbolic communication can be included within its scope" (p. 2). In fact, however, Cicero and Quintilian were unable to resurrect a rhetoric of Isocratean scope, and the narrowing of rhetoric that had already progressed to such an extent in ancient Rome continued. Two major developments in Western history—the triumph of Christian philosophers such as Augustine and the rise of science—added such strength to the Platonic-Aristotelian tradition that the battle for the scope of rhetoric was lost and, as a result, the battle for the stature of rhetoric was lost as well.

4

Christianity, Science, and the Victory of Philosophy

If rhetoric remained the crown of education in ancient Greece and Rome, two powerful movements in Western civilization—Christianity and science—added such strength to ideas that I have associated with Plato and Aristotle (by incorporating them) that philosophy ultimately won its conflict with rhetoric. Both Christianity and science gave force to ideas that promoted withdrawal from human affairs and attacked the stature and scope of rhetoric. Both used definitional exclusion to sever rhetoric from a concern with ethics and other forms of professional deliberation and limit it to persuasive efforts in public speaking. Indeed, the undermining of rhetoric through definitional exclusion proceeded to such an extent that Ramus, in the 16th century, limited rhetoric to a concern for style and delivery alone.

After classical antiquity, rhetoric enjoyed a brief resurgence in the Renaissance, but otherwise its fortunes tended to decline, until, in the 20th century, approaches to many social problems were compromised by the narrowness of human goals, social structures, and methodologies. Important areas of human endeavor progressed without adequate consideration of ethical implications, and too many human institutions ignored major responsibilities because their goals narrowly excluded them. Specialization, hardened into narrow social structures, militated against the full engagement of problems. And, in the absence of adequate rhetorical theories, humans inappropriately used methodologies designed for philosophical identification of unchanging phenomena to address problems involving choice in changing human affairs.

AUGUSTINE AND AFTER

Between the death of Cicero in 43 B.C.E and the birth of Quintilian in 40 C.E., a mythology called Christianity had its origin in the Mediterranean world. Christianity was based on two sets of purported facts, one set associated with Judaism, as understood by the prophets and embodied in a canon of writings called the Old Testament, and another set associated with the life of Jesus, as understood by the apostles and embodied in a canon of writings called the New Testament. As indicated by Kenneth Scott Latourette (1937–1945), in *A History of the Expansion of Christianity*, Judaism had a long history and development before Christianity emerged as one of its sects. Christianity took its starting point from the life of Jesus, who was born about 5 B.C.E. and was crucified in 29 or 30 C.E. Although it adopted part of its scriptural canon as well as its monotheism and much of its ethics from Judaism, it was aggressively missionary and shed many of its Jewish trappings to become more universal in its appeal.

Its remarkable success in attracting adherents profoundly affected the fortunes of the ideas that I have been following. As it spread ever more widely into new cultures, it absorbed ideas from these cultures, one of the results being a variety of Christian sects in a variety of cultures. According to Latourette, the five major regional divisions of Christianity before the end of the 5th century were the following: Syrian-Persian-Nestorian, Syrian-Monophysite, Egyptian-Monophysite, Greek Orthodox, and Roman Catholic (Vol. 1, p. 360). Among the ideas absorbed and supported by European sects associated with the latter division (although certainly transformed by their new settings) were many of those found in the works of Plato, Aristotle, and their followers. The support afforded these philosophers by Christianity in the Middle Ages and afterward militated against many of the ideas that I have associated with Isocrates.

Augustine (354–430 C.E.), one of the major figures in the transition from classical antiquity to the Middle Ages, serves as an excellent starting point for any study of the uses that Christians made of the classical ideas available to them. He not only encouraged Christians to appropriate the ideas of classical antiquity, but also showed them how to do so. He himself was first a rhetorician, then shifted his allegiance to philosophy, and, in the end, supported a Christianity that drew on both of his earlier areas of expertise. Until the end of the 12th century, his influence in the Middle Ages was dominant, and later, after the Reformation, both Protestant and Catholic sects drew heavily on his work for support. His work was critical to the early Christian propensity to reinforce ideas associated with the Platonic-Aristotelian tradition and either ignore or stand in opposition to ideas associated with the Isocratean tradition.

As Augustine (1952) indicated in his *Confessions*, rhetoric played a major role in his early life. As a boy, he developed the ability to write what he wanted, learned to speak better than many others in his class, and mastered and loved Latin (though he had difficulties with Greek)—achievements that led him to be called a "hopeful boy" (I,20,23,27). To enable him to fulfill his promise, he was sent to Carthage to study rhetoric and prepare for a career as a pleader in the lawcourts; he excelled to such an extent that he became "chief in the rhetoric school" (III,1,6). After his studies, he taught rhetoric at Tagaste, Carthage, Rome, and Milan and dedicated one of his books to Hierus, a famous Roman orator.

At the age of 32, Augustine heard a voice (interpreted as a command from God), opened at random his Scriptures, and was converted by his reading to Christianity; he then abandoned his career as a rhetoric teacher and returned with friends to the country where he prepared for baptism (VIII,29,30; IX,7). Although his career teaching rhetoric was at an end, his capabilities, education, and experience in rhetoric held him in good stead in later duties such as preaching; in a letter in 395 to Alypius, Bishop of Tagaste, he described some examples of the extraordinary impact of his preaching on audiences (trans. 1930, pp. 69–92).

Augustine (1952) included his reading of "certain books of the Platonists" (called "Neoplatonists" in the 20th century) as among the events that promoted his conversion to Christianity (*Confessions*, VII,13). While still a teacher of rhetoric at Milan, Augustine was told and learned for himself that the works of the Platonists led "to the belief in God, and His Word" (VII,26; VIII,3). He had no problem appropriating what was useful from the Platonists and other philosophers (*On Christian Doctrine*, II,60). Because Christians could appropriate so much from the Platonists, Augustine concluded that no other philosophers came "nearer to us than the Platonists" and that Plato was "justly preferred to all the other philosophers of the Gentiles" (*City of God*, VIII,4,5). As Latourette suggested, Augustine developed a theology that was "largely a combination of Neoplatonic with traditional Christian views" (Vol. 1, p. 312).

Augustine considered Christian ideas so similar to those of Plato that he felt compelled to support a theory proposed by Ambrose that Plato learned from the Christians rather than the Christians from Plato. Here is the problem Augustine confronted: "the readers and admirers of Plato dared calumniously to assert that our Lord Jesus Christ learnt all those sayings of His...from the books of Plato" because "Plato lived long before the coming of our Lord." In response, Augustine supported Ambrose's theory "that Plato made a journey into Egypt at the time when Jeremiah the prophet was there," showing "that it is much more likely that Plato was through Jeremiah's means initiated into our literature." Clearly, then, "it becomes much more probable that those philosophers learnt whatever they said that was good and true from our literature, than that the Lord Jesus Christ learnt from the writings of Plato" (*On Christian Doctrine*, II,43). Unfortunately, by the time Augustine wrote *The City of God*, he realized that historical chronology made it impossible for Jeremiah to have instructed Plato (Jeremiah was already dead when Plato was in Egypt), but he continued to muse about the possibility of Plato's learning some of the ideas of the prophets through conversation with interpreters (VIII.11).

If Augustine found much in the works of the Platonists that was compatible with Christianity, however, he also found much that was incompatible and rejected it. In fact, as Latourette suggested, one Neoplatonist—Porphyry—wrote *Fifteen Books against the Christians*, an attack that the church regarded as the most dangerous written argument against Christianity. Although the full text has not survived, replies that it evoked reveal something of its arguments. Porphyry raised embarrassing questions about contradictions in the scriptures—different genealogies, different narratives about the death and resurrection of Jesus, and the like (Vol. 1, pp. 20, 133–34). Augustine devoted considerable effort—in *The City of God*, for instance—to delineating the differences between Christianity and not just the ideas of Porphyry, but also those of other Platonists as well. Still, Augustine's work derived so much from the Platonists that A. H. Armstrong (1972) reported: "Most people who have studied St. Augustine would be prepared to accept the description of him as a Christian Platonist" (p. 3). Gilson (trans. 1960) perhaps put it best in citing Thomas Aquinas's statement that Augustine followed Plato as far as the Christian faith allowed (p. vii). At the very least, Augustine's works incorporated enough of the ideas of Plato to further a focus of attention that can be associated with Plato's philosophy.

According to Augustine, he first discovered philosophy while reading Cicero's *Hortensius*, a work now lost. This work "contains an exhortation to philosophy" and, ironically, directed his attention away from the this-worldliness of Cicero and toward the otherworldliness of Plato: "How did I burn then, my God, how did I burn to re-mount from earthly things to Thee" (*Confessions*, III,7,8). He believed that humans could not achieve rest until they contemplated God: "our heart is restless until it repose in Thee" (I,1). Augustine cited Plato in describing the ideal relationship with God as a kind of knowledge or imitation: "Plato determined the final good to be to live according to virtue, and affirmed that he only can attain to virtue who knows and imitates God" (*City of God*, VIII,8). Augustine also described this relationship with God as a kind of union (X,3).

In taking flight from this world to the divine, we move from the material, temporary, and changing to the spiritual, eternal, and unchanging. We need to use this world in order to enjoy the divine: "if we wish to return to our Father's home, this world must be used, not enjoyed, that so the invisible things of God may be clearly seen, being understood by the things that are made—that is, that by means of what is material and temporary we may lay hold upon that which is spiritual and eternal" (*On Christian Doctrine*, I,4). The divinity that we enjoy is the triune God, the Trinity (I,5). The sharp dualism that Augustine established between "corruptible, and injurable, and changeable" this-worldliness and "incorruptible, uninjurable, and unchangeable" otherworldliness accords well with the similar dualism that we find in Plato (*Confessions*, VII,1).

Augustine included in his *Confessions* an example of a mental ascent from the "beauty of bodies celestial or terrestrial" to God or "THAT WHICH IS" (VII,23). In describing this mental ascent, Augustine resembled Plato in dividing humans into body and soul, body engaging this-worldliness through sense, soul engaging otherworldliness through reflection. Otherworldliness is associated with "what is" and is engaged through faculties associated with soul—reason and understanding. Augustine credited the Platonists for their help in his ascent: "having then read those books of the Platonists, and thence been taught to search for incorporeal truth, I saw Thy invisible things, understood by those things which are made" (*Confessions* VII,26). Augustine's mention here that he has learned to search for incorporeal truth from the Platonists is supported by numerous passages in his works. According to Augustine, for instance, when humans attain truth, they are partaking of God: "All truth is of Him who says, 'I am the truth.'" (*On Christian Doctrine*, Preface,8). As in Plato, this apotheosis of truth places value on what is, on identification, on understanding, on knowledge.

Although Augustine found help for his thinking about otherworldly experience in the works of the Platonists, his ultimate authority for preferring otherworldly contemplation to this-worldly action was scripture, the books of the Old and New Testament (*Confessions*, XIII,22). The facts of belief found in the Old and New Testaments—that is, the facts that constitute Christian faith—come from Christ Himself: "This Mediator, having spoken what He judged sufficient first by the prophets, then by His own lips, and afterwards by the apostles, has besides produced the Scripture which is called canonical, which has paramount authority" (*City of God*, XI,3). The authority of the scripture, then, is divine: "Scripture...excels all the writings of all nations by its divine authority" (XI,1).

As a source of belief, scripture is superior to human reason. Reason is limited because humans "walk by faith not by sight" (*On Christian Doctrine*, II,10). Scripture, then, must be preferred to the unaided mind (II,9), and human wisdom is directly dependent on a knowledge of scripture (IV,7). Augustine placed such reliance on scripture and used it to such an extent in his works that Marrou (1957/ 1960) felt compelled to write: "For Augustine, Holy Scripture is the sum total of all truth, the source of all doctrine, the center of all Christian culture and of all spiritual life. His theology is very directly biblical, his instruction is no less so" (p. 56). While Augustine relied heavily on the Platonists, then, he placed the authority of scripture before the authority of their works and devoted considerable effort to distinguishing some of the facts of faith inspired by God and found in the scripture from beliefs of the Platonists (see, for instance, *City of God*, VIII).

Augustine used the existence of miracles as evidence for the authority of scripture. Among the miracles that served as evidence for the authority of scripture were visions of angels, control of the stars, healing of the sick, restoration of the dead to life, and the virgin birth and resurrection of Christ (*City of God*, X,32). Miracles helped promote the view that "Scripture...gives no false information" (XVI,9). If scripture contained no false information, however, it was very difficult to determine what it said. In fact, when Augustine first encountered the scriptures, difficulties of interpretation—along with perceived inferiorities to the work of Cicero—initially repelled him: "they seemed to me unworthy to be compared to the stateliness of Tully: for my swelling pride shrunk from their lowliness, nor could my sharp wit pierce the interior thereof" (*Confessions*, III,9). Only later did he comprehend that God made the scriptures difficult to interpret for important reasons:

> Some of the expressions are so obscure as to shroud the meaning in the thickest darkness. And I do not doubt that all this was divinely arranged for the purpose of subduing pride by toil, and of preventing a feeling of satiety in the intellect, which generally holds in small esteem what is discovered without difficulty. (*On Christian Doctrine*, II,7)

Interpreters of scripture encountered other difficulties besides obscurity. They also encountered passages that seemed either pointless or in conflict with Christian belief. Fortunately, while still a rhetoric teacher at Milan, Augustine learned from Ambrose the art of figurative or allegorical interpretation to resolve what appeared to be problems when scriptural passages were interpreted literally (*Confessions*, V,24). As a result, he later encouraged figurative interpretation when passages appeared to be pointless: "whatever there is in the word of God that cannot, when taken literally, be referred either to purity of life or soundness of doctrine, you may set down as figurative (*On Christian Doctrine*, III,14). Augustine also encouraged figurative interpretation when passages seemed to conflict with Christian belief:

> Those things, again, whether only sayings or whether actual deeds, which appear to the inexperienced to be sinful, and which are ascribed to God, or to men whose holiness is put before us as an example, are wholly figurative, and the hidden kernel of meaning they contain is to be picked out as food for the nourishment of charity. (III,18)

Figurative interpretation could not guarantee accuracy, however. If the scriptures, as divinely inspired, were infallible, interpretations could vary and contain error. Anything stated by an interpreter that history later proved false, then, was not a problem of faith, but a problem of interpretation. When Augustine insisted that the universe was only 6,000 years old (*City of God*, XII,10), later historical and scientific revelations rendered that error an interpretive rather than scriptural problem. Differences in interpretation down through the centuries led to extraordinary divisions in Christianity, many of them bloody. As Latourette indicated, "Christianity has been the most quarrelsome of religions. No other faith has shown so many acrimonious divisions" (Vol. 1, pp. 63–64). The Thirty Years War (1618–1648) was among the more frightening manifestations of these divisions.

If interpreters are liable to error, however, some can be better than others. The best interpreters will be those who read all of the books and remember them even though they cannot fully understand them (*On Christian Doctrine*, II,12). Augustine also recommended a methodology akin to Plato's dialectic for interpreting Scripture, although he ignored synthesis and focused on analysis: "the science of definition, of division, and of partition...is evolved from the reason of things." This science or art, "which deals with inferences, and definitions, and divisions, is of the greatest assistance in the discovery of...meaning" (II,53,55).

Christian education is tied directly to interpretation. Christians should try to acquire only that knowledge that is necessary to help them understand scripture. For instance, since mathematics is useful toward this end, it should not be ignored: "we must not despise the science of numbers, which, in many passages of holy Scripture, is found to be of eminent service to the careful interpreter" (*City of God*, XI,30). With regard to such subjects, however, "we must hold by the maxim, 'Not too much of anything'" (*On Christian Doctrine*, II,58). Only those areas of mathematics directly relevant to the interpretation of scripture should be studied (II,59). Unlike Plato, who encouraged the philosopher to use reason freely to pursue knowledge, Augustine limited the use of reason to the interpretation and understanding of faith. Christians accept from given texts a given set of facts that constitute faith, and the sole function of reason is to understand these facts and their interrelations.

Augustine, then, took from the Platonists what helped him understand his faith and ignored what did not appear to serve this function. For instance, he found useful the concepts of a hierarchical cosmology that descended from God to this world and a spiritual experience that enabled humans to reascend from this world to the contemplation of God. As Paul Oskar Kristeller suggested in *Renaissance Thought* (1955/1961), Augustine also found useful such typical Platonist doctrines as "the eternal presence of the universal forms in the mind of God, the immediate comprehension of these ideas by human reason, and the incorporeal nature and immortality of the soul" (p. 55). But he encouraged Christians to ignore other areas emphasized by Plato, such as astronomy, because they were of such little value in interpreting scripture (*On Christian Doctrine*, II, 46).

If Augustine's focus on scripture inclined him to exclude much that is found in Plato's works, it also inclined him to devote considerable attention to scriptural exegesis or commentary that had no parallel in Plato. *The City of God*, for instance, contains a lengthy commentary on "Genesis." His focus of attention on scriptural and church matters, then, joined his focus on the otherworldly contemplation of God in directing attention away from practical concerns of everyday living. Even a Catholic Platonist such as A. H. Armstrong (1972) wrote:

> I am inclined to think that the lack of any broad human and humane interest and concern with the world around us, which is so often apparent in Christians and has alienated so many good and intelligent people from the Church and contributed so much to the present general rejection of Christianity, is due not so much to other-worldliness as to churchiness. (pp. 14–15)

Armstrong may have placed the blame more on churchiness than otherworldliness, but, clearly, both inclinations direct attention away from this-worldliness.

Still, according to Augustine, at least some attention to this-worldliness is encouraged by scripture. After all, God is "the only and true Creator and Governor of the Universe" (*Confessions*, III,16), and He has made all things good (VII.18). Since humans—both body and soul—are good, then, we need to concern ourselves about helping them: "Let us break our bread to the hungry, and bring the houseless poor to our house. Let us clothe the naked, and despise not those of our own flesh" (XIII,22). Caring for other humans is important enough to be linked with the love of God as the two most important commandments. Augustine referred to "those two commandments on which hang all the law and the prophets: 'Thou shalt love the Lord thy God with all thy heart, and with all thy mind, and with all thy soul'; and 'Thou shalt love thy neighbor as thyself'" (*City of God*, X,3). That the commandment of loving other humans has been taken seriously is evidenced by that extraordinarily strong tradition of altruism that has been part of Christianity down through the centuries and has been such a great source of its strength.

Because humans should love their neighbors, they should devote appropriate attention to human institutions as well. Augustine listed some of the necessary human institutions (*On Christian Doctrine*, II,39) and encouraged Christians to pay attention to such matters: "This whole class of human arrangements, which are of convenience for the necessary intercourse of life, the Christian is not by any means to neglect, but on the contrary should pay a sufficient degree of attention to them, and keep them in memory" (II,40). In Augustine's lifetime, the Christian Church became increasingly important as a source of stability in human arrangements. Augustine witnessed much of the collapse of the Roman Empire; in 410, Alarac and his Visigoths captured and sacked Rome. With the decline of secular authority, the Christian Church—which had largely been a force for protest and a source of hope for poor Romans—became the sole stable institution that strove to maintain social order. As Latourette suggested, the Church remained "the only protector of the weak and the sole refuge of the poor" (Vol. 1, p. 186). It maintained hospitals, hospices for strangers, and houses for orphans, widows, and the indigent. R. R. Bolgar (1954/1958), in *The Classical Heritage and Its Beneficiaries*, wrote: "during the centuries that follow the fall of Rome, the Christian faith" was "treasured not only as the pledge of a personal salvation, but as a social good" (p. 237).

Indeed, much of Augustine's own life could serve as a model for involvement in this-worldliness. As Plato repudiated his otherworldliness in a work such as *Laws*, Augustine repudiated his otherworldliness in his activities as a bishop. In 395, not quite 10 years after his conversion to Christianity, Augustine was selected bishop of Hippo, a town in Africa second in importance only to Carthage. In this post, he occupied himself so much with administration and written rhetoric that W. R. Johnson (1976) made the following remarkable claim: "When Augustine assumed his duties at Hippo, he had Plato in his mind and in his heart, but he had Isocrates in his blood....The rhetorical bishop spent his days in law courts; he talked over what had to be done with politicians; he studied tax legislation and the problems of the economy" (p. 227). Johnson wrote: "The more one reads the *Confessions* and the *Civitas* the harder it becomes to distinguish the philosophy from the theology, the theology from the Isocratean rhetoric" (p. 228). He placed Augustine's words within the Isocratean tradition that I have traced: "Behind these words there lies the powerful and subtle intellectual discipline that extends from...Isocrates, through Cicero and Quintilian, to Augustine himself" (p. 220).

While it is possible to draw some comparisons between Isocrates and Augustine, Johnson's claims are untenable. It is true that Isocrates focused on political rhetoric and that Augustine, as bishop, was forced to concern himself with the politics involved in his post. It is also true that Isocrates used written speeches as the medium for his arguments, and Augustine, too, used written documents to promote his views. But, although some superficial parallels such as these can be found, Augustine's *Confessions*, *City of God*, and *On Christian Doctrine* diverged sharply from the works of Isocrates, and Augustine's rhetoric differed substantially from Isocratean rhetoric in both stature and scope.

Augustine's *Confessions*, *City of God*, and *On Christian Doctrine* accorded well with attitudes toward this-worldliness in Plato's early works and, as a result, stood in opposition to Isocrates's concern for the management of public and private affairs. In *Confessions*, Augustine and his friends so detested "the turbulent turmoils of human life" that they almost resolved "on living apart from business and the bustle of men" (VI,24). Later in his life, from 388 to 391, Augustine actually did withdraw into monastic seclusion, hoping to spend the rest of his life living this way, and only reluctantly was he persuaded to assume pastoral responsibilities at Hippo (Battenhouse, 1955/1956, pp. 38–39). According to Augustine, a soul that was "conformed to the truth" had to "die to this world" (*On Christian Doctrine*, I,19). Only the enemies of the city of God were found "eagerly pursuing earthly joys and gaping after transitory things" (*City of God*, VI,1). While Augustine used the things of this world to direct attention toward the divine, Isocrates used the things of this world to enable better decisions in everyday living. While Augustine restricted our knowledge of this world to what was essential to our relationship with God and the scripture, Isocrates encouraged the widest knowledge of this world possible to enable progress in developing civilization.

Augustine's works reflected the same distaste for such bodily needs as food, drink, and sex as is found in Plato's *Phaedo*. In *Confessions*, Augustine wrote: "I strive daily against concupiscence in eating and drinking" (X,47). God encourages "continency from the 'lust of the flesh, the lust of the eyes, and the ambition of the world'" (X,41). Augustine described his early ensnarement in sex, its great power over him, and excoriated it as the "filth of concupiscence" and "hell of lustfulness" (III,1). In contrast to Plato, however, Augustine did not strive to curb his passion, only to shift it from woman to God—although the language that Augustine used for the love of God has created a happy hunting ground for those who perceive that experience as sublimated sexuality. Augustine's extreme asceticism here, his inclination to despise sexual intercourse (maintained despite his belief that God created all things good, including body), has attracted a substantial following among Christians down through the ages, even into the 20th century.

Although Augustine occasionally encouraged Christians to help their neighbors with food, clothing, and shelter, his works often manifested the same lack of concern for the well-being of humans in this life that can be found in Plato's works. According to Augustine, the good Christian "extricates himself from every form of fatal joy in transitory things, and turning away from these, fixes his affection on things eternal" (*On Christian Doctrine*, II, 10). Christians should not be too concerned about the good and bad in this life because they happen to good and bad men indifferently (*City of God*, I,8). At times, Augustine's indifference toward this-worldly concerns verged on callousness. He considered Christian martyrs "useful to the Church" (X,21). He wrote: "many Christians were slaughtered, and were put to death in a hideous variety of cruel ways. Well, if this be hard to bear, it is assuredly the common lot of all who are born into this life. Of this at least I am certain, that no one has ever died who was not destined to die some time" (I,11). This kind of Christian resignation could militate against an Isocratean drive to improve the human lot here and now.

If Augustine's otherworldliness in his *Confessions*, *City of God*, and *On Christian Doctrine* diverged sharply from Isocrates's this-worldliness, it is hardly surprising to find their rhetorics divergent as well. While Isocrates lauded rhetoric as the crown of education responsible for most of the blessings of civilization, Augustine followed Plato in disparaging rhetoric. Rhetoric is not important enough to engage the attention of men:

> I do not think it of so much importance as to wish men who have arrived at mature age to spend time in learning it. It is enough that boys should give attention to it; and even of these, not all who are to be fitted for usefulness in the Church, but only those who are not yet engaged in any occupation of more urgent necessity, or which ought evidently to take precedence of it. (*On Christian Doctrine*, IV,4)

Indeed, Augustine disparaged even the rhetorical education he received as a boy. Although successful in declamation exercises, he referred to them as "smoke and wind," as "empty trifles, a defiled prey for the fowls of the air" (*Confessions*, I,27). He wondered if "teaching can impart" the "skill of speaking" (VIII,13).

Among the reasons that Augustine's rhetoric lacked the stature that Isocrates gave the area was that Augustine followed Plato and Aristotle in defining the area differently than Isocrates. While Isocrates considered ethical conduct the most important goal of his rhetoric, Augustine considered the pursuit of truth to be his major goal, but excluded rhetoric from any role in that pursuit. Like Plato,

Augustine saw rhetoric as an amoral instrument of persuasion that could be used for either good or bad ends, that could support either truth or falsehood. Augustine did not blame rhetoric or eloquence for "the perversity of those who put it to a bad use." The rules of eloquence "can be used for persuading men of what is false; but...they can be used to enforce the truth as well" (*On Christian Doctrine*, II,36).

While Isocrates included within the purview of rhetoric the invention of what to say, Augustine separated the invention of content from its presentation and limited rhetoric or eloquence to the latter, a separation that had roots in Aristotle and Cicero's Crassus and Antonius. According to Augustine, rhetoric was "not to be used so much for ascertaining the meaning as for setting forth the meaning when it is ascertained" (*On Christian Doctrine*, II,55). In describing his excitement about Cicero's *Hortensius*, he contrasted rhetoric or eloquence with philosophy or wisdom, associating the former with sharpening his tongue or style, the latter with content or matter (*Confessions*, III,7). He preferred wisdom without eloquence to eloquence without wisdom, but believed that the most effective Christian would strive toward both wisdom and eloquence (*On Christian Doctrine*, IV,8). To that end, Christians should not ignore the art of rhetoric: "Since, then, the faculty of eloquence is available for both sides, and is of very great service in the enforcing either of wrong or right, why do not good men study to engage it on the side of truth, when bad men use it to obtain the triumph of wicked and worthless causes, and to further injustice and error?" (IV,3).

In Book IV of *On Christian Doctrine*, Augustine offered a few scraps of the art of rhetoric as a guide to eloquence. For instance, he mentioned the appeal to emotions: "If...hearers require to be roused...in order that they may be diligent to do what they already know,...entreaties and reproaches, exhortations and upbraidings, and all the other means of arousing the emotions...are necessary" (IV,6). He encouraged audience analysis and adaptation: "Now a crowd anxious for instruction generally shows by its movements if it understands what is said; and until some indication of this sort be given, the subject discussed ought to be turned over and over, and put in every shape and form and variety of expression" (IV,25). Toward the end of Book IV, Augustine drew heavily on Cicero in suggesting the use of different styles on different occasions.

If Augustine encouraged Christians to learn the art of rhetoric, however, he also severed the art of imitation from the art of rhetoric and encouraged Christians to learn eloquence by imitation and ignore the teachers of rhetoric: "if a man desire to speak...with eloquence....,I would rather send him to read, and listen to, and exercise himself in imitating, eloquent men, than advise him to spend time with the teachers of rhetoric" (*On Christian Doctrine*, IV,8). On the one hand, he argued that the rules of eloquence were true and useful: "There are also certain rules for a more copious kind of argument, which is called *eloquence*, and these rules are...true" and can be "used to enforce the truth" (II,54). On the other hand, the best men learned through imitation rather than these rules: "men of quick intellect and glowing temperament find it easier to become eloquent by reading and listening to eloquent speakers than by following rules for eloquence" (IV,4).

Prayer is actually more efficacious in oratory than the art of rhetoric. In fact, prayer is broadly effective as a methodology for human empowerment. Augustine condemned magic (*City of God*, X,9), but then introduced his own form of magic—prayer—to control the world. Prayer can teach reading: "Christianus...,without any teaching from man, attained a full knowledge of the art of reading simply through prayer that it might be revealed to him" (*On Christian Doctrine*, Preface,4). Prayer is effective in curing breast cancer, as evidenced by the example of the devout Innocentia of Carthage (*City of God*, XXII,8). And the Christian orator derives so little from rhetorical education that piety in prayer will help him more: "our Christian orator...will succeed more by piety in prayer than by gifts of oratory" (*On Christian Doctrine*, IV,32).

Thomas M. Conley (1990), in *Rhetoric in the European Tradition*, accurately gauged "Augustine's attitude toward rhetoric" as "just short of contemptuous" (p. 75). He cited one of Augustine's letters that suggests that pastoral duties are incommensurate with rhetorical subjects: "these subjects are not in harmony with my current profession" (p. 75). Since Augustine differed from Isocrates in his attitude toward rhetoric, we are not surprised to see his attitude toward poetry follow Plato and differ from Isocrates as well. Augustine lauded Plato, "who, in framing his ideal republic, conceived that poets should be banished from the city as enemies of the state" (*City of God*, II,14). With modest exceptions, then, Augustine inclined Christianity to favor ideas stemming from Plato and to disparage those that I have associated with Isocrates.

To the extent that some of the ideas that I have associated with Augustine inform Christianity, to that extent Christianity can militate against some this-worldly goals, social structures, and methodologies. A belief that this world is only to be used and not enjoyed militates against a belief that this earthly life is all we have and that we should enjoy it as much as possible. An encouragement toward ascetic withdrawal and monasticism—supported by a perception of food, drink, and sex as threats—militates against a desire to embrace as much of the richness of human experience as possible and to develop the social structures to best achieve that end. A limitation of attention almost exclusively to an appreciation of the truths of scripture and the Truth that is God militates against an effort to learn as much as possible about the world and use it in household management, business affairs, and civil governance to make the right choices to improve our lives. An emphasis on textuality directs attention away from the fullest appreciation of realities beyond texts.

A number of attitudes promote resignation in the face of the ills of this life and militate against the motivation of humans to work aggressively toward the betterment of civilization. The beliefs that ills in this life are inevitable, that the only happiness in this life results from the contemplation of God, and that hopes for a better life should be placed not in the present, but in some future after death militate against the drive for this-worldly satisfactions. The attack on the power of human reason, the restriction of education to what is essential for scriptural interpretation, and the tendency toward withdrawal that cuts humans off from this-worldly experience militate against the confidence that humans have the mental power and educational and experiential resources to make a difference in the quality of this-worldly living. The faith in divine intervention exhibited by prayers, miracles, and supernatural voices not only promotes gullibility and vitiates healthy skepticism, but also militates against self-reliance based on talent, education, experience, and hard work.

The diminishment and narrowing of the province of rhetoric militate against the development of a methodology of sufficient scope to enable ethical performance in this-worldly affairs. A pejorative attitude toward rhetoric militates against the devotion of attention to this methodology and the retention of past knowledge about it. The definitional exclusion of ethical choice and the discovery of content from rhetoric limits attention to an amoral instrument for persuasion with primary emphasis on style and militates against the creation of a methodology that concerns itself with all choice, all governance, and all knowledge. The exclusive use of rhetoric to encourage conviction about a limited set of historical facts and to direct attention to what is universal, unchanging, and eternal militates against a concern for a methodology that engages what is unique, variable, and temporary and is directed by different this-worldly problems to different areas of historical awareness.

After Augustine's death, Christianity dominated the medieval world, and Augustinian Platonism remained its leading philosophy until the 13th century (Cassirer, Kristeller, & Randall, 1948/1969). If Christianity primarily absorbed and supported Platonic ideas until the 13th century, it also drew heavily on Aristotle and lent strong support to Aristotelian ideas after that. While, in the early Middle Ages, Augustine sought to understand Christianity largely with the help of Plato, a number of Christians in the later Middle Ages, such as Thomas Aquinas (c. 1224–1274), sought to understand Christianity largely with the help of Aristotle. As Kristeller suggested in *Renaissance Thought* (1955/1961), Aquinas went "farthest among his contemporaries in his attempt to reconcile Aristotelian philosophy and Christian theology" (p. 32). The resulting synthesis, called Thomism, received its greatest impetus in the 19th century when Pope Leo XIII, in 1879, proclaimed Thomism the official philosophy of the Roman Catholic Church. Given the differences between Aristotelian and Isocratean ideas, Thomist Christianity has hardly been a bastion of support for either Isocrates or the rhetorical tradition stemming from him.

For all the strong support for philosophy in the Middle Ages (including not only inclinations to favor Plato or Aristotle, but also efforts to synthesize the two), rhetoric was not entirely ignored. For instance, a work such as James J. Murphy's *Rhetoric in the Middle Ages* (1974/1981) suggested a range of developments in the art of preaching after Augustine. Of particular interest and significance, however, were some developments associated with secular rather than sacred rhetoric, especially in Italy. As Kristeller (1955/1961) suggested, two professions—secretaries of princes and cities and teachers of grammar and rhetoric—devoted considerable attention to the art of letter writing. A professional focusing on letter writing (called a *dictator*) conveyed the principles of writing good letters, applied these principles in specific situations, and composed model letters or formularies that could be imitated in certain contexts. Often, the same person switched hats, becoming a notary, and drew up legal contracts and documents. The notaries, who often included ideas about composition in their work, constituted the largest of the learned professions; in 1330, Florence had 600 notaries, 80 lawyers, and 60 physicians (Seigel, 1968, p. 209). These legal, administrative, and business activities—as Kristeller reminded us—were combined with a strong tradition of public speaking in secular contexts.

These developments in secular rhetoric in medieval Italy are of particular interest and significance because they evolved into a broad movement called Humanism that—together with Platonism and Aristotelianism—constituted one of the three major currents or traditions in the Italian Renaissance (Cassirer, Kristeller, & Randall, 1948/1969). Kristeller (1965/1961) suggested that the vast majority of the humanists, like their medieval forebears, were secretaries of princes and cities and teachers of grammar or rhetoric. He indicated that "Renaissance humanism must be understood as a characteristic phase in what may be called the rhetorical tradition in Western culture" (p. 11). He associated the great resurgence of classical studies in the Renaissance with this rhetorical movement: "classical studies in the Renaissance were rarely, if ever, separated from the literary and practical aim of the rhetorician to write and to speak well" (p. 13). The rediscovery of the full text of Quintilian's *Institutio Oratoria* by Poggio Bracciolini at St. Gall in 1416 and Cicero's *De Oratore*, *Orator*, and *Brutus* by Gerardo Landriani near Milan in 1421 gave great impetus to rhetoric, classical studies, and the Isocratean tradition.

In developing their educational program, as Kimball (1986) indicated, the Renaissance humanists used the terms "*studia humanitatis* or *studia humaniora*, terms that Cicero and Gellius had coined and equated with *artes liberales* and that, by the fifteenth century, had come to mean the disciplines of grammar, rhetoric, poetry, and history, often combined with moral philosophy" (p. 78)—precisely those areas emphasized in the Isocratean tradition. Among the areas excluded by definition from the humanities or liberal arts, as Kristeller (1965/1961) indicated, were "logic, natural philosophy, and metaphysics, as well as mathematics and astronomy...and theology" (p. 10)—areas emphasized in the Platonic and Aristotelian traditions. Perhaps the most crucial factor that identified the Renaissance humanists with the major classical rhetoricians and distinguished them from the major classical philosophers was their attitude toward humanity; the term "humanist" contains the cognate "human," and that terminology highlights the humanist "emphasis on man, on his dignity and privileged place in the universe"

(Kristeller, 1955/1961, p. 20). That emphasis corresponds to the centrality of humanity that we find in Isocrates, Cicero, and Quintilian and contrasts sharply with the otherworldliness that I have highlighted from Plato and the relatively low value ascribed to human problems that I have highlighted from Aristotle.

Research about the ideas of the Renaissance humanists is still in its formative stages, but even a cursory glance at a work such as Lorenzo Valla's *De Voluptate* (trans. 1977) uncovers echoes of the Isocratean tradition. Speech is that human capability "by which almost alone we are superior to the animals" (p. 101). Oratory is "the queen of all [arts]" (p. 221). Philosophy is "like a soldier...at the orders of Oratory, his commander and...queen" (p. 75). Cicero should have recovered "from the philosophers all the oratorical trappings that he found among them (since everything that philosophy claims for itself is actually ours)" (p. 75). He should have "raised against those sneak thieves of philosophers the sword he had received from Eloquence, queen of all," and punished them "as criminals" (pp. 75,77). Aristotle is exposed as "neither godlike...,nor happy...,nor wise" (p. 207). Seigel summarized Valla's attitude toward Aristotle: "Aristotle...could not be easily reconciled with the humanist vision of antiquity. He...could only be regarded as an enemy by Valla....Valla regarded Aristotle with hostility, as he did the rest of pagan philosophy. Plato did not fare much better among the early humanists" (p. 257). If Valla, a university professor of rhetoric, were alive today, he would find strange indeed the highly favorable views of Plato and Aristotle found in the works of so many university professors of rhetoric in the 20th century. Instantly, he would know who had won the centuries-old struggle between the rhetoricians and the philosophers.

If rhetoric had one more resurgence among the Renaissance humanists of the 14th, 15th, and 16th centuries and helped give impulse toward the scope contained in the oft-used expression "a Renaissance man," however, the Renaissance also contained the seeds of a further decline for rhetoric. Cicero's Crassus and Quintilian had already placed great emphasis on style and delivery in their rhetoric, and a number of forces combined in the Renaissance to support that emphasis. Among these forces was the work of Peter Ramus (1515–1572), who defined rhetoric as including only style and delivery. This Ramist approach to definition is discussed in *Literary Criticism: A Short History* (1957), by William K. Wimsatt, Jr., and Cleanth Brooks:

> One of the first principles of Ramist reasoning was a clean separation of each liberal discipline from every other—with no overlapping. Ramus could not tolerate, for instance, the fact that the intellectual activities of 'invention' and 'disposition' had traditionally appeared not only in dialectic (or logic) but in rhetoric....He took invention, disposition, and memory away from rhetoric and gave them securely and univocally to dialectic, leaving to rhetoric proper only elocution (that is, style) and delivery. Since the last of these is a matter of externalization (the actor's part), rhetoric proper might be conceived as consisting only of style. (p. 223)

Although Ramus was hostile toward Aristotle, he shared Aristotle's obsession with definition and further fragmented rhetoric.

The growth in the number of genres of rhetoric by the time of the Renaissance promoted the same emphasis on style. With so many different forms of oral and written discourse covered under the single rubric of rhetoric, as Madeleine Doran suggested in *Endeavors of Art: A Study of Form in Elizabethan Drama* (1954/1964), style came "to be emphasized at the expense of 'invention'...and 'disposition.'" She provided the sound reason: "it was so obviously hard to make the structural form fit a different type of discourse, so easy to deal with the minor forms in common terms" (p. 34). It is a principle that too many teachers fail to understand. If you are discussing discourse in general, as Aristotle would have us do—that is, if you are teaching a varied group of students who will be involved in very different writing situations—you will be able to say more of value to all of them about style than about anything else, which may lead to a disproportionate emphasis on style.

Doran gave other reasons for the disproportionate emphasis on style in the Renaissance:

> The practice of rhetoric was colored by the medieval attitude—itself a heritage from decadent post-classical times—towards rhetoric as primarily concerned with the gorgeous accoutrements of style....Further, the revived interest in classical rhetoric, because it was centered on a not too well understood Cicero, joined hands with the medieval tradition in promoting the cultivation of style at the expense of structural form. (p. 43)

Among the results of a growing interest in the gorgeous accoutrements of style was an ornateness supported by extensive use of rhetorical devices.

Richard Foster Jones (1951), in his article "Science and English Prose Style in the Third Quarter of the Seventeenth Century," described this style: "this style is characterized by various rhetorical devices such as figures, tropes, metaphors, and similes....The sentences are long, often obscurely involved, and rhythmical....The penchant for interlarding a work with Latin and Greek quotations is also apparent. The diction reveals a host of exotic words, many Latinisms" (p. 76). The stylistic ideal is copiousness and ornamentation. Writers were often so caught up in verbal exuberance, so delighted with word play, that they seemed more intrigued with the display of rhetorical devices than other, more important goals.

An ornate style imbued with rhetorical devices was severely attacked by apologists for science in the latter half of the 17th century. With the rise of science, the stage was set for a further decline in rhetoric. Essentially, the rise of science created additional support for the ideas that I have associated with Plato and Aristotle and militated against the Isocratean tradition.

THE RISE OF SCIENCE

A. R. Hall (1954) entitled his important book about the rise of modern approaches to science *The Scientific Revolution 1500–1800*. Hall's idea that the development of modern approaches to science in the 16th, 17th, and 18th centuries constituted a revolution has been widely shared by historians, and considerable effort has been devoted to distinguishing modern science from the broader systems of thought including some science associated with Plato, Aristotle, and their followers. This effort has often highlighted the strong resistance to efforts of the new scientists by Christian contemporaries influenced by Plato, Aristotle, and their followers; among the dramatic events associated with this resistance were those carried out by the Roman Catholic Inquisition—including the imprisonment of Tommaso Campanella, the trial and condemnation of Galileo, and the burning of Giordano Bruno at the stake. In the effort to define what was new and unique about the scientific revolution and to tell the dramatic story of the triumph of science over serious obstacles, however, historians have too often lost sight of the similarities between ideas associated with the new science and those associated with their philosophical predecessors.

A comparison of ideas associated with the new science and those associated with Plato, Aristotle, and the Christians who incorporated their thought can be helpful here. While much in the rise of science was indeed new and represented a change, other ideas associated with the scientific revolution perpetuated and strengthened the Platonic, Aristotelian, and Christian traditions that I have been following. These latter ideas were not necessarily identical with the actual approaches that led to scientific success. Nor were they necessarily characteristic of what scientists believed about their practice. Whether they became associated with science because they were part of the milieu in which science emerged, whether they resulted from the efforts of highly convincing authorities to describe the methods that led to scientific success, or whether, at least to some degree, they actually accounted for some of the successes of science, we find them again and again highlighted as central to the practice of science not just by contemporary apologists but also by scholars of the 19th and 20th centuries.

Twentieth-century historians justifiably drew some sharp contrasts between ideas associated with Plato and his Christian followers and those associated with the scientific revolution. For instance, Charles Singer (1925) rightfully noted that Plato's otherworldliness led to "a complete indifference to worldly happenings" (p. 98). This otherworldliness, absorbed by Christians such as Augustine, came to dominate Western thought in the Middle Ages for over a 1,000 years. Lovejoy wrote in *The Great Chain of Being* (1936/1960):

> The final good for man, as almost all Western philosophers for more than a millennium agreed, consisted in some mode of assimilation or approximation to the divine nature, whether that mode were defined as imitation or contemplation or

absorption. The doctrine of the divine attributes was thus also, and far more significantly, a theory of the nature of ultimate value, and the conception of God was at the same time the definition of the objective of human life. (p. 82)

This ethical ideal militated against such this-worldly or secular concerns as the practice of science.

In the Renaissance and after, however, a large number of changes promoted increasing secularism. Lovejoy suggested a new ethical ideal that replaced the contemplation of God: man's duty was "to keep *his* place, and not to seek to transcend it" (p. 200). Such an ethical ideal led "to the open and unqualified rejection of that otherworldliness which had always been characteristic of the Christian and the Platonic tradition" (p. 202). Other historians have supported Lovejoy's view. M. H. Abrams (1971/1973) wrote: "It is a historical commonplace that the course of Western thought since the Renaissance has been one of progressive secularization" (p. 13). Peter Gay (1966) clarified the nature of this secularism: "To speak of the secularization of life in the eighteenth century is not to speak of the collapse of clerical establishments or the decay of religious concerns....To speak of secularization...is to speak of a subtle shift of attention: religious institutions and religious explanations of events were slowly being displaced from the center of life to its periphery" (p. 338). The new science was one of the areas of attention replacing religion.

Twentieth-century historians have also justifiably drawn some sharp contrasts between ideas associated with Aristotle and his Christian followers and those associated with the scientific revolution. Galileo's works have been especially useful toward this end. In Galileo's lifetime (1564–1642), the synthesis of Aristotelian and Christian ideas called Thomism remained a powerful force in Italy, and this synthesis included a substantial number of scientific ideas that Galileo challenged. Singer (1925) wrote: "Every one of the foundations of the Aristotelian system" was "undermined by Galileo or Kepler" (p. 141). As a result, Galileo was not just attacked by supporters of Aristotelian science, but also condemned by the Roman Catholic Inquisition to stand trial, recant his ideas, and live under permanent house arrest.

Among the Aristotelian ideas challenged by Galileo was the notion of an immovable earth at the center of the universe. Aristotle (trans. 1941) wrote: "it is clear that the earth does not move and does not lie elsewhere than at the centre" (*On the Heavens*, 296b). In 1615, the Christian Cardinal Robert Bellarmine, head of the Roman College, indicated that all Christian interpreters of the Bible echoed Aristotle: "the sun is in the heavens and travels swiftly around the earth, while the earth is far from the heavens and remains motionless in the center of the world" (qtd. in Drake, 1957, p. 163). Bellarmine used scripture to support these interpreters: "I add that the words *The sun also riseth, and the sun goeth down, and hasteth to the place where he ariseth* were written by Solomon, who not only spoke by divine inspiration, but was a man wise above all others,...which wisdom he had from God" (p. 164).

Galileo opposed this view by supporting the belief in a motionless sun at the center of the universe with the earth moving around it (Drake, 1957, p. 177). He echoed Augustine, whom he frequently cited, in arguing that his belief was not contrary to scripture: "I believe nobody will deny that...[scripture] is often very abstruse, and may say things which are quite different from what its bare words signify. Hence in expounding the Bible if one were always to confine oneself to the unadorned grammatical meaning, one might fall into error" (qtd. in Drake, p. 181). Galileo argued that God revealed himself through both nature and scripture and that our knowledge of nature could help us in interpreting scripture (Drake, p. 183).

In detailing such sharp contrasts between ideas associated with the new science and those associated with Plato, Aristotle, and the Christians who incorporated their thought, however, historians have too often ignored important similarities. Among these similarities, the apologists for science did not hesitate to refer to themselves as "philosophers." Galileo continually referred to his activities as the practice of philosophy and compared that practice at one point to the reading of a book: "Philosophy is written in the grand book, the universe, which stands continually open to our gaze" (qtd. in Drake, pp. 237–238). Indeed, when Galileo negotiated for a position in Florence in 1610, he insisted on having the title "philosopher" (p. 222). One of Galileo's adversaries, Lodovico delle Colombe, certainly viewed him as a philosopher, although critically: "Some men,...despairing to understand Aristotle or to say anything that will gain them celebrity in his philosophy, and yet being unable to deny all his truths and show off in any ordinary way, oppose against him all sorts of insincere notions, revealing—or rather dreaming of—a new philosophy and a new method of philosophizing" (p. 223).

The term "new philosophy" was often used by the apologists for science. For instance, in *The History of the Royal-Society, For the Improving of Natural Knowledge*, written by Thomas Sprat (1667/1958), we discover terms such as "*New Philosophy*" (p. 417), "*Natural Philosophy*" (p. 55), and "*Experimental Philosophy*" (p. 393). The adjective *new* in the term "new philosophy" suggests that Sprat believed that he and his colleagues were practicing something original, and, indeed, Sprat devoted considerable space to distinctions between the virtues of 17th-century practice and the errors of earlier practice. But the noun *philosophy* in each of Sprat's three terms clearly indicates that he placed himself in the tradition of Plato and Aristotle. Sprat may have criticized Aristotle severely (pp. 30, 34), but such attacks cannot be allowed to obscure the ideas he shared with Aristotle. When Sprat looked for exemplars from antiquity, Plato and Aristotle were among them: "let *Pythagoras*, *Plato*, and *Aristotle*, and the rest of their wise Men, be our examples, and we are safe" (p. 49).

Sprat followed Plato and Aristotle in other respects as well. He followed Plato in defining his subject carefully to make clear the nature of that subject. He followed Aristotle's advice by restricting his subject to a limited area and focusing on that area alone. In line with Plato, Sprat opposed his philosophy—that is, his science—to activities such as oratory and politics (p. 82). As a result, he excluded from science the very subjects that the Renaissance humanists and rhetoricians of antiquity claimed as their own. His reasons for exclusion are noteworthy; these subjects do not lend themselves to observations by the senses, nor can one attain a high degree of certainty about them. Still, if Sprat was in accord with Plato in opposing his philosophy to oratory and politics, he limited his subject even more than Plato and Aristotle by also excluding morality or ethics (p. 82).

Elsewhere in his work, Sprat evinced positive distaste for oratory or rhetoric. He echoed Augustine's contention that rhetoric is for boys: "a *new Method* of Knowledge...is therefore most proper for Men: they still leave to Learners, and Children, the old talkative *Arts* which best fit the younger Age" (p. 324). Furthermore, for all that he criticized Greek science, he nevertheless contrasted it favorably with the neglect of science and focus on rhetoric that he found in ancient Rome. He described the transfer of power from ancient Greece to ancient Rome: "at last with their Empire, their Arts also were transported to *Rome*: the great spirit of their Lawgivers, and Philosophers, in course of time, degenrating into Rhetoricians....Amongst the Romans, the studies of Nature met with little, or no entertainment" (pp. 9–10). This contrast between ancient Greece and ancient Rome became a staple of modern history and obscured the emphasis on rhetoric in ancient Greece.

Disputatiousness was among the characteristics of politics and oratory that most disturbed Sprat. He claimed that "earnest disputers evaporate all the strength of their minds in arguing, questioning, and debating; and tire themselves out before they come to the *Practise*" (p. 332). He was echoing a point made earlier by Galileo. Galileo wrote: "We meant only to address those men, ancient or modern, who try in all their studies to investigate some truth in nature. We meant to steer clear of those who ostentatiously engage in noisy contests merely to be popularly judged victors over others and pompously praised" (qtd. in Drake, pp. 238–239). He suggested that members of an academy for science "will pass over in silence all political controversies and every kind of quarrels and wordy disputes, especially gratuitous ones which give occasion to deceit, unfriendliness and hatred, as men who desire peace and seek to preserve their studies free from molestation and to avoid every sort of disturbance" (p. 78).

Among other aspects of oratory or rhetoric that Sprat disdained was its overemphasis on stylistic ornateness. He attacked past writers for expression devoid of content; he complained that past writers "wanted matter to contrive: and so, like the *Indians*, onely express'd a wonderful Artifice, in the ordering of the same Feathers into a thousand varities of Figures" (pp. 15–16). He associated rhetoric with decoration, claiming that the Royal Society, the association for scientists first chartered in England in 1662, had to "separate the knowledge of *Nature* from the colours of *Rhetorick*, the devices of *Fancy*, or the delightful deceit of *Fables*" (p. 12). He associated rhetorical devices with obscurity: "Who can behold, without indignation, how many mists and uncertainties, these specious *Tropes* and *Figures* have brought on our Knowledg?" (p. 112). Sprat and other apologists wanted a plain style, a transparent style that enabled readers to grasp reality directly with the least impediment from language. For the early scientific apologists, language had become an obstacle rather than an aid to expression or understanding. They rejected the kind of ornate style popularized by Renaissance writers.

Sprat's exclusion of politics and rhetoric from his definition of philosophy or science was not without an element of withdrawal that has already been associated with Plato and Aristotle. Sprat contrasted the pleasant contemplation of nature by scientists with the disquiets of human affairs: "It was *Nature* alone, which could pleasantly entertain them....The contemplation of that, draws our minds off from past, or present misfortunes, and makes them conquerers over things, in the greatest publick unhappiness: while the consideration of *Men*, and *humane affairs*, may affect us, with a thousand various disquiets" (p. 56). Furthermore, human affairs were a distraction from the practice of science: "the *affairs of State*, the administration of Civil Government, and the execution of Laws" have "drawn away the Inclinations of Men, from prosecuting the naked, and uninteressed Truth" (p. 26).

If Sprat excluded from his definition of science those deliberations about humans associated with subjects such as oratory, politics, and morality, however, other deliberations about them—together with thoughts about nature—are fair game for scientists:

> These two Subjects, *God*, and the *Soul*, being onely forborn: In all the rest, they wander, at their pleasure: In the frame of *Mens bodies*, the ways for strong, health-ful, and long life: In the *Arts of Mens Hands*, those that either *necessity*, *conve-nience*, or *delight* have produc'd: In the *works* of *Nature*, their helps, their varieties, redundancies, and defects: and in bringing all these to the *uses* of *humane Society*. (p. 83)

Sprat combined here what Aristotle separated into theoretical sciences and practical sciences. He combined what we would today call science and engineering. Furthermore, he emphasized usefulness, a goal also emphasized by Isocrates, but expressly ranked below curiosity or wonder by Aristotle.

In addition to his emphasis on usefulness as a goal, Sprat also highlighted truth, as already indicated in his contrast between human affairs and the disinterested pursuit of truth. He indicated that the scientists of the Royal Society have the following goal: "to restore the Truths, that have lain neglected: to push on those, which are already known, to more various uses: and to make the way more passable, to what remains unreveal'd" (p. 61). J. W. N. Sullivan (1933), in *Limitations of Science*, saw a progression in thinking about the goals of science. While usefulness was initially an important goal for some apologists such as Sprat, the dominant motive in the pursuit of science eventually became curiosity, as was the case with Aristotle, and the dominant goal became the pursuit of new truths (p. 240). Like Plato, Aristotle, and their Christian followers, the scientists became primarily interested in identification, description, and the quest for truths about "what is."

As was also the case with their philosophical predecessors, the apologists for science associated their quest for truth with such terms as "contemplation," "understanding," and "knowledge." For instance, Galileo referred to his astronomical observations as "true philosophy" and "important contemplations" (qtd. in Drake, p. 31). Much as Augustine contemplated and sought to understand scripture, Galileo contemplated and sought to understand "this great book of the universe" (p. 127); he described his quest as "the knowledge for which we now search" (p. 123). The knowledge that he acquired often constituted a quantitative increase; he wrote of an "increase of known truths" (p. 175) and described such an increase: "to the three stars in the Belt of Orion and the six in the Sword which were previously known, I have added eighty adjacent stars discovered recently" (pp. 47–48).

Given that truth was a goal of science, Sullivan (1933) claimed that early scientists tended to focus on certain kinds of truth. While prescientific thinkers were said to be satisfied with accepting the diversity of experienced objects as a given, scientific thinkers were said to focus on quantitative abstractions of this experience. What is quantitative became most real: "Bodies, for instance, have for their measurable aspects size, shape, weight, motion. Such other characteristics as they possess were regarded as belonging to a lower order of reality. The real world is the world of mathematical characteristics" (p. 129). Some 17th-century writers about science highlighted the early emphasis on mathematics that Sullivan described. Among them, Galileo argued that the universe "cannot be understood unless one first learns to comprehend the language and read the letters in which it is composed. It is written in the language of mathematics" (qtd. in Drake, p. 238). Apologists for natural philosophy such as Galileo, then, shared the high value placed on mathematics by philosophers of antiquity such as Plato and Aristotle and differed sharply from a philosopher or rhetorician such as Isocrates, who disparaged mathematics.

Another early apologist for science, Fontenelle, is so enamored of mathematics that he recommended that the mathematical approach be applied to other branches of knowledge:

> The geometrical method is not so rigidly confined to geometry itself that it cannot be applied to other branches of knowledge as well. A work on politics, on morals, a piece of criticism, even a manual on public speaking would, other things being equal, be all the better for having been written by a geometrician. (qtd. in Hazard, 1963, p. 132)

As we shall see, mathematics was applied to other branches of knowledge in the twentieth century to a degree that might have astonished even Fontenelle.

According to historians, the emphasis on mathematics led early scientists to focus on areas where quantitative analysis had the greatest success. Sullivan (1933) claimed that the early scientists discovered that science was "strongest in dealing with the material universe," that "the scientific account of our universe appears clearest and most convincing when it deals with inanimate matter" (p. 125). Furthermore, scientists did not explore inanimate matter in all its diversity but tried to discover uniformities. As Galileo suggested, they stripped away such experienced qualities of natural objects as colors, sounds, tastes, and odors by associating them with human subjectivity (Drake, 1957, p. 274). Experienced qualities of natural objects were said to be creations of the human mind.

What was left, according to Sullivan (1933), was the study of matter in motion: "In the absence of mind the universe would be a collection of masses of various sizes, shapes, and weights, drifting, without colour, sound, or odour, through space and time" (p. 130). William Wotton (1694/1697), in *Reflections upon Ancient and Modern Learning*, certainly wrote in accord with Sullivan's view. The first item on one of Wotton's lists of the components of scientific method was as follows: "Matter and Motion, with their several Qualities, are only considered in Modern Solutions of Physical Problems" (p. 364). The study of matter in motion enabled scientists to relate natural objects to one another, to translate them to one homogeneous scheme, to discover patterns behind seemingly different phenomena, to move from the concrete to the universal. The process of abstraction, the movement from concrete to universal, was considered an unmasking of illusion to get at reality.

The new philosophy, then, strove not only to identify stubborn facts, but also to discover universals called laws. Singer (1925) wrote: "Science is the purposeful search for such general laws that can then be used to link together the observed phenomena" (p. 89). As examples, Sullivan (1933) pointed to Kepler's three laws of planetary motion: "Kepler's first two laws are true for each planet individually. It is true of each planet that it moves in an ellipse, and that its radius vector sweeps out equal areas in equal times. Kepler's third law finds a relation between all the various planets" (p. 44). Sullivan suggested that "these laws are purely descriptive laws. They are just statements of fact, like saying that gold is yellow. Kepler gives no reason why these laws should be as they are. The observation and recording of laws is the first step in scientific procedure. Science begins by hunting for uniformities amongst natural phenomena" (p. 44).

As Sullivan suggested, however, "the aim of science is to proceed to the next step, the construction of theories. Just as a law unifies a group of phenomena, so a theory unifies a group of laws. A theory is, as it were, a central principle, from which the various laws belonging to it can be deduced" (p. 45). Sullivan used as an example of this next level of universals what he called the most celebrated of all scientific theories, Newton's theory of gravitation:

Newton knew many isolated laws. He knew Kepler's three laws of planetary motion, he knew the rate at which a falling body increases its speed, he knew that the path of a projectile is a parabola, and so on. He saw that if we suppose that every piece of matter in the universe attracts every other piece of matter we can show that all these diverse phenomena are necessary consequences of this attraction. The strength of the attraction depends, of course, on the masses of the bodies involved, and also on their distance apart. (p. 45)

The positive value placed by apologists for science on laws and theories that are abstract, universal, and unchanging clusters well with the similar valuation that I have highlighted in Plato, Aristotle, and their Christian followers.

The efforts of scientists to discover new facts, laws, and theories were so successful and so revolutionized human thinking about the universe that the science of predecessors, especially Aristotle, was considered so much nonsense. Fontenelle (1688/1970) was typical of the apologists for science in his attack on Aristotle and the scholastics: "When the Authority of Aristotle was unquestioned, when truth was sought only in his enigmatic writings and never in Nature, not only did philosophy not advance at all, but it fell into an abyss of nonsense and unintelligible ideas whence it was rescued only with great difficulty" (p. 369). In his emphasis on intelligibility, Fontenelle seemed to have been influenced by Descartes. Descartes (1637/1956) wrote in his *Discourse on Method*:

The first rule was never to accept anything as true unless I recognized it to be evidently such: that is, carefully to avoid precipitation and prejudgment, and to include nothing in my conclusions unless it presented itself so clearly and distinctly to my mind that there was no occasion to doubt it. (p. 12)

Descartes's notion of intelligibility rested on a skepticism toward the past and a distrust of human judgment. Clearly linked with the rise of modern scientific thinking, then, was an obsession with human limitations. The apologists for science did not want to repeat the mistakes of prescientific thinkers. Many of them disparaged human judgment in much the same way as Plato and Aristotle.

What was essential was increased modesty. Toward the end of better adapting to human limitations, Galileo called for a reduction in the scope of science: "dealing with science as a method of demonstration and reasoning capable of human pursuit, I hold that the more this partakes of perfection the smaller the number of propositions it will promise to teach, and fewer yet will it conclusively prove" (qtd. in Drake, 1957, p. 240). Other apologists attacked authorities such as Aristotle and Descartes for devising grand systems of philosophy. Wotton (1694/1697) included this criticism in one of his lists of the components of scientific method (pp. 364–365).

Among other ways of coping with the inadequacies of the human mind and keeping the scope of scientific effort within reasonable limits, scientific apologists encouraged ever more specialization. As already indicated, the emphasis of the scientific apologists on definition and specialization led to an exclusion of those human deliberations associated with activities such as politics, oratory, and ethics. Later, science itself was classified into limited areas such as physics, chemistry, and botany, and scientists tended to limit themselves to one of these areas. In fact, classification itself very quickly became revered as a part of scientific method. Wotton (1694/1697) certainly included classification as one of his components of scientific method (p. 82). This emphasis on classification resulted in, among other things, the highly successful system of classification in botany devised by Linnaeus.

Many apologists for science believed that another means of avoiding human error was to focus more on the external world. Wotton suggested that this view had roots in Bacon: "My Lord *Bacon* was the first great Man who took much pains to convince the World that they had hitherto been in a wrong Path, and that Nature her self, rather than her Secretaries, was to be addressed to by those who were desirous to know very much of her Mind" (p. 370). This view also had roots in Galileo: "a man will never become a philosopher by worrying forever about the writings of other men, without ever raising his own eyes to nature's works" (qtd. in Drake, 1957, p. 225). Such a stance hardly accorded well with the notion of imitation so widely heralded in the past by rhetoricians.

Two additional ways to avoid human error were experiment and the use of instruments. Wotton (1694/1697) included both among his components of scientific method:

> (2.) To collect great Numbers of Observations, and to make a vast Variety of Experiments upon all sorts of Natural Bodies. And because this cannot be done without proper Tools, (3.) To contrive such Instruments, by which the Constituent Parts of the Universe, and of all its Parts, even the most minute, or the most remote, may lie more open to our View; and their Motions, or other Affections, be better calculated and examined, than could otherwise have been done by our unassisted Senses. (pp. 81–82)

Since human capability was suspect, human judgment had to be corrected by the external world, and our awareness of the world had to be extended by both experiments and instruments. Sullivan (1933) described the kind of experimental testing performed by Newton:

> [Newton] starts by investigating experimentally a simple group of phenomena and disentangling from them their quantitative relations. He then deduces the mathematical consequences of these relations. These deductions, if correct, will cover the behavior of phenomena over a wider field. Newton accordingly brings these phenomena to the experimental test, to see if his deductions are confirmed. (p. 136)

Many early scientific apologists, while always insisting on a skeptical frame of mind, nevertheless assumed that such experimental testing was crucial to achieve not only objectivity, but also certainty.

As we move toward the 20th century, the external world became even more primary and real and the human being a mere effect of it, a creature whose perceptions were misled by the vagaries of sense and mind and whose conclusions could be dismissed as opinion, illusion, or impressionism. To the greatest extent possible, investigators were eliminated from the research process, and scientific instrumentation became even more critical, partially to eliminate human error. Instrumentation evolved from such early instruments as the balance, air pump, microscope, and telescope to such 20th-century developments as the cloud chamber, electron microscope, cyclotron, and computer. To introduce some kind of instrument between a human and the object of that human's attention became increasingly satisfying.

Twentieth-century scientists, however, were skeptical about certainty. Sullivan (1933) suggested the examples of Einstein and Eddington:

> At the present day we have an interesting example of the influence of purely "subjective" factors in the creating of scientific theories in the methods adopted by Einstein and Eddington respectively in their attempts to reduce the laws of electromagnetism to geometry. Judged by the scientific criterion of accounting for phenomena there seems nothing to choose between them. But Einstein has said that he dislikes Eddington's theory, although he is unable to disprove it, and Eddington has said of Einstein's theory that it is a matter of taste. Here we are in a region where the ordinary "objective" criteria fail us. Our attitude towards these theories seems to depend on considerations which are, at bottom, aesthetic. (p. 171)

Sullivan called the aesthetic element "most prominent in mathematics" and "not lacking in the physical sciences." He related this aesthetic element to simplicity: "The search for universal laws and comprehensive theories is indubitably a manifestation of the aesthetic impulse. It is sometimes said that scientific men, in their choice of one of two theories that equally well cover the facts, always choose the simpler. But simplicity is, at bottom, an aesthetic criterion" (p. 165).

The characteristics that I have associated with science have not been uniformly embraced by writers about science. In its earliest stages, for instance, proponents such as Galileo and Descartes might have emphasized mathematics, but that emphasis was absent in Bacon. An early apologist such as Sprat (1667/1958) might have claimed that "a good Method of thinking, and a right course of apprehending things, does contribute towards the attaining of perfection in true knowledge, than the strongest, and most vigorous wit in the World, can do without them" (p. 15). But he would also have been quick to assert that the scientists of the Royal Society "had no Rules nor Method fix'd" (p. 56), that the "true *Experimenting* has this one thing inseparable from it, never to be a *fix'd* and *settled Art*, and never to be *limited* by constant Rules" (p. 89). Scientists have consistently been among the most vociferous in complaining that what is said about science is erroneous, and the flexibility of science has certainly been one of its greatest strengths—not only in the area of research, but also in the area of politics.

Whatever the adequacy of the ideas that have been associated with science, however, nobody would deny their strength, and that strength has been a source of concern to some observers such as Sullivan. Sullivan (1933) cautioned readers about the dominance of science and insisted that science be kept in perspective. As he indicated, any suggestion that the supposed concerns of science were more real than other concerns had to be rejected: "there is no faintest reason for supposing that everything science ignores is less real than what it accepts" (p. 147). Furthermore, he rightfully indicated that science was localized, that the concepts of science would never be broad enough to provide the means for human beings to engage all of their problems (p. 128). He even allowed that the problems of science might be of less interest or concern to humans than problems in other areas (p. 163). Scientific advancements in such areas as medicine and scientific contributions to the development of weaponry in the 20th century—the creation of atomic bombs, for instance—raise serious questions about Sullivan's last statement. But the existence of crucially important areas of human concern outside science cannot be forgotten.

Science is only a part of the realm of human activity. The effort to determine what to do or say includes not only the contemplation of inanimate matter toward the end of describing some aspect of the universe mathematically, but also the pursuit of excellence in such activities as creating a work of art, achieving the best lives possible, fashioning courtroom exchanges, and hammering out governmental policy. It includes not only the achievement of simplicity by moving away from the full concreteness of particular situations toward ever higher levels of abstraction, but also the careful study of all the complexity and richness of a unique situation toward the end of developing the precise expression best for that situation. It includes not only efforts to limit human subjectivity in a process of formulating universal and unchanging statements about the universe, but also efforts to consider the full range of human needs in making judgments in unique situations.

If perspective is maintained and this relationship of the whole to the part is kept clear, difficulties are not likely to arise. If, however, the dominance of science promotes the ideas I have associated with science to the status of an ultimate ideal, an ideal as ultimate as those we find in the works of Plato and Augustine, then a number of troublesome outcomes are possible. Among them, the ideas that I have associated with science have a way of inclining our attention so that we forget areas of concern beyond science, and methodologies associated with this activity are incorporated into other activities where they are inappropriate. In the second half of the 20th century, in industries where science was highly influential, such tendencies became especially troublesome for technical communication.

THE LATER DOMINANCE OF PHILOSOPHY

In the 18th, 19th, and 20th centuries, the ideas that I have associated with Plato, Aristotle, Christian philosophers, and the apologists for science rose to dominance in Western civilization. Although each of these centers of power had a multitude of variations down through the centuries and although the philosophies associated with these centers may have differed in substantial ways from one another, the similarities that they shared mutually reinforced one another and militated against ideas that I have associated with Isocrates, Cicero, and Quintilian. The resulting force—strengthened by a range of other social forces—powerfully shaped modern society, foregrounding goals, influencing social structures, and predisposing problem-solvers toward certain methodologies. By the second half of the 20th century, this shaping was so powerful that it compromised the scope of deliberation essential for ethical and effective performance.

In terms of foregrounding goals, future centuries will find it difficult to understand the obsession for science that afflicted the 20th century. This obsession was accurately suggested by Robert L. Heilbroner in "The Future of Capitalism" (1970):

> Science *is* the burning idea of the 20th century...science carries a near-religious ethos of conviction and even sacrifice....The scientific cadres proper, the social scientists, the government administrative personnel—even the military—look to science not merely as the vehicle of their expertise, but as the magnetic North of their compass of values. (pp. 297–298)

While the practice of science was broader than the ideas that I have associated with it, these ideas powerfully shaped not only scientific pursuits, but also other human activities as well.

Given the similarities between the ideas that I have highlighted from the apologists for science and those that I have highlighted from Plato and Aristotle, it is not surprising to find a book written by Philipp Frank entitled *Philosophy of Science: The Link Between Science and Philosophy* (1957). Frank wrote: "the deeper we dig into actual science the more its links with philosophy become obvious" (p. iv). To buttress his case, he cited extensively from Robert Maynard Hutchins's *The Higher Learning in America* (1936). Hutchins stated that the "sciences one by one broke off from philosophy" (p. 26), and he regretted that philosophy was an isolated department in universities (p. 102). Hutchins insisted that philosophy and science had to be linked (p. 103). Although Frank criticized some of Hutchins's views, he, too, emphasized the need to show the links between philosophy and science: "In the traditional teaching a 'link is missing' in the chain that should connect science with philosophy" (p. xii). Frank longed for "the old unity between science and philosophy" (p. 12).

If Frank longed for the old unity between science and philosophy, Hutchins longed for the old preeminence of theology that had been lost in the growing secularism since the Renaissance. The loss of religious experiences valued for over a millennium did not take place without periodic reactions in the centuries that followed. Among the effects of increasing secularism in the Renaissance and afterward, some humans felt the need to turn back to original Christian otherworldliness; the extraordinary success of Edward Young's *Night Thoughts* in the 18th century, which mystifies so many modern critics, is perfectly understandable in this context. Other humans were inclined to turn to intellectual, emotional, and physical environments associated with this world that helped constitute experiences with characteristics similar to those of otherworldly Christian experiences; the triumph of the sublime in the 18th and 19th centuries easily comes to mind here. Hutchins's longing for theology, then, was part of a long tradition that was not without power.

Hutchins (1936) did not overtly identify with a particular theology such as Catholicism, but he expressed a longing for theology in general (p. 105). He tried to suggest "how much we feel the need of an orthodox theology or a systematic metaphysics" (p. 104). He wistfully recalled how theology unified the medieval university (p. 96) and decried the fate of theology in the 20th century: "Saddest of all is the fate that has overtaken theology itself." It has been displaced "from its position as the queen of sciences" (p. 101). He described the modern situation. "Theology is banned by law from some universities. It might as well be from the rest....To look to theology to unify the modern university is futile and vain" (p. 97). Hutchins had to look elsewhere for his source of unity for the modern university.

Since Hutchins could not turn to theology, he simply relied on the Greek ideas that informed it:

> If we omit from theology faith and revelation, we are substantially in the position of the Greeks....Now Greek thought was unified. It was unified by the study of first principles. Plato had a dialectic which was a method of exploring first principles. Aristotle made the knowledge of them into the science of metaphysics. Among the Greeks, then, metaphysics, rather than theology, is the ordering and proportioning discipline. (p. 97)

Since Hutchins could not have Christianity itself, he would have Plato and Aristotle, who informed it. Much as Frank strengthened philosophy through science, Hutchins strengthened philosophy—especially Plato and Aristotle—through religion.

Plato and Aristotle, however, were not without their own strength in the 20th century. John Dewey (1929), in *The Quest for Certainty*, highlighted their strength in directing attention away from human affairs:

They brought with them the idea of a higher realm of fixed reality of which alone true science is possible and an inferior world of changing things with which experience and practical matters are concerned. They glorified the invariant at the expense of change. It bequeathed the notion, which has ruled philosophy ever since the time of the Greeks, that the office of knowledge is to uncover the antecedently real, rather than, as is the case with our practical judgments, to gain the kind of understanding which is necessary to deal with problems as they arise. (pp. 16–17)

The dominance of Plato and Aristotle in modern philosophy militated against an Isocratean focus on the changing world of practical problems.

Given the strength in the 20th century of the tradition that I have associated with Plato, Aristotle, Christian philosophers, and apologists for science, it is not surprising to discover the pursuit of truth foregrounded as a goal. Basil Willey (1935/ 1953), in his *Seventeenth Century Background*, claimed—astonishingly—that the separation of the true from the false, the real from the illusory, was the task of thought at all times. He indicated that this winnowing process was carried on more actively during the period of Greek philosophy and the centuries following the Renaissance (p. 11). Clearly, Willey identified with Plato, Aristotle, and post-Renaissance scientists. Yet Willey came from the field of literary criticism, which considered itself one of the humanities in the 20th century. Since Willey was clearly in the camp of the philosophers, however, and since he stood at opposite poles from the Renaissance humanists, who identified with the rhetorical tradition, Willey's words can stand as an example of the triumph of the philosophical tradition in the 20th century.

If the philosophical tradition focused attention on truth and directed attention away from human affairs, however, human affairs had a way of calling attention to themselves. Humans were impelled from within toward such goals as survival and love and were driven toward acquiring food, shelter, and companionship and avoiding injury, disease, and conflict. Human needs prompted involvement. Dewey (1929) experienced these needs and decried the depreciation of action that he found in Plato and Aristotle (p. 4). He stressed the importance of knowing in order to live, of using the intellect to obtain greater security about the issues of action (p. 38). He wanted to know what concrete judgments to form about ends and means in the regulation of practical behavior (p. 46).

Dewey longed for a philosophy that could help respond to these needs, a philosophy other than that provided by Plato and Aristotle and absorbed into Christianity:

In spite of enormous extension of secular interests and of natural science, of expansion of practical arts and occupations, of the almost frantic domination of present life by concern for definite material interests and the organization of society by forces fundamentally economic, there is no widely held philosophy of life which replaces the traditional classic one as that was absorbed and modified by the Christian faith. (p. 76)

Dewey was clearly expressing the desire for a philosophy or rhetoric akin to that provided by Isocrates. It was a measure of the strength of the philosophical tradition, however, that Dewey could not escape the siren call of truth himself. Despite the great differences between Dewey's ideas of science and those of the early apologists for science, he limited his role for the university to the same goals as these apologists—discoveries of new knowledge and truths (p. 207). He differed from the early apologists, among other ways, in looking for his discoveries or truths in a different area—social affairs.

In addition to foregrounding goals, the success of the philosophical tradition helped shape social structures. The forces promoting definition, specialization, and the expert—including Plato, Aristotle, and the apologists for science—succeeded in fragmenting society. Bolgar (1954/1958) recognized this trend: "the firms, corporations, Government Boards and Authorities that proliferate around us...exist...to carry out specialised tasks, and the policies of those who direct them are determined...by the pressures of a particular need....The energies of millions are mobilised for fragmentary ends" (p. 391). Among the major social structures focusing on specialized tasks in 20th-century America were industries and universities. These specialized social structures, in turn, were themselves aggregates of numerous specializations. The organization charts of corporations in the 20th century provided some insight into the extent to which the concept of specialization controlled structure.

The emphasis on definition, specialization, and the expert might have been most manifest in those social structures called universities. American universities in the 20th century were divided into isolated entities called schools, which, in turn, were divided into isolated entities called departments. Kimball (1986) suggested that science was not without responsibility for this specialization: "Becoming the key characteristic of American scientific societies between 1866 and 1918, specialization inspired the development of the undergraduate 'major' and 'minor,' in line with the departmentalization of graduate faculties according to fields of specialized scholarship" (p. 163). As Bolgar (1954/1958) indicated, a philosophical pursuit such as science was amenable to specialization and pursuit of the partial (p. 392).

Specialization and departmentalization attracted their critics, however. In 1948, for instance, Arthur O. Lovejoy wrote about the relative isolation of the subjects that were taught in university departments. These subjects were associated with separate journals and learned societies without much in the way of interrelations. However, Lovejoy noted that the lines of division separating some of these distinct disciplines were breaking down because questions raised within the traditional limits of some subjects proved incapable of adequate answer without going beyond those limits. The notion that the subjects under study themselves forced greater scope than departmental lines of division allowed is important.

Bolgar (1954/1958) explored the difference between 20th-century specialization and the undifferentiated knowledge of the Renaissance. He noted the number of subjects in distinct and water-tight compartments in the 20th century that were looked upon as the infrangible province of rhetoric and grammar during the 15th and 16th centuries. Only three specialties in the Renaissance—philosophy, medicine, and law—had the status of independent disciplines. Since Bolgar, like Lovejoy, had reservations about specialization and wrote favorably about an "overall conception of humanity" and "that harmony of purposes and interests which each individual must of necessity try and establish within his own experience" (p. 391), one might have expected him to discover that rhetorical scope in the Renaissance was promoted by the rhetorics of Isocrates, Cicero, and Quintilian and to respond favorably to the classical rhetoricians. As will be seen, however, Bolgar ridiculed Cicero and Quintilian; furthermore, he associated rhetoric with "the persuasive," "verbal jugglery," and "the appearance of truth" and contrasted it with "the cogent" and "the truth itself" (p. 153). Like Dewey, he was troubled by the results of the philosophical tradition, but was still driven by it.

Bolgar's demeaning view of rhetoric was part of a long tradition after the Renaissance. The triumph of the philosophical tradition, after all, affected not only goals and social structures but also methodologies. In the 17th and 18th centuries, John Locke and Immanuel Kant suggested the extent to which philosophers joined their classical predecessors in disparaging rhetoric. In *An Essay Concerning Humane Understanding* (1690/1700), John Locke wrote:

> If we would speak of Things as they are, we must allow, that all the Art of Rhetorick,…all the artificial and figurative application of Words Eloquence hath invented, are for nothing else but to insinuate wrong *Ideas*, move the Passions, and thereby mislead the Judgment; and so indeed are perfect cheat: And therefore however laudable or allowable Oratory may render them in Harangues and popular Addresses, they are certainly, in all Discourses that pretend to inform and instruct, wholly to be avoided, and where Truth and Knowledge are concerned, cannot but be thought a great fault, either of the Language or Person that makes use of them. (III,x,34)

Locke noted, however, that rhetoric still maintained considerable strength: "Rhetoric, that powerful instrument of Error and Deceit, has its established Professors, is publickly taught, and has always been had in great Reputation" (III,x,34).

Immanuel Kant (1790/1968)—who is often attributed a philosophical stature comparable to Plato and Aristotle—was equally severe in his *Critique of Judgment*:

> Rhetoric, in so far as this means the art of persuasion, i.e. of deceiving by a beautiful show (*ars oratoria*), and not mere elegance of speech (eloquence and style), is a dialectic which borrows from poetry only so much as is needful to win minds to the side of the orator before they have formed a judgment and to deprive them of their freedom; it cannot therefore be recommended either for the law courts or for the pulpit. (p. 171)

Kant offered only the Aristotelian and Ramistic definitions of rhetoric as alternatives; for him, the Isocratean alternative had disappeared.

By 1850, even the defenders of rhetoric were acknowledging its weakness. In that year in America, for instance, William G. T. Shedd translated Francis Theremin's *Eloquence a Virtue* (1850/1860), which attempted to restore the high reputation of rhetoric and respond to its detractors, especially "Aristotle among the ancients" and "Kant among the moderns" (p. 55). In an 1878 edition of the introduction to his translation, Shedd noted that all culture in classical antiquity seemed to have culminated in rhetoric and oratory and that American educators continued to view rhetoric as the crown of education, hardly a symptom of weakness. Shedd went on, however, to suggest that rhetoric had been weakened by a separation of content from style. He condemned the neglect of invention and the conversion of the art of rhetoric into a collection of rules relating to expression. As a result, rhetoric had sunk from its pride of place and had become a synonym for the shallow and showy (pp. 99, 104). The great emphasis on style and delivery in the rhetorics of Cicero and Quintilian and the restriction of rhetoric to these two areas by Ramus were clearly still playing themselves out in the 19th century.

By the 20th century, the decline was even greater. In 1936, I. A. Richards wrote in *The Philosophy of Rhetoric*:

> I need spend no time, I think, in describing the present state of Rhetoric. Today it is the dreariest and least profitable part of the waste that the unfortunate travel through in Freshman English! So low has Rhetoric sunk that we would do better just to dismiss it to Limbo than to trouble ourselves with it—unless we can find reason for believing that it can become a study that will minister successfully to important needs. (p. 3)

Wilbur Samuel Howell (1956), in his *Logic and Rhetoric in England, 1500–1700*, reported that "rhetoric" was popularly taken "as a term for the sort of style you happen personally to dislike" (p. 3). Even if the term had no negative connotations, it was perceived as unimportant; Neal W. Gilbert (1960), in his *Renaissance Concepts of Method*, wrote that "rhetoric" was "a subject long out of fashion" (p. 119). In 1971, committee members of the National Developmental Project in Rhetoric suggested the ongoing dismal state of rhetoric: "This art has not been taught seriously and widely for at least two hundred years" (Bitzer & Black, 1971, p. 240).

In the absence of serious and widespread attention to rhetoric early in the 20th century, humans confronting situations requiring rhetorical methodologies too often used other inappropriate methodologies, especially those associated with science. For instance, although Dewey (1929) rejected the philosophical tendency to direct attention away from human affairs and embraced the rhetorical tendency to focus on such matters, the methodology that he foregrounded was not rhetoric, but scientific experimentalism. In *The Quest for Certainty*, he expressed his belief in industrialization as applied science, as "the direct fruit of the growth of the experimental method of knowing" (p. 79). He wanted more extensive "transfer of experimental method from the technical field of physical experience to the wider field of human life" (p. 273). He was concerned that there had been "so little use of the experimental method" to form "our ideas and beliefs about the concerns of man in his characteristic social relations" (p. 271). The adoption of experimentalism as a dominant methodology in engaging human affairs became the ruin of whole disciplines in the 20th century—schools of education in universities being perhaps the best example.

The foregrounding of experimentalism as a methodology—like the trend toward ever-increasing specialization—was not without its critics. For instance, Lloyd Bitzer wrote:

> We need to clarify the relations between scientific and rhetorical methods—the methods of scientific investigation and proof and the methods of rhetorical investigation and proof. The naive view of eighteenth and nineteenth century rhetoricians and theorists of other disciplines that scientific method is all-sufficient has been widely rejected. The methods of inquiry that are relevant and decisive in handling a problem in experimental physics are not equally relevant and decisive in deliberating whether to commit troops to Cambodia. (Bitzer & Black, 1971, p. 203)

Bitzer encouraged theorists to reject "the assumption that there is a single methodology to be used by sensible people in all kinds of investigations and deliberations, namely the methods of empirical science" (p. 203). The implication here was that situations themselves determine the methodologies appropriate to engage them.

As the 20th century progressed, rhetoric increasingly attracted greater attention. Isocrates, Cicero, and Quintilian received some of this attention—they attracted attention in all of the centuries following the Renaissance—but 20th-century discussions of rhetoric were dominated by Aristotle's definition. As has already been suggested, 20th-century scholarship concerning oral communication referred to Aristotle's *Rhetoric* more than any other source. In 1976, in *Rhetoric and Philosophy in Conflict*, Samuel Ijsseling suggested how admiring such references could be: "In its basic structure the Aristotelian system of rhetoric has persisted through the centuries, thereby proving its soundness" (pp. 32–33). Even Brian Vickers, whose work I so often find myself admiring and who, in his *Defence of Rhetoric* (1988/1990), understood perfectly how Plato attacked rhetoric through definitional exclusion, failed to perceive—probably because he neither appreciated nor understood Isocrates—that Aristotle was employing the same technique. Unfortunately, Vickers, like so many of his contemporaries, defined rhetoric as "the art of persuasive communication" (p. 2). He called Aristotle's *Rhetoric* "the most penetrating analysis of speech in its *full* individual and social dimension" (emphasis added, p. 26). Vickers even praised the breadth of Aristotle's *Rhetoric*: "the breadth of his discussion shows how widely rhetoric can be conceived" (p. 25).

Such praise becomes understandable in light of Shedd's criticism in the 19th century that rhetoric had degenerated into no more than a set of maxims about style. Twentieth-century scholars rightfully perceived that Aristotelian rhetoric was broader in scope than such Ramistic approaches, that the discovery of the available means of persuasion in any given case brought more into play than a focus on style. Edward P. J. Corbett found a range of authors in the 20th century who suggested that "the split that developed between matter and form, between thought and expression" contributed to "the decline of rhetoric" (Bitzer & Black, 1971, p. 170). He also found these authors "lamenting the divorce between form and content and recommending, implicitly if not explicitly, a remarriage" (p. 171). If 20th-century scholars rightfully perceived that Aristotelian rhetoric incorporated more than Ramistic rhetoric, however, most did not perceive the extent to which Aristotelian rhetoric reinforced the split between thought and expression. They failed to take the next step of embracing the Isocratean tradition.

Indeed, most were made uneasy by the scope of the Isocratean tradition. Vickers (1988/1990), for instance, understood that Isocratean rhetoric was broader than Aristotelian rhetoric "his, and the Sophists' conception of rhetoric generally, is much wider than Aristotle's" (p. 158)—but he did not pursue the implications of this observation. In fact, the scope promoted by the Isocratean tradition troubled Vickers, as indicated in his treatment of Cicero: "In his major rhetoric-book, the *De Oratore*,...Cicero attempted a wider scope, indeed the widest, bringing into the rhetorician's field of competence everything under the sun....The widest scope is claimed for rhetoric, but it is claimed only, not demonstrated" (p. 29). Vickers failed to appreciate the value of Ciceronian scope: "Cicero's significance in the history of rhetoric may finally be not as a theorist but as a practitioner" (p. 35).

Furthermore, Vickers raised the issue of impracticality when Nizolio, in the Renaissance, adopted Ciceronian scope as an ideal:

> In the mid-sixteenth century M. T. Nizolio, fanatical admirer of Cicero, took over the all-embracing claims of *De Oratore* in an un-Ciceronian spirit, rejecting the logical works of Aristotle as "vicious", expelling dialectic and metaphysics, while making rhetoric the truly universal art, its subject-matter being all human knowledge. Such claims, revealing as they do their own impracticality, do little harm beyond making rhetoric seem ridiculous. (pp. 181–182)

The issue of the impracticality of Ciceronian scope must be taken seriously, and I shall address it when I have adequately built a sufficient foundation to do so.

Vickers was not alone in calling Cicero impractical. Bolgar (1954/1958), for instance, was downright insulting:

> the exact import of the *de Oratore* and the *Institutiones Oratoriae* is difficult to assess. They transport us into a cloud-cuckoo-land of unrealisable ideals; and as we

study the magnificent array of their arguments, marshalled with so much art to arrive at such impractical conclusions, we cannot help feeling ourselves face to face with some remarkable aberration of the human genius. (pp. 30–31)

What we have here are Vickers and Bolgar—both scholars in their university ivory towers—accusing a man of impracticality who was one of the most successful orators in history, who was writing in his full maturity the results of the richest possible involvement in legal and political affairs, including assumption of the highest state office in ancient Rome—the consulship. Is this the kind of man from whom we would expect impracticality?

If the scope of the Isocratean tradition made most uneasy, however, some of the authors of *The Prospect of Rhetoric*, edited by Lloyd Bitzer and Edwin Black (1971), seemed prepared to move in Isocratean directions. *The Prospect of Rhetoric* contains essays, reports, and recommendations of some 40 top scholars in rhetoric involved in the National Developmental Project on Rhetoric. The discussions of these scholars focus on practical affairs: "We conceived of rhetoric in the classical, and richest, sense—as the theory of investigation, decision, and communication concerned particularly with practical, especially civic, affairs" (p. 237). The goal is to formulate an art of choice, "to attempt redefinition and perfection of that discipline as a modern method of problem-solving and decision-making" (p. 237). The dominant recommendation focuses on scope: "*the scope of rhetorical theory and practice should be greatly widened*" (p. 238). The authors called for greater articulation of the nature of this broader rhetoric: "*a clarified and expanded concept of reason and rational decision must be worked out*" (pp. 238–239). They adopted Bitzer's rejection of "the assumption that a single methodology—namely the new science—should be used by sensible people in all kinds of investigations and deliberations" (p. 239). The resulting concept of rhetoric allowed humans "to judge and order competing conceptions of `the aspirations of the human community'" (p. 240).

The results of developing such a rhetoric were considered substantial:

> Were the judgments of our conferences accepted, sweeping changes would be necessary throughout the educational establishment of the nation. In the humanities and in the several fields of social inquiry especially, "scientific models" would be relegated in application to those matters of detail in which "fact-nonfact" judgments are possible, and a "rhetorical model" specifying that human valuation is all that men can attain would control the analysis and presentation of most major data and issues in these branches of learning. To adopt such emphases in research, teaching, and public affairs would be revolutionary. (Bitzer & Black, pp. 243–244)

They added: "to replace the 'scientific stance' and the 'analytic stance' with a 'rhetorical stance' in humanistic and social affairs would be to effect a major cultural change" (p. 244).

Not unexpectedly, many authors presented a retreaded Aristotle as the new, revolutionary rhetoric; Corbett noticed this: "as I study the so-called 'new rhetoric,' I am simply amazed at how much that is proposed as new is just Aristotle in new trappings or new terminology" (p. 169). Some authors such as Samuel L. Becker moved beyond Aristotle: "More than any other need in our rhetorical studies...is the need to take a far broader view of what constitutes a relevant datum in the study of a particular communication situation" (p. 24). Becker called for a scope that extended beyond persuasion: "we have taken too narrow a view of the functions which communication serves; our historical and critical studies...have tended to be built almost exclusively upon an influence or persuasion model. Yet persuasion is only one of the many important functions of communication" (p. 23). Becker called for a new conception of rhetoric but could not detail its nature: "for these times,...new conceptions of rhetoric are needed. I have no such new conception to offer; I wish that I did" (p. 29).

However, Richard McKeon's article, "The Uses of Rhetoric in a Technological Age: Architectonic Productive Arts"—although somewhat limited by McKeon's Aristotelianism—cited his indebtedness to Cicero and promoted a rhetoric of truly Isocratean scope. McKeon's article reflected no awareness whatever of Isocrates's dominance in ancient Greece: "The history of rhetoric has played an important part at some points in the formation of culture in the West, notably during the Roman Republic and the Renaissance" (Bitzer & Black, p. 45). But he understood Cicero's call for scope: "Cicero enlarged rhetoric into a universal productive art...and applied it to resolve what he conceived to be the basic problem of Roman culture, the separation of wisdom and eloquence, of philosophy and rhetoric" (p. 47). Furthermore, McKeon also understood the importance of scope in the Renaissance:

> Renaissance philosophers and rhetoricians sought to rejoin eloquence and wisdom and developed within the new rhetoric they constructed a new universal subject-matter. They sought to make rhetoric a productive architectonic art of all arts and of all products rather than a productive technical art of language and persuasion. (p. 49)

McKeon called for a new rhetoric with roots in Cicero and the Renaissance. This rhetoric could not be more Isocratean, providing "the devices by which to determine the characteristics and problems of our times and to form the art by which to guide actions for the solution of our problems and the improvement of our circumstances" (p. 52). It reunified "eloquence and wisdom, rhetoric and philosophy" (p. 53). It focused on the particular—"particular questions or constitutions in law, particular works or compositions in art, or particular facts or data in experience and existence" (p. 53). It called for abandonment of the divisions promoted by definition, specialization, and the celebration of the expert:

we can abandon the rigidities of accepted classifications of knowledge—institution-alized under headings like theoretical, practical, and productive; physics, logic, and ethics; science, poetry, and history; natural sciences, social sciences, and humani-ties—and return to rhetoric for hints concerning how to construct new interdiscipli-nary substantive fields by the use of the methods and principles formed for the resolution of problems for which new fields are needed. (p. 58)

The present could find its model in the past when "the terms of art, of ethics, politics, and rhetoric merged, and deliberation could be applied not only to ends as well as means, but to theoretic and productive as well as practical problems" (p. 61).

The call for greater scope in *The Prospect of Rhetoric* by McKeon and others was a response to their perception of the needs of the times. In the "Foreword" to the book, the goal of the National Developmental Project on Rhetoric was stated:

The central objective of the Project was to outline and amplify a theory of rhetoric suitable to twentieth-century concepts and needs. At the Project's two major confer-ences, scholars from several fields considered rhetoric's past and future, identified the problems in contemporary life which require application of rhetorical concepts and methods, and recommended lines of research and educational programs needed to bring an effective rhetoric into relation to current and future needs. (p. v)

Samuel L. Becker, in his article, elaborated:

Douglas Ehninger has described the ways in which our conceptions of rhetoric have altered at various periods through history to adjust to the needs of the times. A rhe-torical system, he tells us, 'cannot be merely good or bad; it must be good or bad for something.' It is appropriate that we meet in 1970 to consider the sort of alterations called for by *our* time. It is appropriate that we be concerned with the needs of our time and the conception or conceptions of rhetoric which will be 'good' for serving those needs. (p. 21)

And Wayne Brockriede, in his article, reflected an understanding that a rhetoric is a response to a particular problem situation, that a rhetorical situation or transac-tion must "itself suggest its own analytic categories," that needs and the rhetorics that respond to them cannot be determined without "field studies that utilize the real actions of real people in real situations" (p. 128).

What excited me most about *The Prospect of Rhetoric* was that the modern sit-uations that some of its authors were examining were evoking the same call for scope as the situation that I was examining. I had always felt in the grasp of a strong determinism of needs, and the fact that contemporaries were being driven by the needs that they were examining in the same directions as I was—away from the narrowness of the philosophical tradition and back to the scope of the Iso-cratean tradition—seemed a measure of confirmation that our situations shared similarities, that one way of characterizing these similarities was narrowness, and that the Isocratean tradition could serve as a historical source of liberation from that narrowness. If all this were true, however, the call for scope in the work of someone such as McKeon did not go much further than the call for scope that we find in Isocrates or Cicero. Vickers could level the same criticism at McKeon that he did at Cicero—that the widest scope was only claimed for rhetoric and not demonstrated. Although some general reasons were suggested, no effort was devoted to exploring how an actual problem situation shapes the art of choice that enables decisions. No attempt was made to discover the ways in which a particular problem situation can direct attention to specific areas of its historical context and the kinds of help that can be derived from them. Although the adoption of a rhetoric of greater scope was said to promote revolution, no description of the nature of that revolution was forthcoming. The separation of university scholars from such realms of action as industry and government and the notion that only experts should engage such problems militated against close attention to such matters.

In 1996, on the 25th anniversary of *The Prospect of Rhetoric*, the Rhetoric Society of America held a conference to explore once again the new prospects for rhetoric, and some of the papers were published in *Making and Unmaking the Prospects for Rhetoric*, edited by Theresa Enos and Richard McNabb (1997). In one of the essays, "The Prospect of Rhetoric: Twenty-Five Years Later," Edwin Black reinforced my observation that the essays in *The Prospect of Rhetoric* tended to lack engagement with actual problem situations. According to Black, most of the essays failed to refer to specific rhetorical phenomena (p. 22). He stated: "this vacuity characterizes most of the book" (p. 22). He concluded his essay: "Let us occupy ourselves with phenomena" (p. 27).

It is time now to turn to the particular rhetorical phenomena—a wealth of problems confronting people whom I associate with the term "technical communication"—that directed my attention to the specific rhetorical history that I have presented so far. In the effort to help these people engage their problems and perform well, I was driven again and again to an awareness of the need for approaches of greater scope in both industries and universities. Demonstrating this is particularly important in the light of some recent efforts to narrow the scope of rhetoric. For instance, Lloyd F. Bitzer, in an essay in *Making and Unmaking the Prospects of Rhetoric* (Enos & McNabb, 1996), stated: "The time has come to narrow rhetoric's scope—narrow its territory" (p. 19). The time has really come, however, for humans to realize that they cannot arbitrarily say anything about the scope of rhetoric. Problems themselves dictate the scope essential to successful engagement.

5

The Insufficiency of Ethical and Political Deliberation in Technical Communication in Industry

Among the major forces that increased the importance of the exchange of information in the second half of the 20th century were the military build-ups of World War II and the cold war, and among the major areas of development that resulted were a complex of activities that could be associated with the term "technical communication." In corporations, these activities were performed by two groups—"practitioners" and "professionals." Practitioners included those scientists, engineers, and administrators who generated and distributed information as a supportive activity. They created technical discourse to support such primary activities as research, product development, and management. The history of practitioners extended throughout the 20th century, but their technical communication grew dramatically in extent and importance in World War II and the cold war.

Professionals included those writers, graphics specialists, speakers, trainers, and directors who produced such forms of communication as manuals, online information, talks, educational seminars, and films as a primary activity. They created technical discourse not as a supportive activity, but rather as their primary focus of attention. This technical discourse was sometimes priced independently, sometimes distributed as support for other products without prices directly associated with them. The history of technical communication as a profession had its origin in World War II and the cold war, and the size of this employment force grew until, toward the end of the 20th century, the Society for Technical Communication (the major professional organization) included over 20,000 members.

From the 1950s through the 1980s, corporate administrators discovered serious deficiencies in the technical discourse of both practitioners and professionals. Many practitioners either refused or neglected to carry out their responsibilities to create technical discourse, and too many of those who did make the effort performed inadequately. Because these deficiencies could lead to customer dissatisfaction, product failure, financial loss, and even danger to humans, top administrators were deeply concerned about them. The performance of professionals may have evoked even greater concern. Television, magazines, and newspapers were filled with accounts of the failures of product instructions and the frustrations of customers. At times the damage could be considerable; for example, problems with instruction manuals for one product contributed substantially to the failure of Coleco Corporation in New York with all the resulting adverse effects on employees, their families, and the rest of the people dependent in some way on Coleco's contributions to the economy.

Such contexts of failure prompted practitioners and professionals to focus more on avoidance rather than the imitation so favored in classical antiquity. As projects came to an end and failures all too often materialized, practitioners and professionals had to try to avoid such failures in future projects. They needed to develop rhetorics of avoidance—an approach only nominally mentioned by Quintilian in classical antiquity. Sometimes they tried to address their problems themselves, and sometimes they brought in consultants. In the 1960s and afterward, I engaged a number of these problems first as a practitioner and professional in industry and then as a consultant from universities.

In engaging these problems, I gradually began to realize how many of them were caused or reinforced by narrowness of various kinds. Narrow goals, social structures, and methodologies militated against not only sufficient attention being paid to technical communication, but also, where sufficient attention was paid, the deliberative scope essential to address the needs of situations. When I attempted to determine what caused or reinforced the narrowness of approaches, I was driven back again and again to those areas of the philosophical tradition that I have already explored. In industries, technical communication tended to be most affected by ideas associated with the scientific area of the philosophical tradition—a contrast to the situation in universities where technical communication tended to be most affected by ideas associated with Plato, Aristotle, and the theological areas of the philosophical tradition (although the scientific area had substantial impact as well).

Recognition that narrow approaches of various kinds were causing problems in technical communication in industries prompted a quest for ideas that could serve as sources of liberation. This quest was guided in two ways. First, if narrow approaches were causing problems, then a quest for ideas that prompted greater scope could lead to solutions. Second, if ideas associated with the philosophical tradition were causing or reinforcing narrow approaches, then an effort to explore the ideas of opponents of that tradition might suggest alternatives. Both kinds of guidance led back to the exponents of greater scope in the rhetorical tradition in classical antiquity—Isocrates, Cicero, and Quintilian.

In the same way that problem situations in technical communication could be used to discover helpful materials in history from the philosophical and rhetorical traditions, so ideas associated with the philosophical and rhetorical traditions could be used to reassess problem situations in technical communication and uncover new particulars. An oscillation back and forth between the particulars of problem situations and the history related to them, a process of comparison and contrast involving numerous recursions, could help achieve the goal of the fullest awareness of the particulars with a bearing on a problem and the fullest awareness of history that could help not only assess the problem, but also suggest the best approaches to engaging it. An ideal engagement, then, involved using the particulars of new problem situations and their related histories to generate the approaches appropriate for those situations rather than, as was too often the practice, simply applying approaches derived from the engagement of past problem situations.

Among the discoveries resulting from this process was an awareness of how well the particulars of problem situations in technical communication from the 1950s through the 1980s accorded with an Isocratean orientation. For instance, with technical communication receiving its greatest impetus from the military build-ups of World War II and the cold war, practitioners and professionals were hardly withdrawing from social affairs to contemplate nature or God; on the contrary, they were assuming a role in political conflict. Far from being motivated by wonder alone, they could hardly have been more utilitarian, able to succeed only if they were useful to governments and businesses. And the extraordinary rate of change in their environments called for the use of judgment to make decisions about what was unique, variable, and temporary far more than efforts to acquire certainty about the identification of more stable matters.

Although this Isocratean orientation might have been expected to incline technical communicators to embrace the history of rhetoric as a source of help and to approach their problems with Isocratean scope, they were instead inclined by the dominance of science and weakness of rhetoric to approach their problems in ways shaped by scientific ideas and to narrow the scope of their deliberations accordingly. Practitioners and professionals focused their attention on too few concerns and were too narrow in their approaches to these concerns. They too often carried out the tasks of the practical arts, the arts that I have associated with Isocrates, Cicero, and Quintilian, using the approaches of the theoretical arts, the arts that I have associated with Plato, Aristotle, the Christian philosophers, and the apologists for science.

Technical communicators perceived some of the problems resulting from this misapplication, and responses to these problems promoted a broadening of goals, social structures, and methodologies that could be characterized as an unconscious enactment of Crassus's call for a rhetoric of increased scope. In many instances, however, technical communicators failed to perceive problems resulting from this misapplication, and deliberations remained narrower than contexts required. Among these instances, too many technical communicators failed to perceive and respond to their full ethical and political contexts.

This chapter explores the reasons why ideas associated with science dominated engineering and shows how engineers, by assuming the early role in developing technical communication in this century, encouraged the use of scientific ideas in engaging technical communication problems. This chapter also explores the extent to which the military build-ups of World War II and the cold war swelled the ranks of scientists and engineers in industries, creating industrial contexts for technical communication imbued with the ideas of science, especially since these scientists and engineers were practitioners and, in many instances, professionals. This chapter concludes with the first of a number of examples that will highlight the inappropriateness of an excessive reliance on ideas associated with the philosophical tradition in industrial practice. While the context confronting practitioners and professionals called for ethical and political deliberation, such deliberation remained insufficient, and ideas that I have associated with the philosophical tradition militated against more adequate approaches.

THE DOMINANCE OF SCIENTIFIC IDEAS IN ENGINEERING

Technical communication received its first significant impetus as an important concern in the 20th century in the profession of engineering. Although agriculture played a noteworthy role in technical communication in the early 20th century— see, for instance, *Technical Writing of Farm and Home* (1927) by Beckman, O'Brien, and Converse—practitioners associated with engineering had the greatest influence in shaping this activity because they devoted the greatest attention to it. The greatest number of publications about technical communication in the years before World War II were associated with engineering.

As a result, technical communication was profoundly influenced by scientific ideas not only through the overall dominance of science in the 20th century, but also through its dominance in engineering. The successes of science in this century had such an impact that approaches perceived as associated with that success became virtually unconscious habits and assumptions in approaching all activities. However, the fact that engineering provided the best environment for the growth of technical communication at the beginning of the century also promoted scientific approaches. In the 17th century, natural philosophy or science was valued both for the disinterested pursuit of knowledge and for the ways it could help humanity. In the 19th century, each of these values became a goal for a different branch of science. The disinterested pursuit of knowledge became a goal for "pure science," while the quest for ways that science could help humanity became a goal for "applied science," which was associated with a new name—"engineering." Because engineering considered itself a science, it incorporated and promoted approaches associated with science.

By the end of the 19th and beginning of the 20th centuries, engineering and science were already devoting considerable attention to technical communication. For instance, in a 1904 address entitled "Higher Education for Civil Engineers," J. A. L. Waddell complained about the inability of engineering graduates to express themselves correctly and forcibly in writing and speaking. He indicated that graduates were unable to write letters, reports, specifications, and contracts (Waddell & Harrington, 1911). Waddell emphasized the importance of a command of English to the success of engineers:

> Too much stress cannot well be laid on the importance of a thorough study of the English language. Given two classmate graduates of equal ability, energy, and other attributes contributory to a successful career, one of them being in every respect a master of the English language and the other having the average proficiency in it, the former is certain to outstrip the latter materially in the race for professional advancement. (p. 455)

One of Waddell's proteges, John Lyle Harrington, whom I have not found cited in any histories of technical communication, is my personal favorite among the engineering voices calling for increased quality in communication. Harrington worked as a student intern for Waddell, heard him speak at the University of Kansas, edited *The Principal Professional Papers of Dr. J. A. L. Waddell, Civil Engineer* (1905), and worked with Waddell when both were consulting engineers in Kansas City, Missouri. In 1907, Harrington delivered an address entitled "The Value of English to the Technical Man" to the Technological Society of Kansas City, the Engineering Society of the University of Missouri, and the Civil Engineering Society of the University of Kansas. It was printed in pamphlet form later that same year and was reprinted widely in anthologies at least through the 1920s.

According to Harrington, the technical man was often involved in writing and speaking: "the technical man, that is, the engineer, the architect, and the applied scientist of every kind, finds a sound, accurate knowledge of the language essential to him in every part of his work" (p. 2). Harrington later elaborated on the extent of the writing and speaking tasks of the technical man:

The character of the technical man's language is important in his social and business intercourse; in his business and professional correspondence; in the promulgation of orders, rules, and regulations for the guidance of those under his direction; in the preparation of specifications, contracts, and reports; in writing and delivering addresses and technical papers; and in writing technical books for the advancement of his profession. (p. 13)

But Harrington was appalled by the writing and speaking capabilities of the technical man: "Technical men are peculiarly prone to offend in the use of their mother tongue" (p. 6). Among their deficiencies, they lack a knowledge of rhetoric (p. 10), and the personal cost of ignoring this knowledge can be dear: "Upon whether its teachings be followed or ignored may depend the success or failure of any technical student to attain in after life the highest rank in the engineering profession" (Waddell & Harrington, 1911, p. 49). And the cost to others can also be dear:

Provoking and expensive errors often arise from the misunderstanding of badly expressed orders, rules, and regulations....It is hardly necessary to say that the consequences of a mistake in train orders, in instructions regarding breaking track for repairs or renewals, or for making temporary construction to span washouts, may result in expensive and fatal accidents. (Harrington, 1907, pp. 16–17)

Whatever Harrington's success in promoting the importance of education in technical communication, the need that evoked his address also evoked a number of related books for practitioners not only in engineering but also in science. In the years before and after Harrington's address in 1907, the following were among the books that appeared: T. Clifford Allbutt's *Notes on the Composition of Scientific Papers* (1904/1925), T. A. Rickard's *A Guide to Technical Writing* (1908), George K. Pattee's *Practical Argumentation* (1909), Samuel Chandler Earle's *The Theory and Practice of Technical Writing* (1911), Wilbur Owen Sypherd's *A Handbook of English for Engineers* (1913), and Richard Shelton Kirby's *Elements of Specification Writing* (1913). By 1916, the number of publications in the area had grown to such an extent that it warranted Sypherd's *A Bibliography on "English for Engineers."*

During these same years, Waddell and Harrington published *Addresses to Engineering Students* (1911), which was widely imitated in the 20th century. The first of its kind, to my knowledge, this book was intended to "instruct engineering students in good, modern, engineering English, instead of teaching them mainly from the ancient classical literature" (p. v). It contained engineering addresses that could serve as models of excellent English for students and could be read in classes or independently throughout the student's four years of college. During the rest of the decade, the Waddell and Harrington anthology was imitated by at least three others: Frank Aydelotte's *English and Engineering* (1917), J. L. Eason and M. H. Weseen's *English, Science, and Engineering* (1918), and Ray Palmer Baker's *Engineering Education* (1919).

Many authorities in these anthologies reinforced the view of engineering as applied science. For instance, in an article entitled "The Relation of Pure Science to Engineering," Joseph John Thomson described the aim of pure science: "The physicist endeavors to discover new properties of matter, new physical phenomena, for the sake of extending his knowledge of Nature, and without any thought as to their utility or the possibility of their application to the service of man" (Baker, 1919, p. 31). On the other hand, utility was the goal of applied science or engineering: "The province of applied science, of engineering, is to survey the facts known to science, and to select those which seem to have in them the possibilities of industrial application; to study and develop them from this point of view" (p. 33).

Despite these differences in goals, however, Thomson agreed with others in the anthologies that the methods of science and engineering were similar: "The methods employed by the physicist and the qualities of mind called into play in his investigations are, to a very large extent, the same as those used by the engineer in the higher and more pioneering branches of engineering" (Baker, 1919, p. 31). The similarities between science and engineering suggested by Thomson and others promoted a widespread assumption expressed by Alex C. Humphries in an address entitled "The College Graduate as an Engineer": "No sharp line can be drawn between the man of pure science and the man of applied science. The engineer of today must have a general knowledge of science and he must have a full knowledge of and be capable of practically applying the laws of Nature in at least one little corner of the great field of engineering" (Waddell & Harrington, 1911, p. 177).

At least one highly influential authority suggested that the ideas associated with science were central to practice not just in science and engineering, but in all areas of human endeavor. In 1918, the Eason and Waseen anthology included an address by Thomas Henry Huxley (delivered about 1860) that suggested that scientific method was applicable to all other kinds of thinking. Huxley opened his address: "The method of scientific investigation is nothing but the expression of the necessary mode of working of the human mind. It is simply the mode at which all phenomena are reasoned about, rendered precise and exact" (Eason & Waseen, 1918, p. 28). This address was still included in such anthologies for practitioners and professionals in the 1960s as Everett L. Jones and Philip Durham's *Readings in Science and Engineering* (1961) and W. Paul Jones and Quentin Johnson's *Essays on Thinking and Writing in Science, Engineering, and Business* (1963). Even in the 1970s—in a textbook that I assigned for my first courses in technical communication at the University of Iowa, *Writing Scientific Papers and Reports*—W. Paul Jones (1946/1978) cited the first sentence of Huxley's address (p. 14).

It was not surprising, then, to discover publications for practitioners and professionals from the 1920s through the 1980s not only equating scientific and engineering method, but also encouraging the use of scientific method as an approach to technical communication. In his second book on technical communication, entitled *Technical Writing*, T. A. Rickard (1920)—in a paragraph that expressed indebtedness to Huxley—wrote: "the art of writing is based on scientific method.

Science is organized common sense" (p. 8). In 1961, Martin S. Peterson, in *Scientific Thinking and Scientific Writing*, echoed Rickard: "This book is based on a postulate. The postulate is that you cannot write good expository prose without knowing and applying the general logic of science" (p. iii). As late as 1981, in the preface to an anthology entitled *The Example of Science*, Robert E. Lynch and Thomas B. Swanzey furthered this approach: "In *The Example of Science*, we point out the similarities between the human act of writing and the human act of science, between the methods of the writer and those of the scientist, between the goals of the writer and the aims of the scientist" (p. ix). They later added: "the assumption behind the structure of this book is that the act of writing and the act of science are similar" (p. 2).

An examination of the anthologies by Waddell and Harrington, Aydelotte, Eason and Weseen, and Baker suggests the extent to which science and engineering imbued technical communication with ideas that I have associated with not only the apologists for science, but also Plato and Aristotle before them. The resulting narrowness did not go unnoticed at the time. Charles Proteus Steinmetz, in an address entitled "The Value of the Classics in Engineering Education," published in 1913, complained that ideas current in engineering tended "to narrow the view and to hinder a man from taking his proper position as a useful member of society." He assailed the narrowness of engineering: "By dealing exclusively with empirical science and its applications the engineer is led to forget, or never to realize, that there are other branches of human thought besides empirical science" (Baker, 1919, pp. 95–96).

Steinmetz's call for breadth echoed the call for breadth by Crassus in Cicero's *De Oratore*:

> The greatest problem before the educational world to-day is the method of broadening education to counteract the narrowing tendency of modern life and modern industrialism, and to produce the intellectual development and broadening of the mind which create...citizens capable of taking their proper place in the industrial and social life of the nation. (p. 97)

Steinmetz understood the necessity of approaching science and technology as part of human political endeavor.

POLITICAL CONFLICT AND THE RESULTING DOMINANCE OF SCIENTIFIC IDEAS IN INDUSTRIES

Later in the century, during World War II and the cold war, science, engineering, and technical communication sustained their greatest growth from political conflict and a resulting emphasis on defense. With defense becoming a dominant concern of the country and scientists and engineers assuming a dominant role in defense as bureaucrats, managers, product developers, and researchers, these practitioners used the ideas that constituted their education—those associated with science—to help shape their environments. Since so many engineers became professionals and the practice of technical communication was not infrequently equated with the practice of science anyway, professionals were similarly inclined. When technical communicators engaged their problems in the 1970s and 1980s, then, they worked in environments that were imbued with the ideas that I have associated with the apologists for science.

In *Dismantling the Cold War Economy*, Ann Markusen and Joel Yudken (1992) described the military build-ups in World War II and the cold war—a political conflict with the Soviet Union—that constituted such an important political context for science, engineering, and technical communication. They called the development of the A-bomb the beginning of a new process: "Previously, most innovations in equipment for war were adaptations of domestic or industrial technology; with the A-bomb, innovation began to be conducted in taxpayer-sponsored labs expressly devoted to military endeavors" (p. 102). The Manhattan Project, launched in 1942 to develop the A-bomb, required extensive expertise in both science and engineering and eventually employed "150,000 scientists and technicians" (p. 102). In addition to the Manhattan Project, activities such as aerial bombing, submarine warfare, and computing also mobilized numerous scientists and engineers. In World War II, it became important to win the quality battles of the arms race, and quality depended "upon scientific and engineering expertise" (pp. 103–104).

After the end of World War II, the onset of the cold war prompted the continuation of military build-ups. The United States began the "amassing of an impressive array of permanent institutions dedicated to the harnessing of science and engineering in the interests of war" (Markusen & Yudken, p. 102). The aerospace, electronics, communications, and computing industries were targeted to help develop such military innovations as intercontinental ballistic missiles and communication satellites. Scientific and engineering expertise was "required to generate continual innovation in high-performance weapons" (pp. 14–15). By the 1960s, roughly half of the 1.2 million American scientists and technologists were "supported by the federal government budget, either directly as civil servants or indirectly through contracts with companies, foundations, or universities" (p. 105).

Cold war communities sprang up to support the military build-ups. Markusen and Yudken described the emergence of a "Gunbelt"—"a patchwork of cities and towns strung out along an arc from Alaska to Boston, sweeping down through Seattle, Silicon Valley, and Los Angeles in the West, across the more southerly mountain and plains states, through Texas and Florida, and up to Massachusetts and Connecticut" (p. 172). They suggested that three major centers anchored the complex: "Los Angeles is the undisputed capital of cold war industrial design and production. Washington, D.C., serves as the defense services capital. And because of the disproportionate share of military R&D [Research and Development] funding received by its universities, Boston is the leading military-educational complex" (p. 172). Elsewhere, Markusen and Yudken mentioned the location of two important national laboratories—"the Lawrence Livermore National Laboratory in California and the Oak Ridge National Laboratory in Tennessee" (p. 26).

They might also have mentioned the heavy concentration of IBM computing sites in New York. Markusen and Yudken reported that "the computing industry" owed "its origins and spectacular early growth to military patronage" (p. 49). Most of the main features and key technologies of computing owed their existence to decades of military largesse. IBM benefited from this spending: "over half of its research and development during the 1950s and early 1960s" was paid for by federal contracts, and as late as 1963 the government was "still paying for 35 percent" (p. 50). The Pentagon was particularly interested in such technologies as "super-computers, scientific computing, artificial intelligence, software engineering, high-performance networks, and advanced computer architecture" (p. 50).

The flow of technical discourse prompted by these military build-ups increased so dramatically that librarians met to discuss ways of coping with the new flood of information. In 1953, for instance, the Workshop on the Production and Use of Technical Reports was held at the Catholic University of America in Washington, D.C. At one of the talks at this workshop, Alan T. Waterman (1955), director of the National Science Foundation, described the situation that gave rise to the increase in technical reports: "at the present time approximately 60 percent of the scientific research and development in this country is conducted or supported by the national government. It is largely this circumstance that is responsible for the existence of hundreds of thousands of government technical reports" (p. 3). Among the reasons for this flood of reports, according to Waterman, was the need for increased collaboration and the distance between collaborators. Contracts involving military research on a single problem were often awarded to universities, research institutions, and industrial organizations that were distant from one another—an effort to make use of existing facilities. These institutions used technical reports to enable research groups working on related projects at a distance to inform one another on their progress. Scientists and engineers in these research groups, then, had to perform well as practitioners to insure effective performance in carrying out contracts.

Military build-ups in World War II and the cold war not only promoted growth in the technical communication of practitioners, but also gave impetus to the emergence of technical communication as a profession. In 1958, in an article entitled "Growth of the Technical Writing Profession," Robert R. Rathbone wrote:

> Although the art of technical writing is almost as old as science itself, the profession of technical writing has a recent beginning. In this country, before World War I, the writers were the doers. Scientists and engineers, whether in industry, business, or government, wrote their own copy....The real impetus [for the profession] came in World War II, when a special task force was recruited to deliver the paperwork. (p. 5)

Rathbone attributed the emergence of this task force to a shortage of scientists and engineers and a demand for more technical literature, an imbalance that opened the field of technical writing to specialists.

The growth in the number of professionals resulted in professional association during the cold war. In a bulletin, the Association of Technical Writers and Editors in New York placed the origins of societal organization in 1953–54, when five different American writing societies were formed in Boston, Washington, Los Angeles, Oak Ridge, and New York. It should not escape notice that the locations of original societal organization in the United States were the centers of the military-industrial complex already discussed. In 1957, technical communicators in individual societies joined to form the Society of Technical Writers and Editors. This name changed to the Society of Technical Writers and Publishers in 1960 and the Society for Technical Communication in 1971.

As Siegfried Mandel wrote in a 1959 article, "The Challenge to Writers in Industry," practitioners and professionals producing technical communication in the military-industrial complex were challenged by the Russian threat: "A little more than a year ago, the Stanford Research Institute of California studied the question of how Russia was able to effect military and technological innovations in a shorter 'lead time' than we did" (p. 16). Mandel reported the reason given by the Stanford Research Institute: "In 1952 the Soviet All-Union Institute of Scientific and Technical Information was founded." This institute was "staffed by more than 2,300 specialists" and "supplemented by 25,000 scientists and engineers" (p. 17). The Stanford Research Institute proposed a "National Technical Information Center" as a response to this Soviet threat (p. 17). The arms race, then, included an information race.

The greatest impetus for technical communication, then, came from political conflict between the United States and the Soviet Union. The very existence of the profession of technical communication and the jobs of numerous practitioners had their origins in the need to develop military weapons in World War II and the cold war. The substantial growth of the output of both practitioners and professionals in the second half of the 20th century stemmed from arms and information races. As a result, the activities of practitioners and professionals carried serious political and ethical implications. These technical communicators, however, tended not to deliberate about political and ethical matters. If they ventured into such deliberations, their approaches tended to be too narrow. Ideas associated with science reinforced these deficiencies.

AN EXAMPLE OF THE NEED FOR ETHICAL AND POLITICAL DELIBERATION

Among the examples of situations in the second half of the 20th century that raised political and ethical questions and involved the activities of practitioners and professionals were President Ronald Reagan's military build-ups during the 1980s. The Reagan military build-ups raised serious questions about the ability of business and industrial leaders to seize control of government and transform it into an instrument to serve their ends at the expense of others, both here and abroad. In 1976, in response to presidential candidate Jimmy Carter's expressed intention to negotiate arms control agreements and cut defense spending, wealthy business and industrial leaders, who stood to lose substantial profits from defense cutbacks, helped fund and establish the Committee on the Present Danger (CPD) to work against arms control agreements and increase defense spending (Boies, n.d., pp. 45–63).

Buttressed by the work of such conservative political advocacy groups as the American Enterprise Institute, the Hoover Institute, the Heritage Foundation, and the American Security Council—which were also substantially funded by wealthy business and industrial leaders—the CPD, in 1979, testified 17 times in Congress, distributed 400,000 copies of pamphlets and reports, and made extensive use of the media to promote dramatic reassessments of the Soviet threat, raise fears about Russian superiority, and call for new investments in military hardware, the best source of industrial profits (Boies, n.d., p. 63; Wirls, 1992, p. 24). In that same year, the CPD brought in Ronald Reagan as a member, succeeded in helping block ratification of an arms control agreement (the Salt II Treaty), and helped turn public opinion in favor of increased militarism and military spending, a process that culminated in the election of Ronald Reagan as president in 1980 and the emergence of the Republican Party as the champion of cold war militarism (Boies, n.d., p. 33; Wirls, 1992, pp. 21, 27–28).

To respond to both his business and industrial supporters and the supposed threat of the Soviet Union, Reagan included increased national defense spending as one of the major planks in his 1981 *Program for Economic Recovery* and, during his Presidency, sustained the largest military build-up in peacetime history, exceeding by many measures military spending during the Korean and Vietnam wars (Wirls, 1992, p. 35). Markusen and Yudken (1992) reported the percentage increases: "Between 1980 and 1989, the military procurement budget grew by 54 percent and research and development by 94 percent" (p. 35). Although Reagan consistently attacked big government and argued that government should maintain a *laissez-faire* or hands-off policy toward industry, his military build-up increased the role of big government in American society and established an actual government industrial policy favoring a narrow range of industries focusing on aerospace, computers, scientific instruments, and communications equipment (Wirls, 1992, p. 51). Markusen and Yudken reported the impact: "By the end of the decade, a substantial shift in the composition of manufacturing work had taken place in the United States—away from commercial work and toward military projects" (p. 134). This increase in military projects proved a major stimulant in the demand for such professionals as scientists, engineers, and technical communicators (pp. 140, 143).

To help him develop his defense policies, Reagan appointed representatives from defense industries and laboratories to his advisory committees. These representatives, then, were perfectly placed to insure policies that profited their organizations. Boies (n.d.) cited the example of the advisory committee to the Office of Technology Assessment's task force on antisatellite and ballistic missile defense (BMD) technologies, which had the task of advising on "Star Wars" or the strategic defense initiative (SDI). The Office of Technology Assessment's advisory committee included representatives from AT&T (communication equipment, sensing instruments, software, missile electronics), Rockwell (space shuttle, B-1 bomber, missile propulsion systems, aerospace electronic systems), Lockheed (submarine-launched BMD system), Martin Marietta (missile launchers, missile support systems, electronics), Sandia Labs, Lawrence Livermore Labs, and Los Alamos National Laboratory (the latter three receiving the preponderance of R&D funds for SDI). Boies reported: "The bulk of the expenditures on SDI research have gone to the firms and organizations represented on the advisory committee" (pp. 30–31).

In addition to encouraging military build-ups that led to profitable defense contracts, wealthy business and industrial leaders also called for a rollback of the regulatory controls on their activities, which had increased to such a degree in the 1970s. In response, Reagan called for a reduction in government regulations as a second major plank in his *Program for Economic Recovery*. The establishment of the Task Force on Regulatory Relief, the appointment of agency heads hostile to regulation, and a number of acts that won the support of Congress — including the Garn-St. Germain Act of 1982 — were among the steps taken in this effort (Campagna, 1994). Reagan's call for a shift in power from federal to state and local government was also helpful; if the state of Ohio had regulatory power over its coal-burning utility plants, it would hardly be pressured by its state residents to address acid rain problems in the Northeast and Canada (Steiner & Steiner, 1971/1988).

The efforts to free business and industry from governmental control led to widespread abuse. Campagna (1994) described the abuse resulting from the Garn-St. Germain Act of 1982, which sought to eliminate governmental controls on banking: "Using government-backed deposits, speculators and freeloaders could gamble with risky ventures because they could not lose...the door was open to swindlers, high rollers, speculators, money launderers, and ambitious entrepreneurs" (p. 142). Among the results was the savings and loan collapse involving 747 failed thrift institutions and a cost to taxpayers of $90 billion (Rubin, 1995, p. B–11).

A second example of corporate abuse stemming from the absence of government control—this example involving defense contractors—was described by Wirls (1992). The Pentagon instituted a program allowing contractors to police themselves on procurement ethics and practices (p. 206). The resulting abuses led to investigation and a lengthy string of guilty pleas by defense contractors, including Boeing, Sunstrand, and Hughes Aircraft (p. 205). By the end of the Reagan Presidency, defense contractors had an appalling record: "By December 1990, twenty-five of the largest one hundred Pentagon contractors had been found guilty of procurement fraud during the previous seven years—some more than once" (p. 206).

In addition to increasing defense spending and rolling back regulatory controls, Reagan's *Program for Economic Recovery* contained another plank—a reduction in tax rates (Campagna, 1994). Reagan succeeded in reducing tax rates through the Economic Recovery Tax Act, signed into law in August 1981. Among its provisions were "reductions in the gift and estate tax, the accelerated cost recovery system that allowed businesses to depreciate assets more rapidly, extensions and increases in IRA and Keogh benefits to more individuals, the indexing of the tax code, and the reduction of the top rate on investment income from 70 to 50%" (Campagna, p. 71). The result of these tax cuts quickly became clear: "High income groups benefited at the expense of low income groups" (p. 79). Although reforms were undertaken later in the administration, the Congressional Budget Office noted the following disturbing trend from 1977 to 1988: "the lowest income group saw its effective tax rate rise by 20% while the top tenth saw its rate fall by 9.5%" (p. 82). Wirls (1992) called Reagan's reduction in tax rates "tax breaks for corporations and the rich" (p. 125), and Campagna (1994) summarized the resulting charges made against the Reagan administrations: "In their tax and spending policies, they favored those who needed no help, and turned aside from those who did" (p. 183).

If defense spending was increasing and taxes were being cut, federal spending had to be cut in domestic areas (the last plank in Reagan's *Program for Economic Recovery* to be discussed here) to prevent the federal deficit from skyrocketing. Wirls (1992) wrote: "For fiscal 1982, Reagan negotiated with Congress for about $35 billion in cuts in hundreds of domestic programs....[From] FY 1981 to 1987 discretionary spending on domestic programs *decreased* by 21 percent in real terms while defense outlays *increased* by 45%" (p. 54). Campagna (1994) suggested some of the areas of decreased expenditures from the last Carter administration year through the Reagan presidency: "international affairs (–44%), energy (–73%), natural resources [particularly in pollution control] (–13%), community and regional development (–64%), education and training (–14%), and general government (–48%)" (p. 69). Such decreases in spending could further erode environmental controls by limiting the means for enforcement. Even with such domestic cuts, however, the federal deficit skyrocketed: "The deficit rose from approximately $73 billion in 1980 (excluding off-budget items such as Social Security Trust Funds) to $238 billion in 1986" (p. 65).

These developments in the Reagan administrations raised important political and ethical considerations. A nuclear weapons peace movement raised questions about whether military build-ups were threatening our security rather than defending it. While supporters of military build-ups called for peace through strength and containment, members of the peace movement argued that neither of the superpowers could gain an advantage in strength through military build-ups, that nuclear arsenals had long ago reached the point of overkill, that their existence was provocative and subject to human accident or miscalculation, that their use would unleash such destruction that it was ethically unacceptable, and that negotiation and disarmament were therefore the only appropriate choices for the superpowers. This movement grew until it became the largest peacetime peace movement in American history, and it held a rally in New York City in 1982 that may have been the largest political demonstration in American history (Wirls, 1992).

Some observers moved beyond the issue of security and expressed concerns about other adverse effects of military build-ups. Markusen and Yudken (1992) documented in some detail the extent to which an industrial policy favoring such industries as aerospace, computers, scientific instruments, and communications equipment created problems for other areas of business and industry by diverting investment, research and development funds, and scientific and engineering talent—with a net negative impact on American economic structure in the long term. They called for a new economic order with special emphasis on such areas as health, education, and the environment to counter the adverse effects on these areas by military build-ups, resistance to regulatory controls, and cuts in domestic spending. Furthermore, they explored the adverse effects of the creation of defense-dependent areas of the country, among them, the difficulty of moving defense industries into other areas of activity even after hostilities ended.

Perhaps the strongest reactions were evoked by the contrasting impact of these developments on various income levels. Wealthy business and industrial leaders profited from increased defense spending, tax breaks, and looser regulatory controls, including those over pollution. In contrast, the middle and lower classes found themselves responsible through taxation for the costs of increased defense spending, savings and loan failures, fraud, and pollution. These developments were reflected in a growing disparity in wealth. As Michael Lewis (1995) indicated, "Between 1977 and 1989, the average income of the top 1 percent of American families rose from $323,942 to $576,553—even as the incomes of average families remained essentially flat" (p. 66).

Problems in the Reagan administrations associated with the military build-ups of the 1980s, then, prompted consideration of a number of ethical issues. Wealthy business and industrial leaders transformed government into an instrument for shifting wealth toward a controlling plutocracy at the expense of other humans, undermining industrial and governmental legitimacy. Government funds were diverted away from such areas desperately in need of funds as education, the environment, and health to the development of weaponry, which may have been unnecessary given the weaknesses of the Soviet Union and the possibilities for negotiation and disarmament. Growth in nuclear and other weaponry threatened to escalate into global conflict, and reduction in pollution controls led to global environmental degradation—both with the potential for disastrous effects on humanity throughout the world and both, at the very least, causing fear. And efforts to shift power away from international and national to state and local governments undermined the development of social structures essential to cope with such problems.

FORCES MILITATING AGAINST POLITICAL AND
ETHICAL DELIBERATION

Most practitioners and professionals in technical communication could not avoid the military build-ups and political developments in the 1970s and 1980s. These events provided the context and impetus for a burgeoning increase in the need for technical communication, for the birth of the profession, and for the growing numbers of technical communicators in government, business, and industry. Many technical communicators, then, were deeply involved in actions that were being severely criticized as politically and ethically questionable, and one would have expected them to be involved in political and ethical deliberation about these actions.

After all, Western society has argued that individuals are ethically responsible for the actions they take on behalf of corporations. As the Steiners (1971/1988) indicated, this principle was most clearly formulated in the Nuremberg Trials:

> The strong precedent set by the military tribunal at Nuremberg, which tried Nazis for war crimes, indicates that Western society expects members of organizations to follow the dictates of their conscience and reject forced implementation of unethical policies. Just as no Nazi war criminal argued successfully that he was forced to follow an order in an impersonal military chain of command, so no business manager [or technical communicator] may claim to be the helpless prisoner of competitive forces or organizational loyalties that crush free will and justify unethical actions. (p. 324)

Technical communicators, then, were responsible for the effects that all of their actions might have on other humans.

The scope of their responsibilities, especially in multinational corporations, could be very broad. If technical communicators wished to perform ethically, that is, if they wished to achieve a balance between minimizing the afflictions and maximizing the pleasures in their own lives and helping humans, present and future, do the same in their lives, they needed to consider the impact of their actions on humans, present and future, throughout the world. Their deliberations required a scope that included all of the humans affected by a decision—a group commonly called the "stakeholders" of that decision. Despite such responsibilities, however, anyone involved in the activities of technical communicators in the 1970s and 1980s would have been struck by the relative absence of political and ethical deliberation or, where present, its narrowness.

Among the forces that militated against adequate deliberation were the ideas that I have associated with the philosophical tradition, especially the ideas associated with science that engineers and scientists propagated in both technical communication and industries. At times these ideas played a relatively minor role, reinforcing tendencies that had their origin elsewhere. At other times these ideas played a central role, having a much more direct influence in excluding or limiting deliberation. The resulting inadequacies can be explored through an analysis of three examples of limited social structures in American society—the profession, the corporation, and the nation-state.

Many of the ideas that I have associated with the rise of philosophy and science and the decline of rhetoric assumed a major role in militating against political and ethical deliberation within the profession of technical communication. Among these ideas was the restriction of science to a limited area through definition, a definition that opposed science to politics and ethics. Other ideas inclined professionals to focus on the disinterested pursuit of truth, the identification of what is, rather than the interested pursuit of human welfare, the determination of what they ought to do. They inclined them to value philosophy and the theoretical arts such areas as science and mathematics—over human affairs and the practical arts. They inclined them—like Sprat—to turn away from the disquiets of human affairs and withdraw into pleasant contemplation of the inanimate. They inclined them to disparage and shy away from the kind of judgment required by political and ethical questions, which were too compromised by human limitations, and focus on matters that lent themselves to more exact knowledge, which could bring certainty.

These ideas reinforced inclinations to ignore politics and ethics in the profession of technical communication. For instance, much as Sprat narrowly defined science to exclude areas such as politics and ethics, so Robert J. Gangewere, in 1972, also narrowly defined technical communication to exclude both areas. In the process of defining "technical writing," Gangewere stated: "Technical writing as an academic subject has clear limitations....One limit of technical writing is its non-ideological subject matter—in the sense that ideas about politics, morality,...and other humanistic concerns are irrelevant" (p. 57). Such words are astonishing, given the involvement of technical communication in military build-ups in the 1970s.

To provide one additional example, Patrick M. Kelley and Roger E. Masse, in "A Definition of Technical Writing" (1977), also excluded values: "*Technical Writing* is writing about a subject in the pure sciences or the applied sciences in which the writer informs the reader through an objective presentation of facts" (p. 95). They added:

> *Objective* refers to a state of mind. If a writer is objective, he is free from any bias toward his subject. If he writes objectively, he presents the facts as they are, unaffected by his thoughts and feelings about them. These *facts* are pieces of information that can be proved accurate by simple experience or by scientific observation and experimentation. (p. 95)

The emphasis on objectivity and distancing of subjectivity could not help but militate against political and ethical deliberation.

Of course, not all scientists, engineers, and technical communicators kept their distance from political and ethical deliberation. For instance, Melissa Everett

(1989), in *Breaking Ranks*, cited a view by practitioner Tom Grissom, who was an experimental physicist at Sandia, the weapons lab in New Mexico operated on contract by Western Electric. Grissom resigned from his position as manager of 60 people developing state-of-the-art weapon triggers in the mid-1980s, giving the following reason:

> The present course has become odious and alarming to me, as well as intellectually unsatisfying. I cannot accept the premise that we are any longer engaged in a labor of deterrence, with some measure of moral justification, but rather, it seems to me, merely in the self-serving perpetuation of a military-industrial establishment which by its very nature and staggering enormity must ultimately result in our own destruction. In this I can find no historical solace for my fears. (cited in Markusen & Yudken, 1992, p. 150)

The need for ethical and political deliberation, in some instances, overwhelmed the forces that militated against it.

Grissom was not alone. To their credit, numerous scientists—the major logicians of identification—were among the leaders in recognizing the need for the practice of science and technology to be governed by ethics. Whether concerned about the use of humans as subjects in experiments or the dangers to humans from such scientific and technical byproducts as the instruments of war or pollutants, they were in the vanguard of a push to develop a deliberative system to insure the beneficence of scientific and technical development. They understood, in short, that the dangers of science and technology to humanity had reached such proportions that arts of ethical performance had to govern arts of identification.

But too often, as Grissom reported, scientists shied away from ethical and political deliberation. He criticized his colleagues at Sandia:

> I do not observe individuals straining against their consciences....Instead, I observe people who derive enormous stimulation and personal satisfaction from technically challenging and interesting tasks, and from the exercise of power, content not to examine too closely their own motives and constantly reinforced by other like-minded individuals. (cited in Markusen & Yudken, 1992, p. 50)

If some scientists were inclined toward ethical deliberation, according to Grissom, most were not.

Technical communication professionals, whose vocation took its greatest impetus from military build-ups, devoted as little attention to the ethical deliberations called for by these build-ups as Grissom's colleagues. When professionals turned their attention to ethics in the "Third Quarter" issue of *Technical Communication* in 1980, their special section on ethics and their discussion of the Society's recently distributed code of ethics, called the "Code for Communicators" (Schaefer, 1980, p. 4), contained no discussion whatsoever about ethical choice prompted by such contexts as military-industrial build-ups. While the Society's code of ethics committed the technical communicator to "the highest standards of ethical behavior," its description of these standards was embarrassing in its narrowness ("STC Board," 1995, p. 5). Essentially, the code committed the practitioner or professional to communicate well: "I therefore recognize my responsibility to communicate technical information truthfully, clearly, and economically" (p. 5). The code acknowledged the importance of respecting the work of colleagues and enabling an audience to acquire and understand information, but it made no further mention of any other responsibility to humanity. Although Hitler's Germany was still a recent memory, the code did not envision the possibility of ethical responsibility to all humanity bringing technical communicators into conflict with industries or the nation-states contracting with these industries. Leaders could find such a code ideal for promoting the submission of subordinates.

In the 1990s, some improvement was discernible. While ethics cases in the 1970s and 1980s often focused on such problems of communication truthfulness as the distortion of graphics, examples of ethics cases raising broader issues appeared with greater frequency in the 1990s. For instance, John G. Bryan, in an article entitled "The Need to Know" in the April 1996 *Intercom*, described a sophisticated ethics case that raised questions about an employee's company. Theoretical statements also improved. For instance, Charles E. Beck deserved credit for publishing "Ethics for Technical Communication: A Framework for the Profession" in *Technical Communication* (Beck, Levinson, & Wegner, 1993). This article provided one of the more comprehensive approaches to ethics that appeared in a professional journal.

The article included the ethical codes of four different professional organizations, and the code of one of these organizations—the International Association of Business Communicators—contained the following sentence that proposed greater breadth of ethical responsibility for technical communicators: "Communication professionals will not condone any illegal or unethical act related to their professional activity, their organization and its business or the public environment in which it operates" (p. 530). Such a statement was broad enough to include ethical responsibility to stakeholders everywhere and to raise the possibility of challenging one's own company or nation-state. Still, the article also included an annotation by Mark Levinson of the ethical code of the Society for Technical Communication, and its narrowness was still appalling. Furthermore, as any survey of contemporary journals indicated, the level of professional dialogue about ethics—especially at the industry, national, and international levels—remained inadequate. At the end of the 20th century, ethical and political deliberation in the profession of technical communication had only minimally improved.

In addition to militating against political and ethical deliberation within the profession of technical communication, ideas that I have associated with the rise of philosophy and science and the decline of rhetoric also militated against ethical deliberation becoming the primary goal in corporations—the only way that all of the stakeholders of decisions could be protected. The emphasis on definition, specialization, and compartmentalization encouraged by Plato, Aristotle, and the apologists for science supported divisions of attention in Western culture, such as production, that evolved into narrow social structures such as corporations that placed profit before ethics as their primary goal. Furthermore, the idea found in both Plato and Aristotle that the art of ethical choice could be stripped from rhetoricians so that they could be used for either ethical or unethical ends militated against practitioners and professionals having both the responsibility and right to participate in deliberations about the ethical implications of their actions.

In the last two centuries, substantial progress has been made in the area of human rights. In various geographical areas, we have abolished slavery, eliminated colonialism, defeated apartheid, and struggled to acquire new rights for women, gays, and lesbians. Among the human rights that have remained relatively unconsidered, however, have been the rights of stakeholders of decisions by corporations and nation-states, especially those stakeholders located outside the boundaries of these corporations and nation-states. No system of decision-making can be considered ethical unless it includes all of the individuals affected by a decision, and, so far, these stakeholders have not gotten the attention they deserve.

Far too often, practitioners in industries placed the narrow goal of profit before the wider goal of ethical performance in their decisions, causing widespread harm to stakeholders and raising serious questions about the legitimacy of current industrial governance. Such works as Joseph Kestner's *Government Intervention in Productivity and the Work Environment* (1981), Tom L. Beauchamp's *Case Studies in Business, Society, and Ethics* (1983), and the Steiners' *Business, Government, and Society* (1971/1988) detailed a history of corporations that included the brutal use of children as laborers; the bribery, extortion, and employee abuse of the robber barons; the operation of fatally unsafe mines; widespread pollution through toxic waste; the savings and loan banking failures; and the outrages of the American tobacco industry. The Steiners noted: "*U.S. News & World Report* reported that 115 of the 500 largest corporations had been convicted of a major crime or had paid a civil penalty for 'serious misbehavior' between 1972 and 1982—a rate of 23 percent" (p. 328). The view that managers should narrowly focus on corporate financial success, which has the effect of marginalizing ethical deliberation about stakeholders, certainly had its role in this irresponsibility.

The history of unethical actions by corporations has adversely affected their legitimacy. As James J. Brummer suggested in *Corporate Responsibility and Legitimacy* (1991), if social institutions are not ethically responsible, they lose their support: "if they are seen as legitimate institutions, they will be the recipients of continued support and encouragement by society. But if their legitimacy is seen to wane, the loyalty of members and nonmembers alike will often lessen as well, and...the survival of these institutions will be put in jeopardy or abridged" (p. 73). The Steiners (1971/1988) reminded us of the loss of legitimacy by Union Carbide as a result of irresponsibility in the Bhopal, India, disaster. In 1984, the year of the Bhopal incident, Union Carbide was "the nation's thirty-fifth-largest industrial

corporation" (p. 303). On December 4, however, as a result of irresponsible decisions in its pesticide plant in Bhopal, a poisonous cloud of vapor was released that
killed 2,347 victims. Among the many reactions to this incident were suits and a
takeover bid, and Union Carbide was left "a smaller, weaker company" (p. 315).

The appalling record and continuous threat of irresponsible decisions by corporations prompted calls for control at both national and international levels. As the
Steiners reported, the public was particularly insistent about an increase in
national controls:

> In the 1970s, there was an upsurge in public demand for environmental and con-
> sumer protections. These demands grew out of a rise in the values people held for a
> higher quality of life. There was a significant elevation, for example, in the values of
> a cleaner environment, higher-quality products, more equality in the workplace,
> safer products, and safer workplaces. The result was an unprecedented burst of
> federal legislation. (p. 37)

The resulting changes proved so dramatic that they constituted what the Steiners
and others called a managerial revolution. This "revolution...is identified by the
massive transfer of power from the managerial class to a new class of public servants in the federal government armed with authority to make decisions heretofore
reserved for managers in privately owned and operated businesses" (p. 134).

Because so many corporations were multinational, that is, they sold products
beyond the jurisdiction of any particular nation-state, calls for international control were also insistent, particularly in the developing countries. Among the examples of irresponsibility of multinational corporations in the developing countries,
marketers of prepared infant formula encouraged its use, even though it was likely
to be misused in these countries, causing malnutrition, diarrhea, and death (Beauchamp, 1983). Pharmaceutical products considered unsafe for home consumption
were dumped in the developing countries; the Steiners (1971/1988) described at
length the case of A. H. Robins and its distribution of the contraceptive device
called the Dakron Shield, which—because of its dangers—was withdrawn from
American markets yet was still sold in developing countries. And as Elise Boulding (1988) reported, multinational corporations too often built low-cost, low-wage
factories in the developing countries where working conditions were often poor,
taking a heavy toll in health and life expectancy of the women and men who
worked in them. As an example of the international controls that were established,
a monitoring system for the conduct of multinational corporations was developed
after the call for such a system in the United Nations General Assembly in 1974.

If, however, the calls for control of corporations were insistent and, to some
degree at least, realized, the rhetorical structures for decision-making designed to
avoid problems caused by the irresponsibility of corporations were not nearly as
well-developed as they needed to be. The Misches (1977) wrote: "the development of human institutions has not kept pace with the rapid evolution of global

interdependencies. Today's growing sense of powerlessness—experienced on deeply personal as well as global levels—is related to that structural lag" (p. 5). Epstein and Votaw (1978) cited Earl Cheit as making essentially the same point; Cheit argued "that large corporations are not accountable, that there is no place in the organization structure of the large corporation where society can grasp the levers" (p. 78).

Awareness of corporate irresponsibility, challenges to corporate legitimacy, and calls for increased control over corporations prompted corporate responses. Among them, organizations of industrialists such as the Committee for Economic Development (1971) committed themselves to change from a focus on financial performance to the goal of making the corporation "more responsible to its constituencies and to the larger society—while maintaining the managerial decisiveness that is required for efficient operations in the business world" (pp. 23–24). They committed the corporation to "the same obligation as all citizens to participate in and contribute to the general welfare, and to treat human beings humanely" (p. 28). However, implementation must follow acceptance. The choices of industrial leaders have the potential to affect so many humans so quickly and so adversely that traditional after-the-fact reactions to institutional abuse such as bringing public pressures to bear, developing laws, or punishing offenders no longer suffice. A system of checks and balances needs to be implemented to promote a concern for human welfare at all key decision-making points.

Among the most important characteristics of the new decision-making process, industries must insure that their employees possess a reasonable measure of responsibility for choices that affect the quality of their performance. Employees must have the opportunity to "buy into" decisions that affect their art of choice. Accepting employment in industries must no longer carry the aura of becoming an instrument or abdicating responsibility. Industries must create an environment of participatory management tolerant of reasonable individual challenges to institutional tendencies. As in all institutions, the environment in industries must honor the free expression of ideas toward the end of ethical performance—especially the ideas of reasonable whistleblowers who expose industry choices as ethically irresponsible. Promoting tolerance of whistleblowers adds to the system of checks and balances to insure appropriate deliberations at all key decision-making points.

Technical communication professionals, like other employees, must not exclude themselves or allow themselves to be excluded from the process of ethical decision-making. In the second half of the 20th century, however, professionals were too often inclined by their scientific heritage to perceive their profession as nonideological. This inclination was reinforced by industrial specialization, especially the relative exclusion of professionals from decisions about ends and their restriction to tasks that made them Aristotelian rhetoricians focusing on means. Jay Mead (1998), a technical communicator for Galileo International, suggested how completely he accepted the corporate goal of profit as primary and how thoroughly he perceived his role as an instrument (a means) to achieve this goal:

In a business setting, technical documentation is not an end in itself but rather a means to an end. A technical documentation department, like any activity in a business, exists to add value to the company's product or service. As with any other activity, if technical documentation cannot be shown to contribute to the bottom line, it has no reason for being, regardless of its efficiency or the quality of the documents themselves. (p. 353)

While professionals were accountable for their actions, then, far too many of them were neither intellectually liberated so that they deliberated sufficiently about the ethical and political implications of their actions nor ethically liberated to the point that they had access to decision-making that controlled these actions.

Ideas that I have associated with the rise of philosophy and science and the decline of rhetoric militated not only against political and ethical deliberation within the profession of technical communication and the primacy of ethical deliberation within corporations, but also against sufficient breadth in the ethical deliberation of nation-states. Decisions within a nation-state like the United States often have the potential to affect humans in other nation-states adversely. For instance, if the United States allows widespread combustion of fossil fuels, it can adversely affect humans in other nation-states through acid rain and global warming. Other decisions involving military belligerency, kinds of pollution besides the combustion of fossil fuels, overpopulation, unfair trading practices, resource depletion, and support for unethical multinational corporations can also adversely affect humans in other nation-states.

If decisions in the United States affect humans throughout the world, however, the political system predisposes government representatives to place the welfare of citizens of this country before the welfare of humans elsewhere. The only people who vote in the United States are citizens, and their interests are placed before the interests of other humans. At times, the range of interests considered by federal representatives is even narrower. Some powerful Congressional leaders place the welfare of state and local constituents before the welfare of national constituents. And when wealthy citizens or corporations gain control of government representatives through campaign contributions, then the welfare of a plutocracy assumes first priority.

Since the humans of all nation-states can suffer adversely from decisions in nation-states other than their own, calls for international collaboration to address global problems have been insistent, and international organizations have actually multiplied. As Elise Boulding reported in 1988, the United Nations system—with such well-known units as the UN General Assembly, UN Security Council, Hague International Court of Justice, and UNESCO— included 159 of 167 nation-states. She also described numerous international organizations of lesser scope, including the North Atlantic Treaty Organization (NATO), the Organization of American States (OAS), the Organization of African Unity (OAU), the European Economic Community (EEC), and the Association of Southeast Asian Nations (ASEAN). Boulding also described the work of 18,000 active International Nongovernmental Organizations (INGOs) promoting a new world order.

Strong forces in the United States in the 1980s, however, fought international collaboration. Among these forces was the cold war alliance between industrial managers and Reagan Republicans. The members of this alliance promoted hostile divisions between the United States and the Soviet Union, called for a roll-back of national and international controls, undermined and even attacked the efforts of the United Nations, and advocated a shift of power away from national and international to state and local governments. They used appeals to patriotism as support for their efforts. These efforts combined with a range of other forces to promote the isolation rather than the integration of social structures that had become so essential with the growing interdependencies of nations.

Such factors as geography have had considerable force in promoting isolation. Geography has certainly played a major role in isolationism in the United States at some points in history. But ideas associated with the philosophical tradition have not been without force in promoting isolation as well. The influence of these ideas may have been minor, but the philosophical emphasis on definition, on specialization, on compartmentalization, on the belief that humans can arbitrarily limit their areas of endeavor and ought to do so because of their limitations—these tendencies were not without influence in encouraging the maintenance of narrow nation-states in the face of global interdependencies.

While the contexts for nation-states, corporations, and the profession of technical communication called for ethical and political deliberation, then, ideas that I have associated with the apologists for science reinforced tendencies to ignore such deliberation or approach it too narrowly. Ideas that I have associated with Isocrates, Cicero, and Quintilian could have been helpful in this situation. Isocrates and Quintilian insisted on the primacy of ethics in deliberation—an idea that could militate against irresponsibilities resulting from the primacy of profit or truth as goals in decision-making. The Isocratean emphasis on politics could stand as a strong corrective to practitioners and professionals attempting to distance politics. And the Isocratean and Ciceronian belief that deliberation should have a scope that embraced all of the relations of human existence could militate against all decision-making that was limited in some way so as to exclude stakeholders. With the dominance of the scientific tradition and the absence of any resurrection of rhetoric in industries, however, these ideas were not readily available.

6

Failures and Successes in Industrial Efforts to Address Challenges of the Information Revolution

Some dramatic changes in the second half of the 20th century were associated with expressions such as "information revolution," "information society," and "information age." Among the pioneers who tried to make sense of these changes was Daniel Bell. In *The Coming of Post-Industrial Society: A Venture in Social Forecasting*, published in 1973, Bell traced the shift in this country from a farming society to a manufacturing society and then to an emerging society that he labeled as "post-industrial." His post-industrial society was based on services rather than farming or manufacturing, and what counted was information rather than muscle power or energy.

One of Bell's followers, Marc Porat, gave even greater emphasis to the importance of information in this new age. In his 1976 Stanford University dissertation, *The Information Economy*, Porat claimed that the information sector had become central to the whole economy. He stated, in words echoed by many others since:

"Over half our wages and nearly half of our Gross National Product (GNP) origi-nate with the production, processing, and distribution of information goods and services" (p. 1). Porat highlighted the importance of the creation, communication, and use of language in his new and expanding economy: "the intellectual or infor-mation-processing abilities of people are at a premium. It is the ability to create, use, and share symbols that raises humans above all other animal species; and it is only in this decade that the U.S. economy is predominantly organized around those symbolic activities" (p. 2).

Porat divided his information economy into two parts, and his descriptions of these parts continued to emphasize the importance of language. A primary infor-mation sector included all industries that offered information for sale "as a com-modity" (p. 36). A secondary information sector included the administrative and managerial work forces in business, industry, and government—the private and public bureaucracies. Their work was purely informational in nature. They received commands from the top of the hierarchy, processed them in some routine or creative fashion, and issued commands toward the bottom of the hierarchy. All that passed through their domain were information flows—memos, conferences, decisions, reports—and all that they did during the workday was talk, think, and write. According to Porat, these two sectors had become the sources of power in our society: "Those who accrue knowledge, access to knowledge, information, and communication resources will be more powerful than those who do not" (p. 328).

Among the major forces that contributed to the information revolution were the military build-ups of World War II and the cold war, and among the major areas in which this revolution took place was computing. Emerson W. Pugh's *Building IBM: Shaping an Industry and Its Technology* (1995) conveyed how deeply IBM was involved in military build-ups during World War II; according to Pugh, about two-thirds of the company's production consisted of munitions (p. 117). Another book about IBM, *IBM's Early Computers*, which included Pugh among its four authors, described how the Korean conflict (one of the hot areas of the cold war) led to the first generation of IBM computers, the 700 series (Bashe, Johnson, Palmer, & Pugh, 1986). And work on the first-generation IBM computers helped prepare the corporation for a role precipitated by the explosion of the Soviet Union's first nuclear weapon—the development of the large complex of comput-ers that constituted an air defense system.

For a corporation such as IBM, the flow of information required to perform these activities and build its domestic sales as well was extraordinary. Huge net-works of foreign and domestic information flowed from such external sources as governments (acting as customers and regulators), other businesses (acting as cus-tomers and suppliers), and universities (also acting as customers and suppliers). Within IBM, practitioners had full responsibility for an elaborate flow of informa-tion (both spoken and written) that extended from the time a product was first con-ceived until the information about it was passed on to professionals. For instance, the idea for a new product originating from a military or commercial source could serve as a foundation for feasibility studies, which, in turn, could serve as part of the basis for product development plans and schedules. And these were only a few of the documents that were crucial to product development; Edmond H. Weiss (1986) listed 28 different documents that could emerge from a single project, and his list omitted the hallway conversations, telephone calls, memos, conferences, and meetings that played an equally important role in product development. Many practitioners, then, spent as much time speaking and writing as professionals. The process was highly collaborative with the success of performance at any stage of the process dependent on the success of performance at earlier stages.

After practitioners had developed their documents, they passed on some of them to organizations of professionals—writers and graphics specialists—and assigned them the task of improving their presentation and producing them. William O'Neill of IBM-Poughkeepsie in New York described this division of labor in an article, indicating that in the 1960s and early 1970s, practitioners provided technical specifications (product descriptions) to professionals, who rewrote them to improve their presentation (Hillyer, 1985, p. 35). Roger Grice, a member of a group of professionals in IBM Kingston in New York, concurred, noting in an unpublished interview that writers acted "as clerks, transcribing engineering specifications into grammatically correct English."

This sharp distinction between content and presentation had roots in the decline of rhetoric in classical antiquity. For instance, Aristotle separated subject matter from rhetoric. Cicero's Crassus, despite his call for the reunification of rhetoric and philosophy, spoke of rhetoricians beautifying what already existed. Cicero's Antonius spoke of rhetoricians taking materials that already existed from experts or textbooks and weaving them skillfully into discourse. Quintilian followed Antonius in describing a rhetorician as receiving content from an architect or musician and presenting it better than either. By the 20th century, such distinctions had become social structures, dividing, for instance, the activities of practitioners from those of professionals in most industries.

These ideas, together with others associated with the philosophical tradition, militated against successful flows of information in the primary and secondary information sectors of society. Practitioners, who viewed technical communication as lying outside their profession, often either ignored their communication responsibilities or performed them poorly—tendencies aggravated by demands for secrecy and speed prompted by hostilities between nation-states and competition between industries and other organizational units. In turn, the poor performance of practitioners, together with demands for speed and secrecy and placement at the end of the information development process, confronted professionals with problems so serious that they were forced to try to move from the end to the beginning of the information development process. Their relative success in bridging the division between themselves and practitioners—in effect an enactment of Cicero's call for increasing scope in deliberation—resulted in improved performance.

PRACTITIONERS AND THE NEGLECT OF RHETORIC

The ideas that I have associated with the rise of science and decline of rhetoric inclined practitioners to give short shrift to their communication responsibilities. The call for definition, specialization, and compartmentalization prompted overly narrow definitions of professions and the emergence of social structures based on such definitions that militated against responsible performance. For instance, the definitions of science and engineering excluded rhetoric, and science and engineering students destined to become practitioners were educated in specialized departments in universities apart from the speech and English departments where speaking and writing were taught. These students were inclined by such educational organization to view speaking and writing as lying outside their disciplines, and too many of them—also influenced by the low stature of rhetoric in the 20th century—bypassed education in these areas altogether.

As a result, these students assumed positions in industries with inadequate education in rhetoric, and, as practitioners, either did not perform at all, or, in most other instances, performed poorly. Furthermore, their written job descriptions, on the basis of which they were evaluated, usually omitted writing and speaking responsibilities, leading (at least in terms of accountability) to the virtual invisibility of technical communication in the product development process. In one corporation, documents purporting to describe the product development process only occasionally mentioned technical communication—and then only in passing.

These problems were aggravated by demands for secrecy and speed resulting from hostilities between nation-states and competition between industries and other organizational units. The extent to which military contracts issued by nation-states could mandate secrecy was illustrated by an example provided by Pugh (1995) involving IBM's primary competitor in the 1950s, Remington Rand. In 1950, the engineers in a subsidiary of Remington Rand began work on a sophisticated computer called Atlas II. When these engineers discovered that IBM was developing the 701 computer, they sought permission to announce an unclassified version of their Atlas II computer to compete with IBM. Because none of the top managers had a security clearance, however, work on the Atlas II continued in mandatory secrecy until the managers could be informed in the fall of 1952. When Remington Rand finally placed its new computer in competition with IBM's 701, the company did not have time to develop a business plan, and among the resulting deficiencies was inadequate field support (Pugh, 1995). Government secrecy interfered with the flow of information essential for adequate performance by practitioners.

Pugh also provided an example of the extent to which speed was mandated by military contracts issued by nation-states. In 1955, the University of California Radiation Laboratory (operated for the U.S. Atomic Energy Commission) expressed interest in obtaining a "superspeed computer" (p. 231). The leader of the contract negotiations on behalf of the laboratory, the physicist Edward Teller, let it be known that he was in a hurry. At the end of the bidding process, IBM's offer to build and deliver a supercomputer in 42 months was rejected in favor of Remington Rand's offer of 29 months. The demand for short schedules too often placed enormous pressures on practitioners and further inclined them to minimize the attention that they devoted to communication.

Secrecy and speed mandated by the government were aggravated by capitalistic competition between industries. Although Pugh did not explore IBM secrecy in any detail, apart from references to such matters as Watson's efforts to "protect proprietary information" (p. 248) and potential problems that might arise from IBM's "traditional secretiveness" (p. 207), Judith Bronson, in a 1987 article titled "Unfriendly Eyes," suggested the extent to which not just computer corporations but indeed all corporations attempted to keep information confidential. Bronson opened her article with a statement hardly designed to encourage the free flow of information: "'Information thieves are now corporate enemy no. 1,' said *Business Week* in May 1986" (p. 173). The kind of information that corporations were afraid thieves would steal was called a "trade secret."

Legal and corporate definitions of the term "trade secret" did not lack scope. Bronson quoted two such definitions:

> The American Law Institute offers a generic definition: "any formula, pattern, device, or compilation of information which is used in one's business and which gives [one] an opportunity to obtain an advantage over competitors...." Xerox's definition is beautifully simple: "anything Xerox knows through its own efforts that other people don't know and that is important to its business. (1987, p. 174)

The latitude of such definitions was extraordinary. In effect, almost anything could be considered a trade secret if it helped a corporation gain an edge over competitors.

The rivalry between subunits within corporations could also promote secrecy. In the 1920s, Thomas Watson actually encouraged internal rivalry, which promoted secrecy, as a management technique at IBM:

> Competing assignments were frequently made by Watson without informing the inventors. This policy increased the pressure to excel and the sense of urgency. Inventors never knew whether Watson might have assigned the same product objectives to someone else. Intense rivalry developed, and inventors jealously guarded their work. Those who worked for an inventor were careful not to be seen talking with people from other departments lest they be suspected of passing secrets. (Pugh, 1995, p. 47)

Among the rivalries promoted by Watson in the 1920s was one between IBM's New York City site and its Endicott site.

After World War II, Endicott was involved in another rivalry, this time with the Poughkeepsie site. This rivalry was so intense that sometimes it seemed to exceed the rivalry with external competitors (Pugh, p. 261). The resulting secrecy, however, could have adverse effects. Pugh described the kind of product incompatibility that could result from the unwillingness of Poughkeepsie and Endicott to share information:

> None of the Poughkeepsie machines could run programs written for Endicott machines. In fact, none of the first six IBM computers with transistor circuits could run programs written for another. The lack of compatibility was serious for customers, but it was even more of a problem for IBM. The company had to train sales and service personnel and provide programming support for each of the incompatible systems. The process was costly and chaotic. Economies of scale in engineering and manufacturing were reduced. For example, peripheral equipment designed for one computer could not be used on any other without modification. (p. 267)

Product incompatibilities not only caused problems for customers, but also increased costs in a range of areas for IBM.

If secrecy created problems for practitioners at IBM, so did the drive for speed. Pugh called the rapidity with which new technologies were developed and used in products "remarkable" (p. 222). Furthermore, the emergence of new technologies in competing corporations could cause product changes late in the product development process and put extreme pressures on IBM development schedules. And, as if that were not enough, competition between subunits within IBM could further accelerate the pace. Practitioners in such subunits were involved in not just an arms race and a corporate race, but also a site race. As a result of all these pressures, they frequently overextended themselves to keep pace. One administrator recalled his involvement in the development of a product as "a gray blur of twenty-hour days, seven days a week—never being home" (p. 292).

Efforts to achieve speed were sometimes costly. The demand for speed often prompted administrators to assign large numbers of people to projects, dividing the labor into numerous subgroups. This approach, however, often adversely affected product development. Pugh highlighted such a problem in the development of a software product called OS/360. According to Pugh, the magnitude of the task of developing the proposed operating system was "grossly underestimated" (p. 294). Large numbers of people—over 1,000—were assigned to the project to overcome problems, but, according to the leader of the project, the subdivision of implementation of the project into so many different groups itself became a problem (pp. 294–295). Although the problem was not specified, extensive subdivision in the development of a software product, making collaboration difficult, could create such problems as inconsistency.

For instance, in the development of a software product, let us assume that one software developer begins to work on subproduct A, which enables secretaries to print a document, and, in line with the usual division of labor, another works on subproduct B, which enables secretaries to distribute the document to a number of managers. Without collaboration, these developers might create subproducts that are works of art, but when the subproducts are put together into one product, the secretaries might discover inconsistency. They might discover that answering a "yes" question while trying to print their documents requires them to press the "1" key, while answering a "yes" question when trying to distribute their documents requires them to press the "Enter" key. This inconsistency, compounded by countless others, is confusing.

Clearly, then, hostilities between nation-states, competition between corporations, and rivalries between sites fostered secrecy and speed that militated strongly against the kind of pace and cooperation essential to an effective flow of information through the secondary information sector. Among the problems that resulted were levels of employee stress that could be destructive and product incompatibilities and inconsistencies. Product incompatibilities not only limited economies of scale and increased training and support costs, forcing higher prices, but also complicated the learning process for users. Product inconsistencies further complicated the learning process for users.

Furthermore, demands for secrecy and speed could combine with pejorative attitudes toward rhetoric, beliefs that rhetoric lay outside the disciplines of practitioners, and other factors to militate against such discourse-related responsibilities of the computing revolution as distributing information in the form of printed materials and educational classes. Computer corporations were naturally positioned to assume an important role as a distributor in the primary information sector. At the forefront of innovation in hardware, software, and information development, they were among the first groups to have possession of important information in these areas. They knew about their own problems, and they knew about many of the problems confronting customers. They were uniquely qualified to address many of these problems and enable society to adapt appropriately to their innovations. As was true of all corporations involved in innovation, they had not only the opportunity, but also the responsibility to assume roles as educational leaders in society.

Among the factors militating against their assuming such roles, however, was the emphasis on hardware development during the cold war years. The industrial policy of the United States during the 1970s and 1980s rewarded corporations for the development of military hardware. Although computer contracts for military hardware also called for software and such educational products as manuals and online information, these products were usually perceived as support and their costs bundled into the costs of hardware. Computer corporations were simply not in the habit of looking at education or information as a revenue-generating product, and the cuts of the Reagan Administration in educational funding were hardly encouraging.

Traditional divisions or specializations in society certainly masked possibilities as well. Although computer corporations such as IBM were deeply involved in such educational activities as publishing (providing manuals to customers) and classroom instruction (providing the difference between what employees learned in universities and what they needed to know to perform their jobs), the notion that social institutions limited themselves to certain areas of strength militated against a computer corporation such as IBM extending its range as a scientific or technical publisher or, in effect, becoming a university. Besides, with an antitrust case confronting them until 1982, IBM administrators had to be careful about extending the range of their purview or exploring the possibilities of acquisitions or mergers.

The economic markets for technical and scientific publishing and university education were not particularly promising in any event. Although some technical and scientific publishers were able to develop profitable lines of books, many areas of technical and scientific publishing had to be heavily subsidized just to break even—hardly an encouragement for profit-seeking corporations to become involved. The economic market for university education was even worse, as a comparison with, say, health services could suggest. While health concerns were a lifelong concern and funds for it were provided by the government, employers, and individuals on a regular basis, no comparable financial support structure had yet evolved for university or postsecondary education—even though individual needs for such education, too, had evolved into a lifelong concern. The acuteness of the problem could especially be perceived in universities, which could only survive through sophisticated begging from alumni, governments, foundations, and corporations. Despite the desperate national need for classes on computing, computer corporations eager for profits were hardly encouraged by the examples of universities to seek those profits from classroom education.

A number of conditions within computer corporations themselves militated against increased involvement in educational activities. The need or penchant for secrecy hardly encouraged the spread of information. The speed of hardware and software development was so absorbing that little time seemed left for other activities. Scientists and engineers who administered the corporations matured within a tradition that focused on hardware products made of such tangibles as metal or plastic; it was difficult enough getting used to the software business much less getting more deeply involved in information products, which made them—of all things—publishers and educators. As for looking to the professionals who were already performing the publishing for the corporations, practitioners had difficulty hiring enough professionals to carry out the tasks at hand, and the quality of the publications developed by professionals was hardly promising. In any event, computer corporations too often lacked access both to information in other corporations and, more importantly, to appropriate library facilities.

Even with so many factors militating against extension of such educational activities as publishing and classroom education, however, some computer corporations found themselves drawn into the primary information sector in a very limited way. Initially, for instance, a computer corporation such as IBM rushed out some products with inadequate manuals, and enterprising outsiders improved these manuals and successfully offered their versions for sale. Although IBM traditionally distributed manuals free, it eventually began to follow the lead of these enterprising outsiders and sell some of its manuals. The next step was to sell information independently of hardware or software. In 1984, IBM wrote and published a book titled *An IBM Guide to Choosing Business Software*. This book was made available in regular retail outlets, for example, the B. Dalton and Waldenbooks chains. Not tied to a specific hardware or software product, it *was* the entire product. Information had become a product in itself.

IBM was not the only computer corporation to begin selling information as a product in itself, and the kinds of information multiplied. To the extent that information became a stronger source of economic power, to that extent information about creating information became of increasing importance. In this context, the Digital Equipment Corporation (DEC) published *Screen Design Strategies for Computer-Assisted Instruction* (Heines, 1984). This book was designed to help creators of computer-assisted instruction to prepare messages, helps, tutorials, and the like for effective presentation on a computer screen. The book was, in essence, a textbook on creating online information. Since computer corporations were at the cutting edge in this area of development, they had strong qualifications for publishing such a textbook.

A computer corporation such as IBM was also strongly positioned to sell information through classes. Within IBM, for instance, a headquarters organization offered classes for professionals at sites all over the country. Managers of information groups at various sites "paid" the headquarters organization to enable members of their groups to attend the classes. At one point, the curriculum included two courses on the art of writing, three courses on graphics, and single courses on editing, testing information, information planning, organization, media and online information, audience adaptation, and information management. Individuals and companies outside the corporation inquired if they could pay and attend the courses. In 1990, the corporation did not allow outsiders to attend, but they could have changed that policy in a twinkling and, in effect, become a university.

The president of one computer corporation did found a university. In 1979, An Wang, president of Wang Labs, founded the Wang Institute of Graduate Studies in Massachusetts The immediate goal of the institute was to serve as a professional graduate school for software engineering. The institute offered courses not only to Wang employees, but also to employees from other corporations and the public at large. A degree from Wang had the same status in the view of the Massachusetts Board of Education as those given by Harvard and MIT. While the classes there did not focus on developing information, the possibility for such classes always existed.

If computer corporations were drawn to publish some books and offer some classes in the primary information sector, however, their participation was marginal. Since computer corporations neglected the spread of information about technical communication and since educators outside these corporations were prevented by secrecy from acquiring and spreading this information themselves, no national institution was in a position to perform this task well. The resulting deficiencies hurt not only the public, but also computer corporations. These corporations were dependent on universities for well-educated employees, continuing education, and research, and inadequately informed faculty were not likely to be very helpful. They were not able to prepare students intending to become administrators and product developers—that is, practitioners—for the writing and speaking responsibilities in their future jobs. They were not able to help students intending to become professionals to gain the education necessary to address the tasks they faced. They were not able to provide continuing education to help practitioners and professionals already on the job. And they were not able to perform research needed by corporations to address problems they faced.

Practitioners responded to these problems by encouraging professors in such fields as science, engineering, and business to include more technical communication in their educational programs. While some of these professors attempted to foster the development of this education in their own programs, most asked such university departments as English to respond—a policy more in keeping with university specialization. Among the results was the emergence of the highly popular technical communication course for juniors and seniors in English departments all across the country. Unfortunately, however, practitioners did little to inform teachers of technical communication about their needs, and, as will become clear, the kinds of courses that resulted were inadequate.

PROFESSIONALS AND THEIR QUEST FOR SCOPE

When professionals walked into their plants to begin their work during World War II and the cold war, their freedom to perform well was severely curtailed by the social context in which they found themselves. Among their problems, they were confined at the end of the product development process, essentially attempting to make product descriptions presentable. In classical antiquity, Cicero's Crassus warned against the separation of thinking from speaking, and professionals discovered anew the problems with such a split. It did not take them long to recognize that their isolation at the end of the product development process was a division of labor, a definition separating them from their subjects, that did not work. They quickly perceived that they could not successfully perform the responsibilities assigned to them without participation at earlier stages of the product and information development processes.

Both innovation and failure prompted professionals to increase the scope of their concerns. The project situations confronting professionals contained their own imperatives. Problems involving products, specifications, messages, language, wordless instructions, and time were examples of a substantial number of situations that prompted earlier professional involvement. In response, writers and graphics specialists moved toward the front of the product and information development processes, assuming many of the discourse tasks of practitioners, improving products as well as the discourse associated with them, and acquiring greater power to negotiate with administrators.

Writers were forced by innovation to expand their concerns to include product development. Sometimes the very nature of a product—say, a briefcase computer (now called a laptop)—necessitated their involvement earlier in the product development process. A briefcase computer had to be light enough for executives to carry on trips and small enough to fit in overhead airline bins or under airline seats. The instructions required to operate the computer—if contained in manuals— could make the product too heavy and bulky for its purpose. Information groups had to be represented during the early stages of product development not just to make this point but to help search for a solution to the problem. One solution was to furnish instructions on disks as tutorials. Another, which might be combined with the first, was to furnish instructions as "helps"; if users confronted a problem, they pressed a "help" key, and relevant instructions appeared on the screen. Both solutions involved information groups in "online" or "computer-assisted" instruction as opposed to "hard copy" instructions embodied in manuals.

Writers were forced not just by innovation, but also by failure to move into the world of practitioners. For instance, practitioners often developed inadequate product specifications or failed to develop such specifications at all. Their tendency to disdain writing and speaking, their problem of self-definition (their perception of these activities as lying outside their professions), and the absence of any corrective to this perception in job descriptions inclined them to perform technical communication tasks poorly, or even, in some instances, to ignore them altogether. These inclinations were often reinforced by the demand for speed. Because these failures affected the quality of both products and information, administrators were driven to corrective action. In one corporation, the responsibility for developing the specifications for a product was transferred from practitioners to professionals. Professionals were assigned the task of creating a product specification of high quality that assisted not only professionals in the creation of manuals but also practitioners in the creation of the product itself. At one point, 11 writers worked on the specification, and ultimately the specification consisted of 20 volumes and thousands of pages. The resulting product surpassed all of its performance goals.

Failure also prompted changes in the development of computer messages. In line with the division of labor that assigned content to practitioners and presentation to professionals, product developers created computer messages and then distributed them to professionals to have the style and punctuation corrected. What professionals discovered, however, was that practitioners sent them messages with errors, unnecessary information, and other problems. When professionals revised such messages and returned them, their revisions were frequently ignored, largely because messages required software changes, and the tight schedules of software developers inclined them to resist such changes, resulting in poor message quality. To address this problem, administrators at one corporate site mandated that all messages be sent to groups of professionals where they were rewritten and promoted to databases that practitioners had to use to build their message set. Message creation, then, became much more collaborative than linear. In the creation of messages, too, quality improved.

In the same way that division could contribute to problems in specifications and messages, they could also lead to language inconsistencies. An example was provided by Mary Olsen of IBM-Rochester in an article titled "Terminology in the Computer Industry: Wading through the Slough of Despond," published in a 1984 IBM Technical Report titled "Writing in Response to a Changing Environment." Olsen wrote:

> To most of us who work with data processing documentation, it is common knowledge that the vocabulary of the computer—new words raining down onto a sea of other words—is a muddy and muddled mess....On an industry-wide scale, computer-related terms have proliferated with little regard for linguistic decency. (p. 97)

Olsen (1984) specified some of the problems:

> The typical English-speaking computer novice sitting down in front of a computer is now accustomed to hearing its display screen called, variously, a "CRT" or "cathode ray tube," "screen," "display," "tube," "terminal," "data station," "work station," "display device," "panel," or almost any combination of these terms....The computer's data storage area may be called "main storage," "primary storage," "real storage," "core storage," "core," "control storage," "internal storage," or "memory."' (p. 97)

At times, the vocabulary on a single page could be inconsistent: "One publication, for instance, has a chapter on 'Interval Timer' that opens with a page that refers to the interval timer as a 'feature,' a 'three-byte binary counter,' a 'timer,' a 'time-of-day clock,' an 'interval timer counter,' an 'attachment,' and a 'timer attachment'" (p. 98).

According to Olsen (1984), the problem of inconsistent terminology

> has its source in those abundantly creative people who develop the computers. Their abundantly created words get bounced around in conversation, scribbled on chalkboards, and then printed in initial programming specifications. Before you know it the words are built into the programming of the computer system, at which point they're cast in hard rubber if not concrete and are the very devil to change. (p. 106)

Since these practitioners were all too often isolated from other sites and other corporations, opportunities for the achievement of consistency through collaboration were limited. The resulting inconsistencies could adversely affect the quality of information and create a barrier to adequate performance.

Olsen described the effort at IBM-Rochester to address this problem:

> Not surprisingly, the answer to this predicament lies in our getting involved earlier in the development cycle. And because IBM's interest in developing computer systems precedes its interest in publishing books, it is reasonable to expect a publications group to wade into the developers' world rather than wait for the reverse to happen. In past years we have attended the developers' product review meetings on a sometime basis; now this is happening on a regular basis. (p. 106)

What we had here were professionals aggressively pushing to the front of the product development process to improve the quality of their work.

It is interesting to note, though, the role that Olsen defined for information groups. She placed them in a reactive or critical role. In "product review meetings," she reported, "when we hear terms that hit our ears like fingernails on a chalkboard, we can raise our concerns while the ideas expressed by these terms are still just ideas. And we are finding that the developers are generally very cooperative *if* we can explain to them why the terms as they use them won't be effective" (p. 106). It may be that a critical role was all that Olsen and her colleagues were allowed, yet many writers would insist that someone with linguistic capabilities and a knowledge of computing should be collaborating closely with product developers to fashion the language; writers should assume more than a reactive role. As Paradis (1983) showed us in his analysis of the linguistic work of Linnaeus, a wise selection of terminology could substantially advance a particular field.

IBM-Rochester also developed tools to address the problem of inconsistent terminology. To insure that the terms that were born with a new product and grew along with it remained consistent, IBM-Rochester established and continuously updated a product glossary or dictionary. Developers were expected to know the glossary and avoid departing from it. To insure a measure of consistency from product to product, the IBM site created a *Rochester Dictionary* in 1977 and updated it regularly afterward. As Olsen (1984) suggested, inventers of a new computer system became convinced that their computer was "unlike any computer that preceded it and thus" needed "a vocabulary unlike any vocabulary that preceded it" (p. 101). The *Rochester Dictionary* was intended to serve as a caution light.

Such a dictionary had no impact at other sites or other corporations, however. Inconsistent terminology emerged from many other IBM sites and many other computer corporations, such as Data General, Digital Equipment Corporation, Wang, and Apple. To the extent that we were becoming an information society, such a problem loomed large. If the exchange of words and other symbolic codes is a major economic force in a nation, it is imperative that these words and other codes be as effective as possible. Ideally, some kind of system must be established to monitor developments in different economic units, to compare and contrast these developments, to allow qualified individuals to create effective language, and to subject that language to the stress of continual refinement.

If writers were forced to become involved earlier in the product development process, so, too, were graphics specialists. In the early history of professionals, graphics was a relatively neglected area—despite the fact that professionals had to consider the visual as possibly preferable to the verbal, to recognize the verbal as being visual, and to understand the possibilities of visual thinking as a source of invention. Ideas associated with science and engineering reinforced this neglect. They promoted the exploration of inanimate matter not in its diversity, but to discover uniformities. Major areas of science and engineering supposedly related natural objects to one another in order to translate them to a homogeneous scheme, to discover patterns, and to move from the concrete to the universal. They stripped away such experienced qualities of natural objects as colors, sounds, and odors to get at what was most real—the size, weight, shape, and motion of bodies. In areas where such directions had force, the act of concrete visualization and the practice of graphics were likely to receive far less than their due.

It is not surprising, then, that the few graphics specialists who did make their way into organizations of professionals were even more limited in their responsibilities than writers. Writers placed graphics specialists at the end of the publication development process, between the time that writing was completed and printing began, in the same way that product developers placed professionals at the end of the product development process, between the time a product was completed and the time it was released. The job of graphics specialists, for the most part, was to implement decisions about graphics made by writers. Writers, for instance, came up with crude drawings, and the job of graphics specialists was to improve the appearance of the drawings—straighten this line or perfect that circle.

Innovation, however, drew graphics specialists toward the front of both product and information development processes. The example of the development of wordless instructions at IBM in the late 1970s and early 1980s is suggestive. The story of part of this development was contained in two articles: a 1982 article by Richard Hodgkinson and John Hughes titled "Developing Wordless Instructions: A Case History," which explored the development of wordless instructions for the IBM Selectric II typewriter, and a 1984 article by Charles Gange and Amy Lipton titled "Word-free Setup Instructions: Stepping into the World of Complex Products," which explored the development of wordless instructions for the IBM 5080 Graphics System. These articles documented a pattern of increasing responsibilities for graphics specialists, but also suggested the gap between the responsibilities they assumed and the responsibilities that were ideal.

One of the most significant developments of the 20th century was the growing internationalization of commerce. The increase in multinational corporations was one of its manifestations, and one of the most prominent of the multinational corporations was IBM. When IBM developed products, it had to insure that customers with different languages could use them. Instructions about using products written in English, for instance, might have to be translated into French, German, Spanish, and other languages. Typically, IBM would create multiple-language instruction sheets for products that would be shipped to a country or a range of countries with more than one official language, or IBM would create single-language sheets for products that would be shipped to a country or range of countries with only one official language.

However, IBM was confronted with translation problems. The two IBM articles about wordless instructions described a number of these problems. For instance, it was expensive to hire translators, and, furthermore, these translators were not always expert enough to avoid obscurities, inaccuracies, and even unintended hilarity (Gange & Lipton, 1984). Furthermore, a product's destination might not be known at the time of its manufacture and packaging, so it was difficult to know which language sheets to use (Hodgkinson & Hughes, 1982). Finally, multiple-language sheets were "frustrating to use and expensive to produce" (p. 74). As a result, IBM was pressured to search for alternatives to translation.

One alternative was wordless instructions. A growing trend in the data-processing industry was the option of allowing customers to do the final setup or assembly of a product, and here the use of wordless instructions was promising (Gange & Lipton, 1984). In developing wordless instructions, as the two IBM articles made clear, graphics specialists were not simply improving drawings submitted by writers. Writers did not even serve as intermediaries between product developers and graphics specialists. Graphics specialists began to work directly with product developers—a shift from the back to the front of the information development process.

However, the relationship between product developers and graphics specialists was far from ideal. Gange and Lipton described their relationship with product developers in the creation of wordless instructions for the IBM 5080 Graphics System:

> Many hours of industrial design and human factors engineering were invested to make the IBM 5080 a machine that a customer could set up. The result of this investment was a product where the physical connections that a consumer must make to set up the machine were simple and straightforward. What remained to be seen was whether we could get a consumer through the process by using word-free instructions. (pp. 17–18)

In other words, first the system was built, and then Gange and Lipton tried to determine whether wordless instructions were possible.

Ideally, however, the development of the system should not be prior to and separate from the development of instructions. If the goal of the product developers is to create a system that customers can set up, the instructions for that system are indispensable to their success. It is not enough for a system to be easy for a customer to set up; it has to be easy for a customer to use instructions to set it up. The instructions are as much a part of the human factor considerations as the rest of the system. The possibilities available for instructions—especially wordless instructions—might well affect the design of the product. Furthermore, the expertise of graphics specialists is hardly being used to the fullest if their views on the appearance of the system are not considered. What is essential is collaboration between product developers and graphics specialists in the course of system development. To improve the benefits of that collaboration, product developers need some understanding of technical communication and graphics, and graphics specialists need some understanding of computers.

If practitioners were willing to collaborate with professionals—at least to some degree—to address such problems as the briefcase computer, product specifications, computer messages, language inconsistencies, and wordless instructions, they were less inclined to respond to other problems such as time. Among the most serious problems confronting professionals that stemmed from decisions earlier in the information development process was the amount of time that they had to perform their tasks. Practitioners placed unrealistic demands for speed on professionals. Administrators too often established unrealistic schedules for product development, and these unrealistic schedules could, in turn, be worsened by schedule slippage. Among the results, product developers were frequently late in completing their products. Since the work of professionals took place between product development and product release, administrators had the choice of either cutting the schedules of professionals—often unrealistic already—or delaying product release. In almost all cases, the schedules of professionals were cut. The positioning of professionals, then, led to a situation in which delays by practitioners shortened their already unrealistic schedules and, as a result, further compromised their performance.

Professionals discovered that time seemed to be the single most important reason why they could not perform their tasks well, and inadequate time to prepare information inevitably resulted in failure. One professional in a computer corporation said:

> I know how fallible the information in our manuals is. A lot of our source material comes to us at the last minute, with no time for anything but the most superficial editing, and [is] hurried into manuals as they go to the publisher....Yet our users plod through our books, step by step and page by page, and wonder why their computers don't work. If they knew what conditions were like on the writing end...,I think they'd stop using our products in a minute.

Writers were fully aware of the inadequacies of their manuals, and discontent was rampant.

In addition to creating discontent, the time problem made the lives of professionals far too stressful. More work was demanded of them than was healthy. One writer reported: "People are getting burned out—the stress." Another echoed: "Writers are close to burning out. There's no time." In one corporation in which I was asked to interview virtually all of the members of a technical publications organization, I was astonished by the numerous reports of unreasonable time pressures, excessive overtime, burnout, and even emotional breakdowns. These reports were confirmed by a personnel administrator in the corporation. Afraid that I may not have gotten the message, this personnel administrator—obviously fearful of being discovered—drew me into his office and informed me in hushed whispers about the numerous nervous breakdowns among professionals resulting from overwork. Time pressures were not only compromising performance and any resulting information; they were also adversely affecting the lives of employees.

The problem of time pressures clearly had to be addressed, but assessing responsibility for the problem and determining what to say or do about it was extremely complex. Its causes could stem, for instance, from the overly short schedule demanded by a military contract, a desire to gain the marketing advantage of early product release, a decision to force the maximum labor out of employees to keep labor costs at a minimum, unrealistic schedule estimates by product developers in competition with other sites, and the inefficiency of professionals. The environment was so rich with possibilities that even the acutest judgment had difficulty appraising the balance of responsibility for the time problem.

The time problem was so pressing, however, that it compelled immediate and considerable attention. It had clear priority over most other problems. In this sense, the environment was highly deterministic—more forcing than offering choices. Professionals tried to address as many of the factors creating the time problem as they recognized, but progress was difficult. Among their efforts, they insisted on participation in scheduling and head count decisions early in the product development process; militating against such participation were the relative invisibility and low stature of professionals. They tried to write descriptions of the information development process to make clear to schedulers the amount of time essential for creating quality information; militating against this effort was the lack of time professionals had to work on such descriptions and the frequent changes in the process from project to project. In addition, they recorded the instances when hardware and software groups encroached on the time of information groups; militating against this practice, though, was the conflict it caused—a particular problem for professionals since they were so dependent on hardware and software groups for information.

In situations where practitioners were less likely to help professionals, professionals sometimes operated in an adversarial mode. According to Frederick J. Bethke (1984), this was a matter of escalating, of appealing to higher levels of authority to enforce the writer's demands. For these appeals to succeed, management outside of the publications area had to have two basic perceptions. First, it had to recognize the value of technical publications. Second, it had to understand "how writing takes place, what the job entails" (pp. 158–159). What Bethke was discussing here, of course, was power, and this power could only be acquired if management both understood and valued the tasks of professionals.

A number of developments in the 1970s and 1980s increased the power of professionals. Among these developments, problems with manuals led customers to complain directly to computer corporations. At IBM, according to William O'Neill, it was the 1970s when the corporation began to get the message from customers about the importance of manuals. IBM began to perceive that rewriting technical specifications was insufficient; customers wanted better information and were vocal about it. IBM began to realize that technical information was a very important part of the hardware or software product it was offering (Hillyer, 1985). Computer corporations moved from viewing information as support for a product to viewing information as a major part of the product.

Given the frustrations caused by poor manuals, customers began to evaluate them as an important part of their purchasing strategies. Some advertisers and sales engineers were quick to exploit this customer concern as a way of giving their products a competitive edge. Among a number of examples, Apple launched a massive media campaign—including heavy television advertising—comparing the slim single volume of Macintosh instructions to a stack of large manuals accompanying the IBM personal computer. The increased value placed on manuals was paraded frequently before television viewers.

The discovery that poor instruction manuals resulted in increased support costs was a further spur to action. If a confusing or incomplete manual prevented a customer from carrying out a task, the result was more than dissatisfaction and expensive delays for the customer. The corporation often had to incur the costs of sending someone—at one point called a "field engineer"—to correct the problem. These costs mounted up. Improving manual quality, then, also became a way of reducing costs.

A decision to sell software rather than distributing it free also added to the power of professionals. If you were selling computer hardware, you had something to show a customer—a keyboard, monitor, printer, and so on. But if you were selling software, the instructions on a disk or tape, all that you could show a customer about a product was what a manual said about it. In fact, if a product feature was not described in a manual, for all practical purposes it did not exist. Manuals, then, were crucial sales tools, and manuals needed to exude quality. Andrew Turnbull (1981) wrote:

> Attractive, thoughtfully prepared manuals are valuable sales tools at national sales conferences and in the hands of regional sales engineers, who pass out new product manuals like business cards....The head of software development at a large computer manufacturing firm is fond of stressing the value of reliable software documentation by saying, "Customers are not purchasing our software; they're buying our manuals!" (p. 27)

Software developers with such attitudes were not inclined to ignore the needs of professionals.

A final example of a development that strengthened the power of professionals was their own organization at sites and even at corporate levels. Some professionals wanted to remain part of product development groups with hardware and software specialists. As former hardware and software specialists themselves in many instances, they felt more at home that way; they were closer to their sources of information, and many liked the prestige of these groups. But the proponents of information development groups won the day. They argued for a so-called "matrix" organization that allowed both product and communication loyalties. Writers were assigned to product teams, but an information development group remained their home base. Information development groups were necessary, among other reasons, to avoid duplication of effort, to enable improved management of resources, to insure consistency where it was important, and, perhaps most important of all, to develop a consensus on needs and standards for achieving quality and to acquire the clout to persuade corporate administrators to meet the needs and accept the standards.

Technical communicators organized not just at the site level, but also at the corporate level. At IBM, for instance, the corporate-wide Information Development Council (IDC) was formed in 1979. The IDC resulted from a corporate task force convened, according to Raynor Moore, to study the whole issue of providing the best information to customers and uniting the discipline (Hillyer, 1985, p. 34). One chairman of the IDC, Nelson Johns, reported that the goal of the organization was "to set priorities, set directions and monitor what's going on with the profession" (p. 36). Of course, an unspoken goal of the IDC—at least unspoken in public—was to acquire the collective power to improve performance by persuading corporate superiors to address the needs of professionals.

A whole range of forces, then, combined to give professionals the power to move into the world of practitioners and expand the range of their concerns beyond the presentation of a content provided by practitioners. In some corporations, the acceleration of the movement of professionals toward the front of the product development process was dramatic. William L. Benzon (1981) reported one result at Data General:

> When Data General set out to develop a new programming language, it began by getting its software people and their technical writers together so that both groups could design the language. The implementation of the language must be done by the software engineers; but making the language intelligible to the end user is a job for the technical writer. (p. 109)

Benzon suggested the possibility of the two jobs becoming one: "computer programming and technical communication may converge in the near or middle future" (p. 111).

Bernice E. Casey (1981) reported similar collaboration at GTE Laboratories. She indicated the importance of close collaboration: "it makes sense that we, as technical writers and editors, offer our communication skills to software engineers. We can do this most effectively by stepping out of our cubicles and offices in order to become active members of software development teams" (p. 363). Casey described a procedure at her location: "we write the user's manual for a system before it is actually built. Because the primary audience for the document *is* the user, the designer is asked to respond to the system as a user would, to see it as the user would" (p. 370). The manual, then, became a controlling force during product development, a force that promoted cohesion and militated against inconsistency.

In a dissertation titled "Technical Communication in the Computer Industry: An Information-Development Process to Track, Measure, and Ensure Quality," Roger Grice (1987)—an information developer at IBM-Kingston at the time—described the extent to which information developers were able to involve themselves at the front of the product development process at his site. Grice described four different phases in product development—product review, planning, development, and verification—and suggested substantive professional involvement in each phase. While professionals did not have the levels of responsibility suggested by Benzon and Casey, professionals were far more involved in activities during product development than in previous times.

Clearly, then, the contexts of professionals themselves—including such forces as failure and innovation—directed the attention of professionals toward various problems and encouraged them to expand the range of their concerns. Furthermore, such reactions to failure and innovation as customer complaints, advertisements about manuals, the call for quality prompted by the sale of software, and the desire to reduce support costs increased the importance of information development and made it more visible in corporations, encouraging administrators to devote more attention and resources to the area. As a result, professionals were able to increase the scope of their performance, setting new goals and transforming social structures.

In the 1990s, the trend toward increased collaboration in technical communication continued. By 1998, 60 percent of the members of the Society for Technical Communication worked in computer-related industries (Hayhoe, 1999, p. 23), and advancements in computer technology spurred such collaboration. For example, Tim Berners-Lee, the inventor of the World Wide Web, suggested that the original driving force behind the Web was collaboration (1999) and coined a new term—*intercreativity*—for the kind of invention that resulted from such collaboration. As another example, the development of publishing and graphics software made text layout and graphics creation more accessible to writers and promoted increased collaboration between writers and graphics specialists. Throughout the decade, one increasingly heard of cross-functional teams of software developers, human factors specialists, writers, graphics specialists, marketing specialists, and customers collaborating to develop computer products.

In an important article titled "Design Teams and the Web: A Collaborative Model for the Workplace," Cynthia A. Wambeam and Robert Kramer (1996) described the kinds of changes in goals and social structures that resulted in industry from such collaboration. Initially, industries consisted of sets of isolated social structures—for instance, groups of software developers, writers, and graphics specialists. The goals of each group were limited by a narrow disciplinarity, and work in one group was completed before work in the next group in the information flow began. With the kind of collaboration prompted by work in such areas as the World Wide Web, however, members of teams were not expected to restrict themselves to contributions in narrow disciplinary areas, but rather to meld together their talents and through dialogue to help in all areas. The goals of participants, then, were broader, and the flow of information was no longer linear. Social structures collapsed into each other, and integration rather than separation became the ideal.

Throughout the 1990s, we heard again and again about the growing scope of the deliberations of technical communicators. In an unpublished manuscript titled "Writing to the World Wide Web and the Relevance of Classical Rhetoric" (1999), Daniel J. O'Neil described the increase in scope that he perceived as necessary in a course for future technical communicators:

> My curriculum for WWWW [Writing to the World Wide Web] is thoroughly Isocratean, since only the breadth of scope Isocrates prescribes for rhetoric can encompass the challenges of designing onscreen communication....This breadth of scope permeates the course topics....Our topics range from the staples of expository writing courses, such as consideration of topic, audience, purpose, and tone, to subjects usually found in graphic design and programming courses: the principles of visual design, layout, and typography; usability; storyboarding; image editing and illustration software...; and HTML. (p. 2)

In the 1990s, Cicero's call for increased scope in deliberation had certainly been realized extensively in technical communication.

The advances by practitioners were not negligible, though perhaps not as sweeping as those by professionals. Practitioners certainly deserved substantial credit for increasing collaboration with professionals and enabling professionals to expand the scope of their activities. But nobody could claim that practitioners had come to an adequate understanding of the value of discourse activities in industries; too many professionals like Emily Sopensky (1994) still complained about the lack of respect among practitioners for discourse activities and their inadequacies in performing such activities (p. 713). Industries had still not adequately pressured universities, which were bastions of philosophy, to give rhetoric the value and attention it deserved; as a result, universities had still made little progress in bridging the gap between departments of practitioners and departments where writing and speaking were taught, and students who later became practitioners still had little appreciation of the importance of rhetoric and still received little, if any, education in discourse activities.

Such developments in industries as globalization and mergers expanded the scope of the deliberations of practitioners, but practitioners still neglected the primary and secondary information sectors. A corporation such as IBM expanded its activities in education and publication, but demands for secrecy and speed still militated powerfully against such expansion. Not enough attention was devoted to the impact of such factors promoting secrecy and speed as hostility between nation-states and competition between industries and their subunits. Adequate progress in the primary and secondary information sectors remained a task for the 21st century.

7

Methodological Narrowness in Approaches to Technical Communication Problems in Industries

In the second half of the 20th century, narrow methodologies too often reinforced narrow social structures and goals in compromising the development of technical communication in industries. With the historical narrowing of the scope of rhetoric through definitional exclusion and the decline that necessarily resulted from this process, rhetoric was perceived as so narrow by a number of notable professionals in the late 20th century that they failed to understand how helpful it could be in engaging technical communication problems. Totally unaware of Isocratean rhetoric—or even the rhetorics of Cicero or Quintilian for that matter—they accepted the dominant Aristotelian view of rhetoric and, not unexpectedly, failed to see how an area that focused on oratory, limited itself to persuasion designed to overcome resistance, and rejected the abstruse as too difficult for crowds could possibly be helpful to their broader needs in technical communication. These professionals were cut off by a narrow definition from important history that could have helped them.

With their failure to understand the importance of the Isocratean rhetorical tradition, they had no alternative ideas to liberate themselves from dominant philosophical ideas that militated against methodologies important to technical communication. Without the stimulus of Isocrates and others who promoted the importance of history in engaging human problems, professionals devoted far too little attention to history and, when they did engage it, were inclined by professionalism and disciplinarity to limit their explorations to events and texts exclusively associated with such terms as "technical," "scientific," "writing," and "communication," failing to perceive how other history—for instance, that associated with rhetoric—could have helped them understand and address their problems.

Inclined by the philosophical tradition to take methodologies appropriate for fixing truths about relatively stable phenomena and misapply them in situations calling for choices in changing environments, professionals too often used induction to derive insights from past experience and then used deduction to apply these insights to current problems, making the mistake of using preset methodological approaches rather than using the full particularity of problem situations to generate the unique methodologies appropriate to them. The philosophical emphasis on generality, on what was common to all places and times, inclined professionals to search for rules or universals that held for all situations, unaware of the inappropriateness of such a process when a prior context differed substantially from a current context.

In their quest for rules and universals, professionals adopted mathematical methodologies such as readability formulas to evaluate style, an approach that ignored too much of the context of a problem situation to be viable, and used experimental methodologies to justify choice, an example of an inappropriate leap from description to prescription. They were reinforced in this quest by their philosophical predisposition to acquire certainty about what was universal, unchanging, and permanent rather than use judgment to make decisions about what was particular, changing, and temporary. They were also reinforced in this quest by the emphasis on science in industries and the all-too-frequent tendency to see scientific methodologies and technical communication methodologies as identical.

THE DISPARAGEMENT AND DISTANCING OF RHETORIC

In an article in the May 1997 issue of *Technical Communication*, Patrick Moore cited Carliner's (1995) claim that rhetorical theories had nothing to do with anything useful and presented an elaborate argument that such theories were inappropriate for engaging technical communication problems. Moore's statements about rhetoric exemplified the extent to which Aristotelian views of rhetoric had triumphed over those of the Isocratean tradition—to the extent that the latter had become invisible. As might be expected, then, they also exemplified the tendency to define rhetoric too narrowly and, as a result, obscure ways in which rhetorical theories could help in engaging technical communication problems.

Unaware that rhetorics could be as varied as the situations used to generate them, Moore accepted the notion of a "standard" rhetoric, a single kind of rhetoric that could be defined as a preset methodological approach to problems (pp. 164–165). Unaware that classical rhetoric included a group of highly varied theories, he based his standard rhetoric on a supposedly monolithic classical rhetoric that was equated with Aristotelian rhetoric (pp. 164–165). As a result, he limited rhetoric to oratory designed to persuade an audience.

Having used Aristotle to define rhetoric so narrowly, Moore then went on to show the extent to which technical communication lay outside rhetoric. He argued that many kinds of technical communication did not involve persuasion but rather informed users how to perform tasks; he called such discourse "instrumental" rather than "rhetorical" (p. 165). Unlike rhetorical discourse, instrumental discourse governed human activities (p. 166). Instrumental theories of discourse engaged problems that rhetorical theories did not—"managing time and money, keeping teams of workers happy, finding the best technology, planning projects, developing standards, and managing other resources" (p. 167).

If Moore had been aware of the full history of rhetorical theory, he would have understood that the rhetorical theories of writers such as Isocrates had sufficient scope to include all of the problems that he listed. Isocratean rhetoric could have served as a source of support for Moore's critique of the narrowness of Aristotelian rhetoric. It included not only the preparation and delivery of speeches, but also deliberation about all human endeavor, not only persuasion, but the administration or governance of tasks in any line of work. Were Moore fully aware of the teaching approaches being used in university programs across the country, he would have been surprised how many were using rhetorical theory to engage not just the technical communication problems he listed but many more as well.

If writers such as Moore and Carliner overtly disparaged and distanced rhetoric, others reflected similar attitudes by ignoring it. In the fourth quarter of 1985, *Technical Communication*, the major journal of professionals in the field, published a special issue on research that was notable for its silence on rhetoric. As might be expected from the emphasis on science in industries and the all-too-frequent tendency there to see scientific methodologies and technical communication methodologies as identical, the editor of the journal, Frank R. Smith, and the guest editor of the issue, Thomas E. Pinelli, both insisted that technical communication problems should be approached using ideas associated with science.

Smith (1985) compared past research processes in technical communication with those in science and encouraged technical communication researchers to move toward controlled experiments as a means of engaging problems in the field (pp. 6–7). Pinelli (1985) argued that technical communication had to become an academic discipline and suggested how this could be accomplished: "members of this field or profession must begin to apply the scientific method to analyze relationships and solve problems" (p. 6). Both men focused solely on scientific methodology as the ideal research process in the field.

The first article in the special issue, by Myron Glassman and Pinelli (1985), was titled "Scientific Inquiry and Technical Communication: An Introduction to *the* [italics mine] Research Process." The authors limited research to scientific method: "Research is the formal, systematic application of scientific inquiry to the study of a particular problem" (p. 8). The equation and limitation of research to scientific methodology led to the misapplication of this methodology to problems that called for other methodologies. Two examples can be suggestive—the use of mathematical methodologies such as readability formulas to evaluate style and the use of experimental methodologies to devise ideal standards in graphics.

MATHEMATICAL APPROACHES TO STYLE

In the early history of professionals, writers focused most of their attention on style—a focus that had roots in the decline of rhetoric. Even in classical antiquity, when rhetoric was the crown of education, Cicero's Crassus claimed at one point that the essential concern of an orator was a style that was dignified and graceful. Quintilian called style the chief object of study, worthy of the energies of a lifetime. In the Renaissance, Ramus limited the definition of rhetoric to style and delivery, assigning invention, disposition, and memory to dialectic. While many rhetoricians after Ramus rejected his narrow definition, the tradition of associating style and rhetoric remained so strong that Shedd (1878) lamented that the entire art of rhetoric had been converted into a collection of rules about style. This preoccupation with style still remained strong in corporations in World War II and the early postwar years.

Furthermore, if the decline of rhetoric inclined writers to focus their attention too narrowly on style, the rise of science inclined them to use an overly simplistic approach to style. In classical antiquity, as has already been suggested, Isocrates, Cicero, and Quintilian attacked efforts to devise universal rules for all rhetorical situations, arguing that different situations required different approaches. Counter to their wisdom, however, writers tended to approach style with a universal rule so inadequate that historians will look back on it with no little amusement. This tool—called a "readability formula"—had so little going for it that its widespread acceptance could only have resulted from a strongly supportive complex of ideas that inclined people toward it. The readability formula was essentially a mathematical tool, and its appeal no doubt rested on the extraordinary effort in the second half of the 20th century to find mathematical solutions to even those problems that did not lend themselves to such solutions—applications of mathematics that might even have astonished Fontenelle.

Readability formulas were among the communication specifications imposed by armed services agencies such as the Naval Air Services Command on defense industries through contracts. John Mitchell (1976), in an article titled "It's a Craft Course: Indoctrinate, Don't Educate," suggested the extent to which government communication specifications became a standard for all industries. Mitchell argued that industries adopted government communication specifications as a standard for themselves because so much of their product went to the government:

> Now these corporate style guides are essentially product oriented. We have only to analyze where the product goes to see the forms the guides must take. For example, Republic Aviation is 100% contract supported. Mil Spec's [military specifications] determine the forms there....And GE, which we tend to think of as consumer-oriented, gets 65% of its gross from federal contracts. The happy solution at GE has been to train all the writers to write for government. (p. 4)

Although Mitchell did not mention computer corporations, these industries—as has been indicated—were also heavily involved in contract work for government agencies, and these contracts mandated military specifications.

Some of these specifications were no doubt reasonable. For instance, nobody would object to specifications such as the standardization and placement of industry identifying marks (logos). But government agencies—and the industries that followed them—went too far in their prescriptions. For instance, in 1976, the Naval Air Systems Command mandated that its publications pass a Comprehensibility Assurance Test that measured twenty-one comprehensibility criteria, including such calculations used in readability formulas as number of words per sentence and number of polysyllabic words. Each criterion was assigned a mathematical ideal. Some corporations serving the Naval Air Systems Command and organizations like it developed computer programs to measure a publication against comprehensibility criteria. In these corporations, if a publication failed to attain a certain numerical grade on a comprehensibility assurance test, it was sent back to the writer for revision.

In turn, corporations performing contractual work for the government were as concerned about mathematical measures as government agencies. For instance, one early IBM document outlined three steps for professionals striving to achieve information quality: "1. Amass....standards that address quality....2. Decide which quality factors pertain to us....3. Determine metrics for the factors." The term "metrics" referred to mathematical criteria for measurement. Another sheet from IBM insisted that all information plans include "countable criteria for measuring quality." Given this preference for mathematical standards, industries were as receptive to readability formulas as government agencies. Furthermore, their writers, strongly nurtured by the tradition of science, tended to be receptive as well, although some opposition was invariably voiced. The attention attracted by readability formulas—both positive and negative—was suggested by George R.

Klare's 1963 study titled *The Measurement of Readability*. Klare listed 31 different kinds of readability formulas published between 1923 and 1959. His bibliography on the subject ran to 482 items.

An example of one readability formula, used in a computer corporation in the 1980s, can suggest the nature of most such formulas. The first task in using this formula is to select a passage of at least 100 words from the text under consideration. The next task is to determine average sentence length by dividing the number of words by the number of sentences. The third task is to count the number of words of three syllables or more and then determine the percentage of difficult words in the passage by dividing the total number of words into the number of polysyllabic words. The final task is to calculate the reading grade level by adding the average number of words per sentence and the percentage of difficult words and multiply the total by 0.4. The result is a reading grade level.

Clearly, readability formulas had even more in common with the ideas that I have associated with Plato, Aristotle, the rise of science, and early engineering than an emphasis on mathematics. In applying these formulas, writers often focused attention not on the entire communication situation—including the history that led up to it and projections such as audience needs and a writer's purpose—but only on a part of that situation, say a passage of 100 words. They placed instruments—readability formulas—between themselves and the artifacts they were analyzing to extend human capability and limit human error. These instruments translated all texts to one homogeneous scheme by moving from the concrete to the universal, by selecting and abstracting the quantitative from the diversity of the experienced artifact. These quantitative results represented an intelligible, simple, and uniform order achieved through the use of reason. They were compared to a preexisting set of quantities to determine identity along a mathematical scale that represented reading grade level. If the appropriate mathematical match were achieved, writers proved undeniably that their prose was of the highest quality. Readability formulas could be used forever for all texts; they were certain, unchanging, and eternal.

Furthermore, readability formulas could gain credibility in other ways. Let us consider a sentence that I found in a hardware manual some years ago: "The capability of performing the report printing function is provided by the 3211." In its context, what this sentence really means is: "The 3211 prints reports." The second sentence, superior to the first, has fewer words and, unlike the first, no polysyllables. When we develop guidelines for excellent writing, what we often do is examine some example of excellent writing in the past and try to determine the source of its virtues. We then work toward these virtues in the future. If we compare the excellent second sentence here with the first, we might easily decide that number of words per sentence and frequency of polysyllabic words are decisive factors in the analysis of style. The problem is that they often are not, and all it takes is two sentences to show it. Compare the following two sentences:

As I sat down at the computer, I was not eager to begin hitting the keys but rather wished I were out enjoying the beautiful fall day, strolling through the leaves, smelling their rich scent, and feeling the warm sun on my skin.

An SNA terminal, such as 3767, is represented by a physical unit type 1 (PU-T1).

If a reader knows nothing about computer networks, the second sentence, although shorter, is incomprehensible, while the first, over 25 words longer, is easy to understand. The decisive factor here is not number of words per sentence, but computer knowledge.

The same principle holds for polysyllables. Many readers would stumble over at least one of the following monosyllabic words: *quark*, *ploce*, *tort*, and *merle*. I cannot imagine many having difficulty with these polysyllabic words: *happily*, *apartment*, *television*, and *automobile*. The decisive factor here is not number of polysyllables, but, again, knowledge in a specialized area.

No doubt a mathematical formula that encouraged information groups to write sentences of fewer words and words of fewer syllables was sometimes successful in promoting an improved style. That was a half truth that contributed to the widespread acceptance of readability formulas in industry. But situations were often complex, and accurately conveying that complexity may have actually required longer sentences and polysyllabic words. Any effort in these situations to break up sentences and find word equivalents of fewer syllables would have weakened the writing. The ideal approach to a writing situation was not a flimsy tool involving word count and syllable count, but a judgment that incorporated as full a knowledge of audience, subject, and the rest of the writing context as possible.

What made the emphasis on readability formulas and other mathematical measures worse was that they absorbed so much of the attention of technical communicators—and still do in some corporations. As the modern philosophers of science have taught us, our instruments affect our observation. Readability formulas throw syllable count, word count, and style into high relief but leave other aspects of writing in the shadows. As a result, information groups often focused on syllables, words, and style when other concerns should have taken precedence. Situations as a whole should have dictated the major concerns of writers, not prescriptions about some part of these situations. Writers should have engaged their situations with a set of approaches comprehensive enough to suggest all of the shaping forces inherent in these situations.

EXPERIMENTAL APPROACHES TO GRAPHICS

If approaches to style compromised the quality of manuals during World War II and the postwar years, these problems were likely to pale before the problems professionals faced in the area of graphics. Among the sources of many of these problems were standards or specifications established by either the government or corporate practitioners. For instance, in the early history of professionals, when manuals were distributed to customers free of charge, practitioners set specifications for graphics to insure that professionals did not spend too much money on manuals. Cheap grades of paper were mandated, color was forbidden, and margins were kept at a minimum to crowd as much information on the page as possible. The early manuals, then, not only *were* cheap; they *looked* it as well.

Improving the specifications was hardly easy, however. It was difficult to translate a vague feeling that the manuals looked cheap into concrete recommendations for improvement; professionals were woefully ignorant about graphics. Furthermore, even if a concrete recommendation were drafted and professionals tried to gain the authority to change a specification, administrators resisted. Whatever their motives, they wanted empirical evidence that the old specification was inadequate and the new specification an improvement. This empirical evidence was to be acquired through experimental testing.

As might be expected, given the dominance of the ideas that I have associated with science in the second half of the 20th century, the insistence on empirical evidence as a mandate for change was not unusual during this period. Experimental testing required a sharply defined situation in which single variables could be isolated and controlled. The testers attempted to discover a truth. Ideally, they used instruments that limited human error and extended human awareness. They attempted to discover a consistency, a pattern, an order that proved beyond all doubt that their deductions were confirmed. These deductions could be used as a permanent guide.

In this context, in 1981, a major computer corporation asked three professors— I was one of them—to undertake a joint research project. The project called for us to work with seven students to compile descriptions and evaluations of all the empirical research on graphics in the 20th century. Characteristically, the corporation insisted that we limit the scope of our project to research based on experimental testing; no other research could be trusted as valid. At the time, I saw the project as a means to learn more about both graphics and experimental testing. I felt vaguely uneasy about the limitation to empirical research, but I certainly was not as disillusioned about the usefulness of this research as I later became. Helping to conduct the project increasingly enhanced my awareness of the shortcomings of misapplied experimentalism.

As I delved into the history of 20th-century empirical research on graphics, I was staggered by the amounts of time and money that were devoted to efforts such as measuring reactions to kinds of typefaces as a means of making universal legibility recommendations. This research was caught on the horns of a dilemma. On the one hand, research methodologies required controlled conditions so that single variables could be isolated and observed. When experimenters were not careful about control, their research design was criticized. For instance, in 1966, G. Harry McLaughlin announced the results of an experiment comparing the impact of a technical pamphlet on one group of undergraduates with the impact of a revision of this pamphlet on another group of undergraduates. Since the two groups of undergraduates were picked randomly, McLaughlin had no way to account for differences arising from the differences in his undergraduates. Furthermore, the revision differed in many ways from the original, including amount of information, pamphlet size, column format, type size, illustrations, and kinds of paper and ink; McLaughlin simply assumed that all changes in the revision were improvements and declared the original inferior and the revision superior—sublimely indifferent to the possibility that some of the changes might have been negative. As part of our 1981 study, a colleague of mine—a highly regarded social scientist—reacted very simply to McLaughlin's work: "Research design problems."

On the other hand, some researchers conducted experiments that were highly controlled. In 1940, in a book titled *How to Make Type Readable*, D. G. Paterson and M. A. Tinker announced the results of 45 different experiments on typography. They administered a total of 66,062 Chapman-Cook Speed of Reading Tests in different formats to 33,031 persons and then tested them for reading comprehension. These tests typically required subjects to read pieces of text that were short enough to finish in fewer than 2 minutes. In one example, subjects read one piece of text in all capital letters and the same piece of text with a mixture of both capital letters where normally expected (such as at the beginning of sentences) and lowercase letters. This kind of experiment was a classic example of empirical research using simplified stimulus material with each variable controlled in standard laboratory conditions. Paterson and Tinker announced a clear result for this experiment: material set in all capital letters was read more slowly than material set in a mixture of uppercase and lowercase letters.

However, the research design of such highly controlled experiments was also criticized. In a book titled *Graphics in Text: A Bibliography*, Michael Macdonald-Ross and Eleanor Smith (1977) severely criticized the application of the results of experiments such as those conducted by Paterson and Tinker to educational materials. They listed over 30 issues that must be resolved by the typographer or book designer and noted that all items on the list interacted with other items. According to Macdonald-Ross and Smith, these interactions "make nonsense of the one-variable tests that make up so much of the classical literature" (p. 41).

Therefore, the horns of the dilemma were quite pointed. If, on the one hand, a research project engaged an actual communication situation, the methodology proved inadequate. If, on the other hand, a simple enough communication situation were contrived for the methodology to be valid, the results were not applicable to actual communication situations. All too often, the response to such discoveries was a call for more research. However, what was needed was a careful delineation of what empirical research could or could not do. The fruitlessness of the empirical research in graphics that we surveyed raised serious questions about the negative impact of misapplied empirical research on productivity. The waste in money and human energy in the 20th century was extraordinary.

The dilemma of research design was not the only difficulty, however. The use of instruments posed another problem. Lorraine A. Demilia (1968), in an article titled "Visual Fatigue and Reading," described some of the early instruments used in efforts to record eye movements. One researcher attached a tiny microphone to the upper eyelid. As Demilia suggested, such instruments could be either harmful or unnatural in the reading situation. While the instruments that Demilia described were used in very early experiments, the charge of artificiality was also leveled at many of the instruments used in the experimental tests that we surveyed in the early 1980s. A number of these tests involved the use of tachistoscopes (instruments for the brief exposure of visual stimuli), and critics charged that their use in experimental tests was artificial and therefore invalid.

Even if the use of these instruments had been valid, however, the scope of what they were measuring was very limited. Demilia reported that they were measuring "only the rate of reading" (p. 11). Among other possibilities, they were not measuring "accuracy of comprehension" (p. 11). Since normal eye movement could be maintained with little or no comprehension, eye movement could not be used as an indicator for comprehension. Since comprehension was crucial to the reading process, however, the value of experiments that excluded it from consideration seemed highly questionable.

Among other problems with the experimental tests that we surveyed in the early 1980s, the results of one test were often in conflict with the results of others; this conflict hardly supported the view that experimental testing yielded absolute truths or certainties that could serve as permanent guides in all situations. For instance, E. C. Poulton (1960), in an article titled "A Note on Printing to Make Comprehension Easier," compared the recommendations of three sets of authors growing out of experimental research. These recommendations were intended to improve decisions about type style (for instance, American Typewriter), type form (for instance, italics), boldness, size, leading (spacing) between lines, line length, and color of print and paper. The conclusion of Poulton's comparison was startling: "Considering the relatively small range of conditions within which the optimal style of printing must necessarily lie,...there could hardly be greater disagreement between the different authors" (p. 245). Such a conclusion hardly built confidence in the validity of experimental research in the area of typography.

Not only did different research projects yield conflicting results, but researchers often had difficulty replicating or confirming research. In 1975, in an article titled "Typographic Cueing as an Aid to Learning from Typewritten Text," P. Coles and J. J. Foster performed three experimental tests similar to tests reported by J. H. Crouse and P. Idstein in 1972. Crouse and Idstein concluded that underlining was a helpful cueing device, but their research design was criticized because it included an abnormal reading situation. Coles and Foster included a more normal reading situation in their research design. In their first experimental test, subjects were not alerted in advance that they would be reading cued text, and underlining did not help them to recall important information. In their second test, subjects were alerted in advance that important points in one of their texts were underlined, but, again, underlining did not prove helpful in enabling subjects to recall important information. In a third test, subjects were asked to employ a reading improvement strategy; they surveyed a text, asked questions about it, read the text more slowly, recalled the important points, and reviewed the text as a check or recall. The results of this third test supported the view that underlining was a helpful cueing device. It is hard to avoid the impression that Coles and Foster believed that Crouse and Idstein were correct, could not get the same results in their first test, continued to manipulate the testing situation until they got the results they wanted, and then attributed them to cueing devices. Even if that were not the case, the conflicting results undermined confidence in experimental testing as surely as the tests that Poulton surveyed.

Even if the research performed by Coles and Foster were valid, however, their proof that underlining was a helpful cueing device was hardly a dramatic discovery anyway. Our 1981 review of empirical research on graphics in the 20th century failed to turn up a single instance where the research did anything more than confirm what was already known by the unaided reason. I do recall one research report—an article by C. M. Christensen and K. E. Stordahl (1955) titled "The Effect of Organizational Aids on Comprehension and Retention"—that piqued my interest. The report concluded that organizational methods such as outlining, underlining, summarizing, and using headings were not useful in helping readers to comprehend and retain information. Now here was something dramatic—counter to centuries of belief about organization, perhaps as counter to intuition as the fact that the earth revolves around the sun. But the maze of testing procedures and absence of controls led critics to discount the research.

In their 1977 overview of research on typography, Macdonald-Ross and Smith rightfully contrasted the results of empirical research in science with the results of the same methodology in typography. They suggested that science carried authority when it led to surprising and novel truths and deep and interesting principles and theories. The knowledge acquired through empirical research in typography, however, had been the stock-in-trade of the master-printer for centuries. According to Macdonald-Ross and Smith, the use of empirical research in this area was nothing more than "a kind of `aid to rhetoric' whereby educated people (who don't understand or won't accept the experiential basis of craft knowledge)" would take heed of advice if it had "a 'scientific' seal of approval" (p. 42). Therefore, empirical research in graphics was a relatively fruitless response to a distrust in judgment.

Even if empirical research in typography had been fruitful, it would have been difficult to generalize results. To use the argument of Isocrates, Cicero, and Quintilian once again, concrete communication situations—with their varying subjects, media, audiences, and creators—often differed substantially from one another, so insights in one situation were not necessarily helpful in another. For instance, empirical research in typography typically confronted subjects with a relatively short piece of text for the first time in a laboratory. These subjects used the text for only a few minutes, almost always less than an hour, and then their reaction was assessed. This situation differed substantially from the situation involving many computer users, who waded through libraries of lengthy manuals over long periods of time, sometimes referring back to the same material again and again. Humor and cute visual devices could be fun for experimental test subjects, but cloying or even a nuisance to computer users in normal working conditions. Liking for a particular graphic technique could be high initially, but familiarity developed through use could change such liking.

Researchers in the area of typography, then, made a fundamental mistake. They committed what, in my reading, has been one of the most prevalent mistakes in modern thinking: they identified "what is" and then used it as a standard for "what ought to be"; they made description prescription. Tinker created a highly controlled communication situation, made a determination in that situation, and then issued that determination as a guideline for other situations, ignoring the extent to which differences in communication situations could affect recommendations.

My criticism of the social scientists and their research on typography is hardly anything new. Social scientists have been the target of severe criticism from scientists and humanists for decades. What is surprising is their persistence in the face of that criticism. Part of the reason for this persistence lies in the faith that greater sophistication in research methodology can overcome past inadequacies, and there is no doubt that research methodologies in social science have improved over the decades. What this persistence does not acknowledge, however, is the fundamental incompatibility of a methodology that calls for highly controlled circumstances and a reality that remains rich and highly complex. Furthermore, it has not sufficiently addressed the fallacy of using the conclusions about one communication situation as recommendations for another.

Macdonald-Ross and Smith (1977) seemed to have seized on the truth of the matter. Too many people in the 20th century were afraid to accept the results of experience and judgment; they demanded a scientific seal of approval. They suffered from a failure of nerve. They were incapable of making any decision without running some kind of empirical research to confirm it. The diminishment of human capability went too far. Everywhere, people strove to substitute inferior instruments—pathetic little methodologies—for a superior instrument—an astute, informed, wise human being. Even if a methodology could have fixed a truth about a situation, judgment could not be avoided in any effort to apply that truth to another situation. Judgment had to be used to explore the comparability of the situations. The persistence of empirical testing in the area of typography was a testament to the strength of the complex of ideas associated with science that I have been following.

In retrospect, the inadequacy of those approaches that I have associated with Plato, Aristotle, and apologists for science should not be surprising. They proved most useful for contemplating relatively stable phenomena in the physical universe and formulating truths about them. They were sharply differentiated from approaches used in what has been called the active life, the art of making choices in highly changing human affairs, such as governance. Certainly, the differences between these sets of approaches buttressed the divisions between the philosophers and rhetoricians in classical antiquity. As we have seen, apologists such as Sprat used these differences in the late 17th century to define science, contrasting it from such activities as ethics, politics, and oratory—in short, the art of governance. Furthermore, these differences seem to have some basis in reality, for instance, the degree of change in the phenomena under consideration. When technical communicators used approaches associated with science for engaging industry problems, they neglected to perceive the extent to which their actions were part of the governance of the corporation and the extent to which the governance of a corporation resembled the governance of a state. They imported approaches devised for contemplation into the realm of action.

No doubt the activities of professionals were various enough to include considerable contemplation. An effort to participate in governance cannot succeed without acts to determine truths or fix realities. But the scope of their activities extended beyond these acts, and their performance was compromised when the methodologies of contemplation were used in situations that were inappropriate for their use. In situation after situation, professionals engaged problems without sufficient scope in their methodological approaches to achieve the highest possible level of performance.

If professionals were prompted by their contexts to overcome some of the divisions between themselves and practitioners and successfully addressed some of the problems confronting them, nothing in their contexts seemed to prompt them to an awareness of the methodological inadequacy of such approaches as mathematics and experimental testing to many of their problems. Indeed, relatively few of the full range of inadequacies caused by the misapplication of ideas associated with the rise of philosophy, science, and engineering were addressed. Project situations were too often insufficient in themselves to indicate where change was necessary.

For instance, professionals had no way of knowing from their project situations that a major source of help in improving the quality of their performance lay in the awareness of a history of conflict between rhetoricians and philosophers. On the contrary, ideas associated with philosophy and science that influenced them—the focus on what is, the withdrawal from the tumult of human affairs, and the disparagement of prescientific thinking—all militated against a concern for history. Even if professionals had such a concern, history was hardly accessible in the miniscule library that typified most computer corporations—if they had a library at all—and many of these corporations were not close to a university library.

The resulting problems confronting professionals so overwhelmed them that failure was too often the result. Users were among those experiencing this failure, as evidenced by an article by John Greenwald in the June 18, 1984, issue of *Time* magazine. The article raised the following question in a headline: "How Does This #%c@! Thing Work?" A subhead responded: "No matter what happens, do not look at the manual." The article went on:

> Today...the owner of... some...electronic wonder must turn to an instruction manual to get his machine working. But that is often when the trouble begins: the consumer opens a booklet to find a compilation of jargon, gibberish and just plain confusion....Bad instructions are bad business as well as a torture to read. A maddening manual can cripple sales of products that might have been successful. (p. 64)

The *Time* article directed attention to failure associated with one area of technical communication: product user manuals. The negative attitudes of users were frequently echoed by the professionals who created these manuals; the following blunt statement by one professional was typical: "We write rotten manuals."

If, in classical antiquity, the practice of imitation assumed a dominant role in methodological approaches to oratory, then, the contexts confronting professionals in the years after World War II made avoidance a more dominant methodological approach than imitation. As projects came to an end and failures all too often materialized, sometimes leading to customer complaints and other problems, professionals had to try to avoid such failures in future projects. Unfortunately, they too often remained unaware of the ways to do so, and some turned to universities for help.

Problems in recruitment forced them to seek help from universities in any event. Professionals received highly technical information from product developers, and they had to be knowledgeable enough and good enough writers to use this information to create materials for both novice and technically proficient audiences. However, finding graduates from universities who combined technical proficiency and writing capability was exceedingly difficult. Engineering departments turned out technically proficient graduates and English departments turned out graduates with some writing proficiency, but graduates combining these proficiencies were rare. Aristotelian specialization now frozen into university social structures confronted recruiters with problems.

A few universities began to respond to this need for graduates with both technical and writing proficiency, but as late as 1980, the demand was still extraordinary and the response in universities weak. Paul Anderson (1980) accurately summed up the situation: "These are boom years for technical communication. The demand for technical writers and editors seems insatiable; some companies in the computer industry are even reported to be offering bounties to employees who give the personnel office the names of people eventually hired as technical communicators" (p. 271). To some degree, the lack of qualified personnel could be traced to the relative newness of the profession and the numbers of parents and college students who were unaware of its opportunities. Also significant, however, was the inability of technical communication education to gain much of a foothold in universities—largely because so many university English professors prevented that education from growing and thriving.

Thomas Connolly, a manager of information development at IBM-Kingston, and Roger Grice, one of his subordinates, were among the professionals who turned to universities for help. In the course of their efforts, they encountered two major problems. Although the leading college major of professionals was English, Connolly and Grice discovered that most English departments were uninterested in developing programs to address problems in technical communication. Furthermore, in those few departments where some interest did exist, faculty knew very little about conditions in corporations. These two problems and others could be at least partially traced to the impact of the decline of rhetoric and rise of philosophy in universities.

8

Resistance to Technical Communication in Universities and Schools of Humanities

At the end of the 20th century, an observer of universities would have been struck by the stated openness to change in university mission statements. To suggest just one example, Hugo Sonnenschein (1999), president of the University of Chicago, noted that the spirit of his university would "manifest itself in forms ever-new and ever-changing." The scope of studies sounded Isocratean: "the world of the mind knows no nationalism." The University [of Chicago] was organized so that "ideas, no matter how diverse," could be exchanged. One of the attractions of the university was its "commitment to interdisciplinary endeavor and the permeability of traditional departmental and divisional boundaries." Scholars broke through boundaries separating the university from the rest of society and engaged "non-academic audiences" and helped those who made and enacted "important [public] policy decisions."

Such theories of the university seemed ideal for the development of areas of endeavor such as technical communication, and at many universities—especially in the 1990s with the impetus of Internet communication—technical communication flourished. But as recently as the 1970s and 1980s, as Connolly and Grice discovered, most English departments (where technical communication was most likely to be taught) either ignored or actively opposed technical communication. Younger teachers of technical communication today would be astonished by the roadblocks confronted by their forebears in earlier decades.

In the 1970s and 1980s, the tendency of literature faculty in English departments to either ignore or frustrate development in technical communication was as rooted in the philosophical tradition as the narrowness in industries just explored. While the philosophical tradition gained strength in industries through the influence of science, however, it gained strength in English departments largely through the influence of classical philosophies and the theologies that incorporated them. Science was not without its impact on English departments (particularly on literary critics such as Northrop Frye, the experimentalist branches of first-year composition, and those areas of technical communication that were allowed to develop), but English departments in the 1970s and 1980s were far more influenced by theories of the university, humanities, literary criticism, and rhetoric that had their origin directly in Plato, Aristotle, and their theological successors. These theories militated not only against the development of technical communication, but also, where it was allowed to develop, against its attaining sufficient scope.

Literature faculty exercised control over technical communication because they managed English departments. As William Riley Parker (1967) reported in an article titled "Where Do English Departments Come From?" departmentalization had its origin in the need for local management in the late 19th century. University administrators made the department the basic organizational structure of their institutions and delegated to department faculty the power to judge the suitability of courses and programs; recommend appointments, promotions, and salaries; and seek money or equipment. After departmentalization, then, professors had considerable control over decisions about curriculum, personnel, and funding in their disciplines.

A number of forces converged to strengthen the impetus for departmentalization. Among them, Plato relished definition, and Aristotle took this concern for definition, developed an elaborate system of clear divisions in the world (many of which became divisions in the modern university), and encouraged specialization. As Bruce A. Kimball (1986) suggested in his important work *Orators & Philosophers*, science also lent its support to department formation. Specialization became the key characteristic of American scientific societies between 1866 and 1918 and inspired departmentalization according to fields of scholarship (p. 163).

By 1973, when Thomas Wilcox published *The Anatomy of College English*, departmentalization had flourished to such an extent that the department of English was a separate organization at 81.1 percent of all four-year colleges and universities (p. 1). At almost all of these colleges and universities, English was either the largest or tied for the largest department in number of full-time members

(p. 2). These members were mostly literature professors who tended to regard first-year composition and technical communication with condescension and hostility. For instance, in 1979, Norman S. Grabo—a specialist in American literature—delivered a scathing attack on technical communication at a summer seminar for English department chairs, later published in a special issue of the *ADE Bulletin*.

Grabo referred to technical communication as "work for turkeys" (1979, p. 67) and sent us back to Socrates, who taught us

> that writing is a low, trivial, and rather sneaky art, a knack, a technology essentially irrelevant to truth...that if technique is taught apart from truth, if writing and rhetoric are taught apart from literature and philosophy, we create the modern demagogues that Socrates feared—advertising men and women, corporate and government lackeys, the writers of press releases on the beauties of the DC-10, the safety of nuclear power plants. (p. 67)

Grabo seemed unaware that inadequacies in the art of writing could be rectified by an improved rhetoric, that literary critics and their philosophical predecessors were responsible for separating truth and literature from rhetoric, that rhetoricians were also concerned about institutional servants who placed the interests of their institutions over the welfare of humanity, and that the nip of a Socratic gadfly might not be the best way to prevent such behavior.

Literature professors used their control over hiring to reinforce such attitudes and marginalize first-year composition and technical communication. At major private and public universities, administrators such as deans, provosts, and presidents had to approve appointments for English departments, but a general policy of departmental freedom in such matters gave any majority of the members of a department virtual control over hiring. Since most, if not all, of the members of English departments were literature professors, these professors chose the chair, controlled all the important committees, and performed all the hiring. Given their attitudes toward composition and communication, they hired literature specialists for permanent faculty positions and tended to staff first-year composition and technical communication with student teaching assistants (who were working toward their Ph.D.'s in literature), temporary adjunct teachers, younger literature faculty, and "deadwood," the poor performers in the department.

As a result, English departments had more professors in literature than other areas, and these professors were able to control the approval of departmental courses and programs. They were not opposed to their departments teaching many sections of first-year composition—so long as they did not need to teach it themselves. The same situation usually held for sections of introductory technical communication, although, at some universities, specialists in literature registered 100 percent intense disapproval rates of such courses and excluded them entirely from their departmental offerings (Rivers, 1985, p. 53). Part of the reason why some literature professors approved sections of freshman composition and technical communication was self-interest. Ph.D. students in literature could obtain tuition and other financial support by teaching such courses, and these students populated the graduate courses and programs of literature professors.

Another reason for the approval of introductory writing courses was external pressure. For instance, when I was Assistant Director of Freshman English at Texas A&M in 1974–1975, I received a number of letters from industry administrators urging improvement. Robert E. Rodman, General Manager of the Personnel Department at Standard Oil of California, wrote: "Career progress is closely intertwined with oral and written communication skill. These areas should be given priority attention by every student who points toward a business career" (personal communication). G. J. Eisele, Manager of Employee Relations at Mobil Pipe Line, called for specific improvements: "We are not fully satisfied with the communication skills of the college graduates we have recently hired. We believe graduates should have a better understanding of grammar, punctuation, sentence structure and report writing" (personal communication). Literature professors did not want to appear totally unresponsive to such pressure—even when their theoretical positions justified unresponsiveness.

As a result, growth in first-year composition and the standard technical communication course for juniors and seniors was often substantial. The growth in technical communication was confirmed by Rivers's 1985 survey of the members of the Association of Departments of English. According to Rivers, nearly half (46 percent) of the 568 departments responding taught business writing, and nearly two-thirds (63.5 percent) taught technical writing. Of the departments with these courses, nearly two-thirds (64.9 percent) had moderate or dramatic increases in the number of sections offered in the preceding five years. A dramatic increase ranged "from 4.04 sections per term to 13.44 sections per term over 4.4 years" (p. 51). Rivers reported several schools with surges in enrollment that were truly dramatic: "from 16 to 50 sections per term in two years; from no sections to 20 sections per term in one year; [and] from 1 to approximately 75 sections per term in four years" (p. 51).

The growth in introductory writing courses in first-year composition and technical communication resulted in many English departments teaching as many or more courses in writing as in literature. A survey published by the Association of Departments of English in 1984 reported: "Roughly two thirds of the classes the profession teaches are in writing and one third in literature" (Young, Gorman, & Gorman, 1984, p. 53). The survey indicated that 81 Ph.D., 119 four-year, and 67 two-year institutions—a total of 267 departments—taught 65 percent of their classes in writing and 35 percent in literature (p. 53). Even in Ph.D. institutions, English departments taught as many students in writing as in literature: "Ph.D. institutions teach writing and literature to about the same number of students; all other schools have more writing students than literature students" (p. 53).

The spectacle of a discipline that spent half, if not more, of its efforts on writing—usually the result of promptings from outside the discipline—yet focused its attention almost exclusively on literature did not go unnoticed. In a 1972 article titled "Public Hostility to the Academy: What Can Chairmen of Departments of English Do," John C. Gerber (1972) wrote:

> Those of us in English hold that our main function is to teach literature; the public, including in this instance some of our colleagues in other departments, believes that our main function is to teach writing....What we consider to be our main function, in short, is to many others a frivolous activity, and what we increasingly neglect is what others think to be our real and maybe our total excuse for being. (p. 18)

A similar theme ran throughout Richard Ohmann's *English in America*, published in 1976.

The neglect, and often hostility, of literature professors was manifested most clearly in their resistance to degree programs in rhetoric, composition, and technical communication. In 1971, in the first issue of the *Journal of Technical Writing and Communication*, Marguerite F. D'Amico of Western Electric expressed a prevailing attitude among technical communicators in the 1970s and 1980s:

> Unfortunately, formal education providing the preparation and theoretical framework for the profession has been lagging, or more properly, lacking. The result is that, since its inception, the field of technical communication has been notorious for its practitioners coming into it any way but by design. Why, with few exceptions, has there been no serious effort to educate for the field of technical communications? (p. 11)

In 1979, some 8 years later, Martha Eckman of Bowling Green State University was still writing: *"The most recent survey* identified by the Society of Technical Communication showed a demand for 3,000 graduates annually in technical communication—and only 47 graduates around the nation with technical communication degrees" (p. 87).

Literature professors kept the development of bachelor's and master's programs in technical communication at a minimum either by simply ignoring all efforts in the area or, when an advocate or advocates became too insistent, by blocking development through votes in committees. Still, some programs emerged. For instance, the first master's program in technical communication was announced at Rensselaer in 1953, and, by 1982, Thomas E. Pearsall was able to report finding 10 additional English or humanities departments across the country that offered degree programs in the field.

The emergence of Ph.D. programs was particularly slow. Teachers of first-year composition had long found it almost universally impossible to develop Ph.D. programs in rhetoric and composition in English departments, so it should not have come as a surprise that technical communication teachers would experience similar difficulties. Still, the lockout here was not complete either. In 1965, Rensselaer instituted a Ph.D. in Rhetoric and Communication, and, 15 years later, in 1980, it announced a major track in "Technical Communication"—the first Ph.D. program in the country with a major emphasis in the field. Another Ph.D. program with a similarly strong but unformalized emphasis on technical communication developed at Carnegie Mellon.

By the 1970s and 1980s, teachers of first-year composition and technical communication strongly resented the many ways that literature professors marginalized both them and their subjects. They voiced their resentment at the annual Conference on College Composition and Communication (CCCC), where people who were isolated on their campuses could join a force of thousands. This resentment not infrequently assumed the form of bitterness. Participants at the conference sometimes pounded tables and shouted in uncontrolled rage about the literature professors in their departments—outbursts of Juvenalian vituperation that shocked even the sympathetic listeners present.

Among responses to the continuing intransigence of literature professors, Ross Winterowd (1977) wrote: "It is obvious that I do not understand the particular madness of the English department: composition is our sustenance, but virtually all of our commitment and authority are devoted to literature" (p. 28). Wayne C. Booth (1981) argued: "'Literature' programs that leave prospective teachers ignorant about rhetoric, indifferent to all literature except novels, plays, and poems, and contemptuous of any job that requires them to teach writing—such programs are not programs at all but frauds" (p. 14).

John Gerber (1975) attempted to show how the scope of English departments had narrowed in the 20th century. He presented a dialogue between Socrates and an English professor in which Socrates elicited information about all of the areas progressively excluded by English, creating what he called "a curiously narrow field" (p. 22). At the end of the dialogue, Socrates stated:

> To summarize, do I understand that you English teachers, having largely given up the great works of religion, philosophy, and rhetoric, after limiting your literary interests substantially to English and American writings (and only fiction, poetry, and drama among these writings), after having largely given up linguistics, comparative literature, creative writing, journalism, American Studies, the theater, and oral reading, after having eliminated or partly eliminated all of these valuable studies from your English curriculum, you are now in the process of eliminating training in writing as well? (p. 23)

When the English teacher agreed, Socrates concluded that "English teachers have developed the most over-sized deathwish that I have seen in the last twenty-four centuries" (p. 24). He then invited the English professor to share in a drink—hemlock.

Despite these strong reactions, however, the pejorative attitudes of literature professors toward composition and technical communication continued. These attitudes derived support from the ideas that I have associated with Plato, Aristotle, and their theological successors. On the one hand, these ideas informed theories of the university, humanities, and literary criticism that militated against rhetorical activities such as composition and technical communication. On the other hand, these ideas shaped composition and technical communication so that these areas were inadequate to the tasks that confronted them and, as a result, were deserving of criticism.

UNIVERSITY THEORIES MILITATING
AGAINST TECHNICAL COMMUNICATION

In 1986, in his *Orators & Philosophers*, Bruce A. Kimball located what he considered to be the major thrust of American higher education in the second half of the 20th century:

> It has seemed to me that, by and large, American higher education in the second half of the twentieth century holds Socrates, rather than Cicero, as its paragon; that the purpose, rationale, structure, and content of its liberal education are, in a fundamental sense, Socratic and Platonic; and that the history of liberal education that it prefers to report concerns exclusively the philosophical ideal of liberal education: the continuing, ever-critical search for truth. (p. 11)

To the extent that Kimball was referring to the complex of ideas that I have associated with Plato, I could not agree more, although I would extend the range of forces beyond Plato to include the related sets of ideas in Aristotle, Augustine, Aquinas, science, and engineering. These forces converged in the 20th century with profound effects, especially on the humanities and English departments. Among these effects was the rejection of not only the art of management or civilization that I have associated with Isocrates, Cicero, and Quintilian, but also manifestations of that art, such as technical communication.

Kimball claimed that American writings on liberal education always cited three major figures and three major universities—"Aydelotte, Meiklejohn, Hutchins; Chicago, Columbia, Harvard" (1986, p. 3). Of these figures and universities, certainly Hutchins and Chicago can serve as an example to illustrate those concepts of the university that militated against technical communication. Robert Maynard Hutchins became the fifth president of the University of Chicago in 1929, and he published his most influential book—*The Higher Learning in America*—in 1936. In 1950, present and former members of the faculty of the University of Chicago, in a book titled *The Idea and Practice of General Education: An Account of the College of the University of Chicago*, claimed that "The Higher Learning in America...had an impressive influence upon educational thinking throughout the United States" (p. 56).

George Dykhuizen (1973), in a biography of John Dewey, referred to two of Hutchins's primary sources and raised an important consideration: "his frequent references to Aristotle and Saint Thomas as well as his close association with Mortimer Adler, a professed Neo-Thomist, led his readers to believe that some version of Neo-Thomism underlay his thinking" (p. 279). It would have also been relevant for Dykhuizen to note Hutchins's references to John Henry Newman (1801–1890), the first rector of the Catholic University of Dublin and author of *The Idea of a University* (1852/1959). A comparison of Hutchins's *Higher Learning* and Newman's *Idea of a University* suggests the affinities of the two works with the ideas that I have associated with Plato and Aristotle and the extent to which they militated against technical communication.

Like Hutchins, Newman leaned heavily on Aristotle and Aquinas. Aristotle was "the oracle of nature and of truth" (1852/1959, p. 135). Since Aristotle was a pagan, however, Aquinas—"the champion of revealed truth" (p. 354)—had to adapt him for Catholicism (p. 425). Newman agreed with Aristotle and Aquinas that theology was the highest of sciences. His Catholicism, informed by Aristotle and Aquinas, controlled his vision of the university, and he affirmed, of course, that theology should be taught there.

Unlike Newman, Hutchins did not overtly identify with a particular theology such as Catholicism, but, as I have already indicated, he expressed a longing for theology in general. He stated how much he felt the need for an orthodox theology or a systematic metaphysics. He wistfully recalled the unification of the medieval university by theology and decried that theology had been displaced as queen of the sciences in the 20th century. He reported that theology was banned by law from some universities, that moderns no longer accepted revelation, and that it was futile to look to theology to unify the modern university. Consequently, he had to find his source of unity for the modern university elsewhere.

Since Hutchins could not turn to theology to unify the university, he relied on the Greek ideas that informed it. According to Hutchins, if faith and revelation were omitted from theology, the philosophies of Plato and Aristotle remained. These philosophies constituted the unity of Greek thought (p. 97). In positing a unity in Greek thought, however, Hutchins was unaware of the fundamental differences between Isocrates, on the one hand, and Plato and Aristotle, on the other. He was also unaware of Isocrates's dominant position in ancient Greece. He placed himself in the camp of the philosophers, and Platonic and Aristotelian metaphysics became the ideal source of unity for his university, a unity with close affinities to that of Newman.

Newman limited the scope of the university to "thought or reason exercised upon knowledge, or what may be called philosophy" (p. 160). This knowledge was "not merely a means to something beyond it...but an end sufficient to rest in and to pursue for its own sake" (p. 130). The object of knowledge was truth, which, in turn, was equated with facts (p. 83). The contemplation of truth or knowledge was really nothing more than the medieval ideal of the contemplation of God (p. 87). In its emphasis on knowledge, truth, and contemplation, Newman's philosophy was Platonic or Aristotelian rather than Isocratean.

Hutchins, while not as detailed as Newman, oriented the university similarly. Knowledge and truth were primary (p. 66). Indeed, the scope of the university was limited to the pursuit of truth (p. 95). The teacher or scholar strove to unify or systematize the multitude of truths about the universe: "Real unity can be achieved only by a hierarchy of truths which shows us which are fundamental and which subsidiary, which significant and which not" (p. 95). This unity or hierarchy could be found in the philosophies of Plato and Aristotle and could be achieved "by the study of first principles" (p. 97), which was called metaphysics. Hutchins agreed with Newman and cited Aristotle to the effect that the study of first principles and the causes of things ultimately led to God (p. 98).

Both Newman and Hutchins rejected the useful as a goal for the university. Newman called his focus on truth and knowledge "liberal education" (p. 171). He opposed those who insisted that instruction be useful or have utility (p. 171). His liberal education shaped the intellect for its own sake rather than for a specific trade (p. 171)—a stance that accorded well with Aristotle's condescension toward utilitarian goals and his glorification of studies prompted by wonder alone. Newman excluded professional education from his purview because professional education focused on the particular, while liberal education concerned itself with the general. Newman shared the preference of Plato and Aristotle for the abstract over the concrete.

Newman contended that there were "two methods of education": "the end of the one is to be philosophical, of the other to be mechanical; the one rises towards general ideas, the other is exhausted upon what is particular and external" (p. 138). He excluded the particular from the university: "I only say that knowledge, in proportion as it tends more and more to be particular, ceases to be knowledge" (p. 138). One could move away from the particular and utilitarian toward the general and liberal through a "study of the classics" (p. 177)—which included, of course, Aristotle (p. 179). In the 17th and 18th centuries, the apologists for natural science rejected Aristotle and his systems, but Newman reversed that move, distinguishing his liberal education from natural science and reaffirming the importance of Aristotle and systems. In this way, Newman's source of educational principles—Aristotle—also became its end, and nothing could be more tautological and self-perpetuating.

Although Newman contended that his liberal education had no end other than itself, it had the happy result of being "truly and fully a useful...education" (p. 180). A

general culture of mind is the best aid to professional and scientific study...; and the man who has learned to think and to reason and to compare and to discriminate and to analyze, who has refined his taste, and formed his judgment, and sharpened his mental vision, will not indeed at once be a lawyer, or a pleader, or an orator, or a statesman, or a physician, or a good landlord, or a man of business, or a soldier, or an engineer..., but he will be placed in that state of intellect in which he can take up any one of the sciences or callings I have referred to...with an ease, a grace, a versatility, and a success, to which another is a stranger. (pp. 1810–182)

Therefore, a general education that emphasized mental discipline best prepared humans for their professions.

Hutchins, unlike Newman, called his focus on truth and knowledge "general education" rather than "liberal education," choosing to emphasize Newman's distinction between the general and the particular. Hutchins stated that he was "interested in the attributes of the race, not the accidents of individuals" (p. 73). He focused on "drawing out the elements of our common human nature" (p. 73). A course of study based on the elements of our common human nature would be "the same at any time, in any place, under any political, social, or economic conditions" (p. 66).

Hutchins placed as much emphasis on mental discipline as Newman; according to Hutchins, appropriate mental discipline was equally effective in all fields (p. 63). Hutchins went beyond Newman, though, by suggesting a kind of thinking that was better for cultivation of the intellect or mental discipline than all others: "Correctness in thinking may be more directly and impressively taught through mathematics than in any other way" (p. 84). After all, mathematics "exemplifies reasoning in its clearest and most precise form" (p. 83). Since mathematics was an abstraction of the concrete world, it accorded well with Hutchins's emphasis on the general. It should not be surprising that Hutchins cited Plato and Aristotle as support for his emphasis on mathematics.

Hutchins was as insistent as Newman in rejecting the quest in universities for results or utility. The university's "only excuse for existence...is to provide a haven [note the Platonic and Aristotelian idea of withdrawal] where the search for truth may go on unhampered by utility or pressure for 'results'" (p. 43). He followed Newman in associating utility with professionalism, which he called "vocationalism." Hutchins was far more visceral about his distaste for the vocational than Newman. He sharply contrasted general education and vocational education: "There is a conflict between one aim of the university, the pursuit of truth for its own sake, and another which it professes too, the preparation of men and women for their life work" (p. 33). Since vocational education could not be intellectual, it had to be excluded from the university (p. 91). The goal in a university was understanding, but vocational education diverted a student's attention to practice: "the vocational atmosphere is ruinous to attempts to lead the student to understand the subject. By hypothesis he is learning to practice the profession" (p. 38). In effect, Hutchins reserved the role of the university to efforts to determine what is—the focus of Plato and Aristotle—and excluded efforts to determine what to do—the focus of the rhetoricians Isocrates, Cicero, and Quintilian.

Hutchins proposed only three divisions in his ideal university—metaphysics, natural science, and social science. The faculty in these three divisions, like those in Newman's university, were to teach the great books—"those books which have through the centuries attained to the dimensions of classics" (p. 78). Highlighted among these classics, of course, were Plato and Aristotle (p. 81). Like Newman, then, Hutchins's educational principles had the same source and end, resulting in a tautological and self-perpetuating system.

In teaching the classics, universities were to focus on "the best that man has thought" (p. 77), not the problems of modern society:

> Our erroneous notion of progress has...made education the servant of any contemporary movements in society, no matter how superficial. In recent years this attitude has been accentuated by the world-wide depression and the highly advertised political, social, and economic changes resulting from it....We have felt that it was our duty to educate the young so that they would be prepared for further political, social, and economic changes. Some of us have...even thought that we should decide what changes are desirable and then educate our students not merely to anticipate them, but also to take part in bringing them about. (pp. 65–66)

Here, Hutchins explicitly excluded the management or art of civilization, the very concerns that were central to Isocrates, from the concern of the university. However, such an exclusion did not mean that society's problems would be ignored. Happily, like Newman's liberal education, Hutchins's general education, while not designed to be useful, nevertheless helped students prepare for intelligent action: "any plan of general education must be such as to educate the student for intelligent action" (p. 67).

The concepts of the university embodied in Newman's *Idea of a University* and Hutchins's *Higher Learning*, then, represented efforts in an increasingly secularist world to preserve the spirit of Catholic theology. Newman overtly identified the Catholic framework within which he delineated the role of the university, while Hutchins sought to preserve his theology by secularizing it. Newman forthrightly indicated his indebtedness to Aristotle and Aquinas, while expressing both positive and negative views about Plato. Hutchins expressly relied most heavily on Plato and Aristotle, while referring positively to both Aquinas and Newman. Since Plato, Aristotle, and the Christian philosophers militated against Isocratean rhetorics, it is predictable that the ideas of Newman and Hutchins militated against technical communication, which shared so many characteristics with these rhetorics.

Both Newman and Hutchins limited the university to the pursuit of truth for its own sake, accepting the glorification of truth in both Plato and Aristotle. The appropriate exercise of the intellect led, in Newman, to a set of theological truths called Catholicism and, in Hutchins, to the same set of truths stripped of "faith and revelation"—what amounted to the metaphysical ideas of Plato and Aristotle. According to Newman and Hutchins, the university should strive to determine what is and exclude efforts to determine what to do to be useful in society. Hutchins specifically excluded efforts to determine what political, social, and economic changes were essential to avoid human problems such as the Depression. He excluded efforts to enable us to lead the best lives possible by improving the art of civilization. As directly as Plato, Hutchins opposed the life of philosophy or metaphysics to engagement in public affairs. He supported the notion of the university as a haven for withdrawal, an ivory tower.

Given the divisions that Newman and Hutchins drew between the university and the society beyond it, their view that universities should not prepare students for their future jobs—a kind of education called "professionalism" by Newman and "vocationalism" by Hutchins—followed accordingly. Among the reasons for excluding this education, both Newman and Hutchins cited its concern for the particular or individual. Following the lead of Plato and Aristotle, both carried on the tradition of preferring the abstract or general over the particular, a preference that turned attention away from the particulars so crucial to decision-making in practical affairs and inclined Hutchins to favor mathematics as an ideal subject. Both Newman and Hutchins believed that a focus on what was common to all times, places, and conditions—a liberal or general education—would best prepare students for professions or vocations.

Newman's *Idea of a University* and Hutchins's *Higher Learning*, then, contained strong arguments that militated against technical communication, and these works strongly influenced American higher education in the 20th century. Newman, Hutchins, and their followers joined the scientists and became a powerful joint force to direct attention in the university toward the pursuit of truth for its own sake and away from other goals. At least theoretically, these two groups with roots in Plato and Aristotle, virtually divided the university world between them. With rhetorical theory dormant, the study of human affairs too often seemed to be theoretically barren.

Liberal or general education not only proved influential at Chicago and such Catholic universities as Notre Dame and St. Mary's, but also at other institutions such as St. John's; as Kimball (1986) noted, "In 1937, several individuals who came from the University of Chicago reorganized the curriculum of St. John's around a prescribed program of reading great texts" (p. 220). The impact on professors around the country was profound, and echoes of Newman and Hutchins could be heard everywhere. To cite just one example, Frank W. Fletcher, a professor of geology at Susquehanna University, wrote favorably about the tradition of liberal education in *The Chronicle of Higher Education* on April 23, 1986:

> We professors...see ourselves as the symbolic, if not blood, descendants of Plato, Erasmus, Castiglione, Cardinal Newman, and their like. We see ourselves as the current torchbearers and even the guardians of the educational ideal, which views knowledge as an end in itself, to be pursued for its own sake. Dedicated to things of the mind, we place little stock in the notion that knowledge should have imme-

diate and practical utility. Indeed the very lack of practical purpose, together with a dash of good manners and ceremony perhaps, defines liberal education. It's heady stuff. (p. 92)

Similar passages elsewhere often lambasted vocational education, and technical communication was among the areas that suffered as a result.

A HUMANITIES THEORY MILITATING AGAINST TECHNICAL COMMUNICATION

Even before Hutchins wrote *Higher Learning*, he set about as president at Chicago to reorganize the university. On October 22, 1930, he proposed to the University Senate an organization called the "Chicago Plan," which divided the university into four academic areas: Division of the Biological Sciences, Division of the Humanities, Division of the Physical Sciences, and Division of the Social Sciences, each administered by a dean (*Idea and Practice*, 1950, p. 50). The organizational division called "the Humanities" is of interest here because it contained English, the area in which technical communication was most likely to emerge in this country.

English was often called one of the most important areas in the humanities. In 1982, for instance, Walter Jackson Bate, in "The Crisis in English Studies," wrote that English was the flagship of the humanistic fleet for two reasons: "sheer size in number of students and (though less large proportionately) of faculty" (p. 46). As such, he continued, "English is a barometer and measure for other humanistic fields" (p. 47). According to Gerald Graff (1987/1989), in *Professing Literature: An Institutional History*, the great emphasis in English on literary criticism after World War II not only at Chicago but throughout the country was strongly influenced by Hutchins's ideas: "No development had more influence in securing the fortunes of criticism in universities and secondary schools than the movement for general education revived and restated by Robert Maynard Hutchins of Chicago in the 1930s and institutionalized after World War II" (p. 162).

Actually, even if it was true that Hutchins had a strong impact on English, it could also be argued that English had a strong impact on Hutchins. John Erskine, an English professor at Columbia, taught a required course in the 1920s on "the classics of the Western World, the Great Books" (Graff, 1987/1989, pp. 133–134), and Lionel Trilling wrote that it was from Erskine's course "that the movement of General Education in the humanities took its rise and established itself not only in Columbia College but in numerous colleges throughout the nation" (Graff, p. 134). Graff traced a direct line of influence from Erskine to Hutchins:

> One of Erskine's students and fellow instructors in the twenties was Mortimer J. Adler, who went on to the Philosophy Department at the University of Chicago, where he convinced the young president, Robert Maynard Hutchins, that the great books course could be the model for a general education curriculum which would counteract the entrenched forces of...vocationalism (p. 134)

Of significance here are the affinities between Hutchins's general education and certain ideas about the humanities and literary criticism that militated against the development of programs in technical communication after World War II.

One of the major figures in English who can illustrate the extent to which ideas associated with the humanities and literary criticism could militate against the development of programs in technical communication was Ronald S. Crane, one of the exponents of the movement in literary criticism that came to be called the New Criticism. In 1938, John Crowe Ransom, in *The World's Body*, claimed that Crane was the first of the great professors to advocate literary criticism as a major policy for English departments, although he noted that Crane limited his approach to an application of Aristotle's critical views (pp. 330–331). Crane set forth his ideas about criticism and the humanities in a wide array of works, including *The Idea of the Humanities and Other Essays Critical and Historical* (1967), *Critics and Criticism: Ancient and Modern* (1952), and *The Languages of Criticism and the Structure of Poetry* (1953).

In *Critics and Criticism*, Crane (1952) grouped himself with five other Chicago professors—W. R. Keast, Richard McKeon, Norman MacLean, Elder Olson, and Bernard Weinberg—who proclaimed their affinity with Aristotle: "The writers would not wish to minimize their admiration for the *Poetics* and, indeed, for the other basic works of its author [Aristotle], for whose characteristic approach, as they interpret it, to problems of knowledge, action, and art they feel a strong temperamental affinity" (p. 12). These professors were often called the "Chicago Aristotelians," and at least in their allegiance to Aristotle they were not in conflict with Hutchins and Adler.

Crane's affinity with Aristotle did strange things to his history of the humanities in *The Idea of the Humanities* (1967), although he began impressively. According to Crane, the first mention of the humanities could be traced back to the use of "humanitas" in the *Attic Nights* of the second-century Roman Aulus Gellius. There it was equated with education and training in the good arts and associated with Varro and Cicero. For the earliest discussions of the humanities in any detail, Crane referred us to Cicero and Quintilian (Vol. 1, p. 23). In these authors, the humanities were associated with the arts best designed to form the character and direct the activity of the Roman public man or orator. They were intended to address the needs of the virtuous and public-spirited Roman rhetorician. They were associated with the rhetorical and practical and distinguished from the theoretical and speculative (p. 156). The humanities, then, were those arts best suited to help orators or citizens in public affairs determine what to do and what to say.

So far, Crane's historical work was in accord with the scholarship that has succeeded it. For instance, Kimball (1986) followed Paul O. Kristeller and other scholars (as I do) in relating the Renaissance humanists to Cicero and Quintilian:

> what united the Renaissance humanists was primarily their common commitment to an educational ideal based on the classical literature of antiquity, especially the writings of Cicero and Quintilian. Appropriately, this understanding of "humanism" coincides with the original meaning of *humanitas*, defined by Varro, Cicero, and Gellius as "learning and instruction in the *bonae artes*." (pp. 77–78)

This education could be equated with the liberal arts: "For their program of education, the Renaissance humanists took the name *studia humanitatis* or *studia humaniora*, terms that Cicero and Gellius had coined and equated with *artes liberales*" (p. 78). And the liberal arts included the major goal of practical administration: "The first characteristic of the *artes liberales* ideal is the goal of training the good citizen to lead society" (p. 37).

But, as might be expected, Crane somehow wanted to get us to Aristotle, and he found a way. He asked us to consider the sources of the arts central to Cicero and Quintilian:

> Without exception they were all arts which, before the Romans, had been cultivated by the Greeks and which, in the Greeks of the best period, had been formulated with great rigor and theoretical precision in the context of total philosophies. The Greeks did not talk about the humanities as such, but they developed, in the dialogues of Plato and in the treatises of Aristotle on logic, rhetoric, and poetics...devices for dealing with human accomplishments in the arts and sciences which were at once humanistic in their concern with criteria of excellence, and philosophical in the manner of their statement and derivation. (Vol. 1, p. 157)

Since both Cicero and Quintilian were influenced by Plato and Aristotle, Crane was justified in citing them as sources. But he seemed unaware of the criticisms of Plato and Aristotle in Cicero and Quintilian, and he was unaware as well of the dominating presence of Isocrates in ancient Greece and his dominating influence on Cicero and Quintilian.

As a result, Crane made a dramatic mistake. He assumed that Cicero and Quintilian had taken all of their materials from Plato and Aristotle. They had diluted these materials and misdirected them from understanding and appreciation for its own sake toward the guidance of actions and the construction of speeches:

> Now it was upon Greek culture and education that Romans like Cicero undertook to build a culture and education suitable for Rome, and part of their task consisted in

restating in Latin such portions of the Greek tradition in the sciences and the arts as seemed best adapted to their aims. Their aims, however, were predominantly practical and rhetorical; and so it was that from Greek philosophy and science they tended to select the systems and doctrines that could be related most directly to action and practice and to the needs of the orator, minimizing or neglecting what was speculative or theoretical. The result was that in constituting the "good arts" of discourse they tended, while retaining their normative character, to simplify their content; to reduce what, in Aristotle, for instance, had been the consequences of principles, to rules and precepts; and to orient the teaching of the arts not primarily toward understanding or appreciation for its own sake, but rather toward the guidance of actions and the construction of speeches. (Vol. 1, p. 157)

Crane concluded his argument by reasoning that we should hardly go to the dilution (the Roman rhetoricians) when we could get the real thing (the Greek philosophers). The final recommendation of his essay on the humanities was to encourage the humanists to pursue the "theoretical and philosophic spirit" of the Greeks.

History could hardly go more astray than this. As Kimball (1986) suggested, a substantial tradition of scholarship has clearly indicated that Isocrates was the primary source of the ideas about the humanities or liberal arts that we find in Cicero and Quintilian:

> Whether one holds the normative curriculum of *septem artes liberales* to be formulated in the first century B.C.E., or in the fifth century C.E., or at some point in between, the rationale of the program was grounded in Isocratean Hellenism, which the Romans wholeheartedly perpetuated. Plato and Aristotle were certainly not excluded from the curriculum of the seven liberal arts....But the rationale behind the *septem artes liberales* involved something different from the pursuit of critical speculation and learned contemplation, for "on the whole it was Isocrates, not Plato, who educated fourth-century Greece and subsequently the Hellenistic and Roman worlds." (p. 31)

It is, after all, only what we would expect. Isocrates, Cicero, and Quintilian clustered well together, focusing on the public and practical activity of oratory, not the more withdrawn activity of contemplation. They concerned themselves with changing things, not the permanent or stable. They were trying to determine what to do, not formulate truths about what is. Their primary interest was human affairs, not theology, science, or mathematics. And they valued what was human more than Plato and Aristotle, an important attitude for an area of work called "the humanities."

The implications of Crane's analysis were profound. He reinforced the misguided notion of a sharp split between ancient Greece and ancient Rome. He perpetuated the dominance in Western civilization since the Renaissance of the ideas of Plato and Aristotle, who disparaged rhetoric and promoted its decline. He himself clearly reflected the Platonic and Aristotelian preference for understanding and appreciation for its own sake over the guidance of actions and construction of speeches. He directed attention away from Cicero and Quintilian, who could have become part of the basis for the development of improved theory about practical action. In the absence of such theory, practical action was either superficially grounded or misdirected by dominant Platonic or Aristotelian ideas.

Crane's history of the humanities in classical antiquity also affected his analysis of later history, as his selection of Vives to exemplify humanists between the 14th and 16th centuries attested. Instead of selecting someone like Valla—a rhetorician in the tradition of Isocrates, Cicero, and Quintilian—Crane focused on someone who clearly perceived himself as a philosopher (*Vives*, 1913, p. 7). For Vives, Platonic and Augustinian otherworldliness was central; man was created not for material things or troublesome knowledge but to know God and participate in His divine nature (p. 18). Furthermore, Aristotle was the ancient whom Vives revered most: "Aristotle for whose mind, for whose industry, carefulness, judgment in human arts, I have an admiration and respect, unique above all others" (p. 8). Clearly, if humanism in Cicero and Quintilian was mainly diluted Platonism and Aristotelianism, it was not amiss for exemplars of humanists in the Renaissance to be philosophers in the Platonic and Aristotelian traditions.

When Crane (1967) turned to the humanities in his own day, then, he reacted much like Hutchins. He indicated that the 20th century had inherited the quarrels surrounding the humanities in the 19th century and perceived the humanities as under seige: "the humanities...are still in danger—or rather, if we may judge from the words of their many defenders, they have never before had so many or so powerful enemies" (Vol. 1, p. 161). Crane included vocationalists among these enemies. It should not be surprising that Newman was one of Crane's choices as a 19th-century defender of the humanities against vocationalists.

For Crane, much as for Newman and Hutchins, the alternative to vocationalism was the study and appreciation of the great texts of literature. He approvingly mentioned a conclusion of one of his defenders of the humanities: "Education...must be primarily a matter of studying texts" (Vol. 1, p. 142). To be great, these texts had to be among "those human achievements...to which we agree in attributing that kind of unprecedented excellence that calls forth wonder as well as admiration" (Vol. 1, p. 8). This emphasis on great texts accorded well with the strong tradition of imitation in the rhetorics of Isocrates, Cicero, and Quintilian, but it also proved limiting. An emphasis on great texts directed attention away from the observation of experience unmediated by a particular text. It also directed attention away from the study of failure, the formulation of ideas for performance that led to avoidance, and those areas of study that had no great texts.

What was crucial for Crane was the way critics engaged the great texts, that is, "the nature of the methods or arts by which their values are to be realized" (Vol. 1, p. 163). One way that Crane clarified his ideal approach to texts—what he called "criticism"—was by suggesting approaches that he excluded. Crane's ideal criticism was not an effort to use texts to understand authors or their times; it avoided analysis of audience enrichment, ethical impact, and personal reaction (Vol. 2, p. 12). Furthermore, despite the fact that the humanities had their origin in the works of rhetoricians, Crane was especially careful to distinguish his criticism from anything that he perceived might be associated with rhetoric. He rejected, for instance, past approaches to humanistic objects that could be called rhetorical (Vol. 1, p. 169). He attacked those who would "substitute rhetoric or sectarian polemic for disinterested inquiry" (1952, p. 4). He accurately reflected pejorative attitudes toward rhetoric that we find in Plato and Aristotle. What remained was what Crane (1967) called "aesthetic analysis" (Vol. 2, p. 16). He described this analysis in *Critics and Criticism* (1952). Authors who attempted to write works that fell into a particular genre were confronted by generic demands that they tried to satisfy. Ideal critics tried to analyze the extent to which these works satisfied the demands of their genres. They tried to understand and appreciate the coherence of these works, the relation between the whole and its parts.

At the point of final analysis, Crane (1967) wanted to strip away the context of a work. Critics did not need to analyze texts in the light of their historical contexts; they had to consider texts "with respect to those qualities which can truly be said to be timeless...in the sense that they can be adequately discerned and evaluated in the light of general principles quite apart from any knowledge of their origin or historical filiation" (Vol. 2, p. 18). The object of consideration, then, was permanent and unchanging—precisely the kind of object favored by Plato and Aristotle. Critics also avoided an analysis of the usefulness or instrumentality of texts; texts were considered in regard to their "final rather than instrumental value" (1952, p. 13). In effect, texts were isolated from their environment; they were decontextualized, that is, studied without reference to external context. As Graff (1987/1989) suggested, they were approached "in a vacuum" (p. 174).

Crane's ideas about the humanities, then, clustered well with Newman's and Hutchins's ideas about the university and militated against a useful rhetorical vocation such as technical communication. Although the rhetoricians Cicero and Quintilian were acknowledged as the originators of the humanities, literature faculty who agreed with Crane's ideas rejected rhetoric and areas associated with it, such as technical communication. Although Cicero and Quintilian focused on useful and practical affairs in the state, literature faculty imbued with the ideas of the New Criticism were inclined to view a useful vocation such as technical communication with contempt and hostility. Little wonder that literature faculty in English departments ignored or frustrated the development of programs in technical communication.

Furthermore, to the extent that the student teaching assistants, adjunct teachers, younger literature faculty, and poor performers assigned to teach technical communication were educated in the New Criticism (and that was usually the case), they approached their teaching with a complex of ideas shared with Crane that militated against ideas that could be helpful in technical communication. While both Cicero and Quintilian called for increased scope in human deliberation, Crane and his fellow New Critics severely limited the focus of their deliberation, excluding such contextual considerations as ethical impact and audience analysis that were crucial to performance in technical communication. They dismissed the need to know Cicero and Quintilian, directing attention away from areas of history that could have helped technical communication. Their restriction of education to the great books excluded other areas of history that lay outside these books—for instance, histories of failure or histories unassociated with great books crucial to technical communication. Indeed, their emphasis on the permanent and unchanging aspects of texts and rejection of the analysis of texts in their historical contexts militated against history itself—at a time when the study of history was essential for the liberation of technical communication from the constraints of ideas associated with the tradition of philosophy.

9

Another Theory of Literary Criticism Militating Against Technical Communication

In the 1970s and 1980s, literature professors confronted a crisis that inclined at least some of them to consider the friction between literary criticism and composition and technical communication. A few literature professors even attempted to find a basis for uniting these areas and eliminating friction. Their ignorance about these areas and their unwillingness to take the time to find out about them, however, doomed these efforts to failure. The effort of J. Hillis Miller, one of the leaders in the literature area, can serve as an example.

In 1986, the *New York Times Magazine* carried an article by Colin Campbell, "The Tyranny of the Yale Critics," which highlighted J. Hillis Miller. According to Campbell, the elevation that year of Miller to the presidency of the Modern Language Association (MLA), the primary professional organization for university literature teachers in the United States, represented the conquest of the field of literary theory by what had been called "deconstruction" (p. 20). Deconstruction was a kind of literary theory that received much of its impetus from a group of critics teaching at Yale—Harold Bloom, Paul de Man, Jacques Derrida, Geoffrey

Hartman, and J. Hillis Miller—who published a 1979 manifesto called *Deconstruction and Criticism*. Campbell suggested that Miller was—in several ways— "the most formidable of the Yale critics" (p. 48). In a book about deconstruction called *Deconstructive Criticism*, Vincent B. Leitch (1983) called Miller "the leading spokesman" for deconstruction in the 1970s (p. 49) and the "point man" for the school of deconstruction (p. 193). Miller, then, is a good example of a proponent of a major area of literary theory in the 1970s and 1980s.

Miller and deconstruction were on the rise in America at a time when English departments at major universities were confronting crisis. At the undergraduate level, enrollments in literature were shrinking, and enrollments in writing were growing. In a 1983 article titled "Composition and Decomposition," later collected in *Theory Now and Then*, Miller (1991) cited statistics showing that from 1969 to 1979, the number of college freshmen choosing to major in English declined from 6.1 percent of the women and 1.1 percent of the men to 1.2 percent of the women and 0.6 percent of the men. He reported that programs in writing had proliferated and were flourishing. He argued that teachers of English literature seemed to have been relatively less able than teachers of composition to accommodate themselves to current social, economic, and ideological realities (p. 228). As a result of these undergraduate developments, the profession needed a reduction in literature teachers and an increase in writing teachers. Furthermore, Ph.D. education had to shift from an almost exclusive focus on literature to a more balanced approach that included appropriate attention to writing.

Other statistics confirmed the need for such a shift. In the 1970s, English departments were graduating far more Ph.D.'s in literature than there were jobs available. In 1979, in a special issue of the *ADE Bulletin* titled "The State of the Discipline 1970s–1980s," Ward Hellstrom made the following statement: "the services of only about 10% of the Ph.D.'s [in English] produced are needed by the society that is taxed to produce them" (p. 96). He quoted figures from a previous *ADE Bulletin* to suggest that the situation was already deteriorating: "Of Ph.D.'s in English 'almost 40% of the classes of 1977 and 1978 were unable to find full-time teaching positions of any kind, and almost 60% were unable to find positions that offered some possibility of tenure'" (p. 96). Hellstrom saw overproduction as the source of the problem and recommended a solution: "The only reasonable solution to the problem of overproduction...is to reduce that production" (p. 95). What Hellstrom did not report was that, at the very moment that he was writing, the demand for Ph.D.'s in rhetoric, composition, and technical communication—both in universities and industries—was extremely strong.

Hellstrom was not optimistic that English professors would reduce Ph.D. production in literature. Among the reasons, graduate faculty

do not willingly trade a graduate course in their traditional area of interest [literature] for a section of freshman composition. They realize that a reduction in graduate programs would on the one hand necessitate a reduction in graduate courses and on the other create, through the loss in teaching assistants, openings in the freshman program that graduate faculty would be expected to fill. (1979, p. 96)

English professors wanted to maintain graduate programs at current levels, then, to enable them to continue to teach literature. After all, many graduate faculty went into English in the first place because they loved literature. At the 1985 ADE Summer Seminar at West Point, one English chair stated, "What we go into this [literature] for is the enjoyment. I'm not afraid to admit that. I indulge myself. Why not?"

Given the decline in literature and the demand in composition, rhetoric, and technical communication, Miller (1979) argued in the same special issue of the *ADE Bulletin* that change was needed:

If only forty percent of the new Ph.D.'s in 1977 got jobs with a future, and if fifty-seven percent of the tenure-track positions open to new Ph.D.'s in English and listed in the *MLA Job Information Lists* in 1977–78 were in expository writing, linguistics, rhetoric, or creative writing, it behooves the graduate programs in English not only to reduce in size but to begin in one way or another to prepare new Ph.D.'s to be qualified for those positions that exist. (p. 12)

According to Miller (1991), current Ph.D.'s were not qualified. They were trained to teach only literature; they received minimal training in teaching composition (p. 172). Miller did not make this point, but Ph.D.'s had to be educated in composition), rhetoric, and technical communication to prepare not just for future jobs, but also for their current jobs. Most of these students were teaching composition, rhetoric, and technical communication as graduate assistants.

Miller (1979) saw a threat on the horizon for English departments resistant to change. He expressed his awareness that traditional departments focused on English literary history had been in existence for less than a 100 years. He understood that they could atrophy, becoming small and marginal like departments of classics. Their place could be taken by expository writing if professors of literary history remained inflexibly committed to maintaining things as they were (p. 11).

According to Miller, one of the catalysts that could precipitate the marginalization of literature departments was the departure of writing programs, and he strongly encouraged literature professors to work against this possibility. He stated that deans, provosts, and presidents assumed that the real function of departments of English was to teach good writing, and they were not inclined to fund the study of literature if literature enrollments went down. English departments that cut themselves off from expository writing would be punished for it and would atrophy (p. 12).

In the same way that literature needed writing, according to Miller, writing also needed literature; learning to write well could not be separated from learning to read well (p. 12). Miller indicated that this claim held for technical and scientific writing: "one cannot write well, even write well a business letter or a scientific report, unless one can read well the best that has been thought and said in our language" (p. 13). Since literature needed writing and writing needed literature, Miller saw the integration of the two as the most important task confronting English departments (p. 12). The key to integration was what he called "rhetorical study" (p. 13).

The kind of rhetorical study that Miller proposed as the key to integrating literature and writing was that practiced by his own school of literary criticism—deconstruction. He defined deconstruction as "an attempt to interpret as exactly as possible the oscillations in meaning produced by the irreducibly figurative nature of language" (p. 13). He saw the study of figurative language as one of the two major branches of the history of rhetoric:

> Rhetoric has been a two-branched discipline ever since the Greeks. On the one hand, it is the study of persuasion, of how to do things with words. On the other hand, it is the study of the way language works. In particular, it is the study of the function of tropes, the whole panoply of figures, not just metaphor, but metonymy, synecdoche, irony, metalepsis, prosopopoeia, catachresis—the works. (p. 13)

It should perhaps be noted that this summation of the rich, highly variegated, and complex history of rhetoric was as unfortunate as many of the statements about rhetorical history made by Miller's fellow deconstructionist de Man, severely critiqued by Brian Vickers (1988/1990) in his *Defence of Rhetoric*.

Miller's call for change, then, was not directed to deconstructionists, who already focused on figurative language. It was directed to all those other literary critics, who, according to Miller, by no means fully accepted that the center of the discipline was "the teaching of reading" and that the center of that was "expertise in handling figurative language" (p. 13). Miller listed the schools of criticism—those other than deconstruction—which were among those that had to change to address the crisis confronting English departments. If the professors in these schools of criticism did not teach reading and expertise in handling figurative language, they would continue "to have a furtive and guilty air, as though they were doing something not altogether justifiable in the present context" (p. 12).

Literary critics of all kinds, then, had to become deconstructionists to solve the crisis confronting English departments. If Miller had his way, three things would have been accomplished. First, since literature professors were addressing the need to teach writing, deans, provosts, and presidents would no longer threaten English departments with cuts. Second, all literary criticism would become nothing more or less than deconstruction, with Miller and his fellow deconstructionists leading the profession. Third, deconstruction would actually address current problems in writing.

The threat of cuts in literature positions was not wholly without substance. In the 1970s and 1980s, some deans, provosts, and presidents actually made such cuts, but the numbers of these cuts across the country were not many. The forces promoting inaction were too strong. Among them, administrators were confronted by such serious financial problems—stemming from inadequate maintenance, poor salaries, inadequate research funds and equipment, and higher costs in a range of areas—that fund-raising from the state, industry, and alumni was virtually an all-consuming task. The little energy left over was likely to be consumed by a raft of other problems such as the role of minorities and women on campus, town-gown relationships, the increasing threat of crime, the growth of legal suits, problems of censorship, and day-to-day governance. These problems were not likely to encourage administrators to create others by proposing cuts in English departments, usually their largest single constituency and an articulate one to boot. Besides, universities generally held to the philosophy that departments should guide themselves according to the best lights of their disciplines. One is almost tempted to believe that the threat of cuts was more of an argument that Miller could use on recalcitrant literary critics in schools other than deconstruction rather than a source of serious concern.

Miller's arguments encouraging literary critics to concentrate on deconstruction as a means of integrating literature and writing certainly appealed to the self-interest of these critics. In addition to averting the threat of literature cuts and the atrophy of English departments, English professors would be able to go on teaching literature as they always had. They had no need to teach composition. All they had to do to attain these goals was to change their critical orientation to deconstruction, the kind of critical theory that could integrate reading and writing.

Miller's claim that deconstruction addressed current problems in writing was only weakly supported. As has already been indicated, Miller claimed that writing well—even in technical and scientific contexts—was dependent on reading well. Elsewhere, he made strong claims about the value of deconstruction in engaging social problems. He claimed that deconstruction responded to the actual nature and needs of the society within which colleges and universities functioned; its new forms of rhetoric and poetics led the way toward that taking of responsibility for language, for literature, and for the role of these in society and history that was called for (p. 336). Since technical communication was confronting some of the more pressing problems in society, since it was primarily the responsibility of English departments in universities, and since writing was such an important part of technical communication, an examination of the extent to which deconstruction addressed problems in technical communication could serve as a check on Miller's claims.

Apparently, for Miller, the problem of writing well was disposed of entirely by deconstruction, that is, by reading well. Except in those contexts where he used a concern for writing as a means to move other literary critics toward deconstruction, he ignored the improvement of writing as a goal for English departments. In a column written as president of the MLA, Miller proclaimed: "Our main business in the coming years will be to teach people to read" (1991, p. 304). In another president's column, he wrote: "this vast institutional and professional activity...is all for nothing unless it supports the activity of reading." He added: "Our professional vocation, with all its responsibilities, begins and ends in that joy of reading....All our meetings, commissions, publications, and so on are for the sake of that" (p. 295). Deconstruction seemed to have taken care of the writing problem, and it now could again be safely ignored.

Miller certainly ignored it in determining what was necessary for an integration of reading and writing. One might expect that a scholar attempting to formulate an appropriate integration of two fields would hold himself responsible for both fields, but Miller never concerned himself with learning about the scholarly fields associated with writing—even though these fields had done more in Miller's chosen area of integration—rhetorical study—than literary critics. Miller even suspected that this was the case: "I have the impression that much more [rhetorical study] has been done already on the side of expository writing than on the side of the study of reading or interpretation" (1979, p. 12). But the phrase "I have the impression" suggested how thoroughly Miller had studied the scholarship about writing. Two tendencies in the modern university reinforced the propensity of literature professors to ignore this scholarship. First, the continuing emphasis on specialization promoted a tendency not to move outside one's chosen area of study. Second, a mature field (such as literary criticism) had a tendency to ignore the publications of an emerging field (such as writing).

Miller's ignorance about writing made it difficult for him to demonstrate that deconstruction solved current writing problems; his arguments could hardly have been weaker. For instance, Miller believed that the writing discipline emphasized "*praxis* as opposed to *theoria*." He thought that the teaching of composition was "primarily a practical matter." Writing well was "learned gradually as an acquired habit, like speech itself." Consequently, literary theory such as deconstruction could help composition teachers understand that *praxis* could not "really be taught in detachment from the *theoria* it presupposes, unless we think students can learn to write blindly, by rote" (1991, pp. 228–229). Miller had apparently forgotten his suspicion that composition specialists had done more in rhetorical theory, his chosen area of integration, than literary theorists. If he had glanced in a previously published bibliography such as Gary Tate's *Teaching Composition: 10 Bibliographical Essays* (1976), he would have discovered the wealth of rhetorical theory that informed composition studies.

Miller's arguments were no stronger when he claimed that deconstruction would help composition teachers in particular areas of rhetorical theory, such as style. For instance, Miller believed that deconstruction, with its emphasis on figurative language, could help composition teachers understand the metaphoricity of language. In 1983, Miller wrote: "insofar as the teaching of composition suggests that the student should write a literal version first and perhaps add metaphors later; insofar as it still assumes that figures are adventitious adornment;...it still has much to learn from that form of the rhetoric of reading called...deconstruction" (1991, p. 241). However, by 1983, the notion of the metaphoricity of language was a commonplace in the composition community. This notion had been strongly reinforced three years earlier, in 1980, by George Lakoff and Mark Johnson's excellent book *Metaphors We Live By*, which was widely read and discussed in composition circles. Early in the first chapter, the authors wrote: "Our ordinary conceptual system, in terms of which we both think and act, is fundamentally metaphorical in nature" (p. 3). This concept was elaborated in the book. Miller was unaware of such developments because he apparently ignored the research community in the field of composition.

Miller's inability to formulate convincing arguments in no way invalidated his claim that deconstruction solved writing problems, however. Only an analysis of what Miller meant by deconstruction and an exploration of the extent to which this theory actually solved writing problems could suggest whether his integration of reading and writing was viable. What Miller meant by deconstruction was shaped by where he looked. In some contexts, such as Miller's "Presidential Address 1986," he seemed to suggest that deconstruction called for the reader to look at "all the signs that surround and penetrate us, all images visual and sonorous" (1991, p. 327). Such breadth of scope was encouraging.

When Miller discussed the integration of reading and writing, however, the reading he referred to was the study of literary texts, he spoke of deconstruction promising "that integration of expository writing and the *study of literature* which I believe is the main task facing our profession at the moment" (emphasis added, 1979, p. 13). Furthermore, much like Crane, Hutchins, and Newman, he did not focus on all literature; he focused on "the great works" (p. 12), "the masterworks" (p. 13), "the best that has been thought and said in our language" (p. 13). As he himself suggested, his idea of what constituted the great works was "conservative" (p. 12): "I believe in the established canon of English and American literature and in the validity of the concept of privileged texts" (p. 12). With such a focus, as has been suggested in the discussions about Crane, Hutchins, and Newman, Miller was directing attention away from concerns important to my community—failure, experience unmediated by texts, and texts that were not failures but were not great either.

For Miller, reading was an experience conducted in isolation from other people; reading was "outside the institution, allergic to institutionalization, private, solitary" (1991, p. 296). It could provide a form of escape from the anxieties of reality: "That is one of the things we need novels for, to assuage our anxiety about a subject by allowing questions to be raised about it and perhaps lead us, as *The Egoist* does, to a happy ending, thereby calming our fears" (p. 199). Since Miller was seeking an integration of reading and writing, writing was solitary as well: "Writing, I claim, is in fact intrinsic to the vocation that begins with the more or less private joy of reading. Writing too remains rooted in that solitary transaction with the words on the page" (p. 300). What Miller meant by writing in this context was writing about "the poems, novels, and plays we read and teach" (p. 300), that is, literary criticism. Miller's attention was focused on writing about the great works of English and American literature.

If writing about such works could be a private, extra-institutional act, that was certainly not the case with all writing in technical communication. For instance, writing in computer corporations, far from being always private or solitary, required extensive collaboration throughout the product development process with such diverse groups as administrators, hardware and software developers, and other communicators. The need to collaborate was so extensive that the ability to do so was an important qualification for excellence in performance. A methodology such as Miller's deconstruction, which promoted solitary engagement with texts, would hardly prepare his students for the interpersonal collaboration that they required in institutional frameworks.

Miller believed that the motive for teaching the great books came from the great books themselves, not from anything external to them. This motive did not come "from any transcendent source, nor from any subject or subjectivity, for example that of the author or reader, nor from society and its institutions—universities, departments, curricula, programs, courses....The call, the imperative to teach, does not come from anywhere but from within the text itself" (1991, p. 306). Education was free of external constraint. Miller perceived reading as "detached from `the real world'" (p. 306). His notion of education, like Crane's, accorded well with the liberal education of Newman and the general education of Hutchins; education was conducted for its own sake and refused to be informed by any notion of usefulness. Miller's educational methodology began with an act of disregarding everything but a stance of disinterested contemplation.

Such a methodology was irreconcilable with the needs of teachers preparing writers in the 1970s and 1980s to become technical communication professionals. These teachers could not close off everything but the siren call of great texts. On the contrary, they had to hear the call of people before the call of great texts. They had to explore as thoroughly as possible the impact of their choices in teaching, research, and other activities on not just students, but all other humans as well. Far from disregarding a large number of considerations, they had to acquire the richest possible awareness of their environments in an effort to determine how their choices might affect humans positively or negatively. Only such an awareness could prompt the best actions or procedures for a particular project. Teachers, like their students, had to realize that a world of ever-changing contexts necessitated the engagement of each new project as an act of discovery that included the perception of the fullest range of external constraints that helped define project procedures.

Miller's goal in engaging the great texts was to formulate truths about them. He was committed "to a rigorous truth-telling about the nature of language, about the meaning of major texts in the Western tradition" (1991, p. 379). He was as concerned about the acquisition of truth as Plato, only he perceived himself as more skeptical about the possibility of attaining it; he saw "referentiality as a problem rather than as something that reliably and unambiguously relates a reader to the 'real world' of history, of society, and of people acting within society on the stage of history" (pp. 313–314). In fact, there could be no certainty about the referentiality of texts: "neither reader, nor teacher, nor student...can ever be certain whether or not the text is truly referential" (p. 307). Undecidability was the only correct response to reading: "Deconstruction...presupposes the indefinability or, more properly, 'undecidability' of all conceptual or generalizing terms" (p. 231).

All readers, then, had to explore the undecidability of their texts, and Miller criticized literary critics who did not approach their texts in this way. For instance, he criticized the critic M. H. Abrams for "his most common mode of citation, which is to illustrate some straightforward point with a quotation which is not 'interpreted,' in the sense of being teased for multiple meanings or implications, but which is taken as the confirmation of the 'point' which has just been made" (1991, p. 89). He challenged Abrams's assumption "that a text has a single meaning which is more or less independent of the play of relations, repetitions, and differentiations within the work itself" (pp. 89–90). According to Miller, "Abrams perhaps takes his writers a little too much at face value,...fails to search them for ambiguities or contradictions in their thought" (p. 90). The meaning of a text "is multiple, vibrating, ambiguous. It cannot be reduced to a single, univocal statement" (p. 92). Correct reading "leads to a suspension of fully rationalizable meaning in the experience of an aporia or boggling of the mind" (pp. 175–176). Such reading was characterized primarily by joy, which Miller described as "the feeling or state of being highly pleased or delighted" (p. 295).

Miller's focus on referentiality and undecidability may have been fruitful in engaging some rhetorical contexts. For instance, it could serve as a valuable approach to literature, such as Wallace Stevens's "The Rock," which was richly multivalent. It complemented the value of earlier critical work, such as William Empson's *Seven Types of Ambiguity*, also a work about multivalence that Miller called a grandsire or great-uncle (p. 174) and labeled "deconstructionist" (p. 193). It could help writers attempting to create essays about difficult literary works and passages. But the virtues of a focus on referentiality and undecidability could not be extended to all rhetorical contexts. Miller went too far when he titled his essay about integrating reading and writing "*The* [italics mine] Function of Rhetorical Study at the Present Time."

Resurrecting one of my favorite sentences—"Push the F9 button."—can be helpful here. Professional writers in the computer industry, confronting this directive in the course of their work, would indeed focus on referentiality as part of their experience with this passage. They would read "F9 button" as referring to a particular button on their computer keyboards. But successfully understanding a representation is only one facet of the experience writers are expected to have with the full sentence "Push the F9 button." They are also expected to act, that is, to respond to the directive "Push." Furthermore, these goals of understanding and acting might be part of a larger matrix of goals that include the desire to help users, to promote the quality of their corporations and communication groups, to avoid the writing problems of the past, and to earn money. A methodology that focuses on intellect, referentiality, understanding, and knowledge is insufficient for technical communicators engaging writing problems in computer corporations.

Equally insufficient is the focus on undecidability. Miller was no doubt correct that readers could never be certain that they were adequately experiencing the texts that they were engaging. Linguists have accumulated numerous examples of failures to grasp the simplest of texts—even a text as simple as "Push the F9 button."—in some environments. But it would be ridiculous for professional writers to engage all texts—including those as simple as "Push the F9 button."—by teasing out multiple meanings or implications; exploring the play of relations, repetitions, and differentiations; searching for ambiguities and contradictions; and achieving a boggling of the mind that is joyful. They do not have the time, they would be out of a job in a hurry, and people would be hurt in the process. The wisest writers attempt to determine the probabilities of the effort required to decide about texts and then act accordingly. Some texts are difficult and call for a skepticism about human judgment; other texts are obvious and call for bold, aggressive, innovative, and/or swift action. The wisest writers inevitably judge wrong on occasion, but their degree of success is greater than that of others. And at times—for instance, after pushing the F9 button—the machine might well react in a way that reinforces the conviction of success.

Miller's deconstruction was not without modest help for technical communication. For instance, Miller raised questions about certain acts of modern pigeonholing such as the dividing of literary history into periods: "We write of medieval literature, the neoclassical period, the baroque, the eighteenth-century, romanticism...and so forth. By what right, according to what measure, guided or supported by what reason, is this framing performed?" (1979, p. 14). To the extent that deconstruction militated against frozen definitions in changing institutions such as universities and industries, it could help my community in improving its performance. But the idea was hardly new—for instance, Lovejoy's critique of the divisions of intellectual history was far earlier (1948)—and Miller's distance from the writing community limited its impact.

Miller's attack on Western metaphysics could also have been helpful. He contrasted metaphysical approaches derived from Plato and Aristotle with his own antimetaphysical deconstruction:

> By "metaphysical" I mean the system of assumptions coming down from Plato and Aristotle which has unified our culture....A metaphysical method of literary study assumes that literature is in one way or another referential, in one way or another grounded in something outside language. This something may be physical objects, or "society," or the economic realities of labor, valuation, and exchange....An anti-metaphysical or deconstructive form of literary study attempts to show that in a given work of literature, in a different way in each case, metaphysical assumptions are both present and at the same time undermined by the text itself. (1991, p. 175)

It is in keeping with Miller's methodology that he found the origin of his deconstruction, which challenged the metaphysics of Plato and Aristotle, in Plato's
Phaedrus and Aristotle's *Rhetoric* (pp. 232–233).

To the extent that Miller's criticisms of traditional metaphysics could have
encouraged a search for alternatives to the ideas that I have associated with Plato,
Aristotle, and certain apologists for science and engineering and to the extent that
they could have promoted a concern for rhetoric and ideas that I have associated
with Isocrates, Cicero, and Quintilian, to that extent they could have helped my
community to improve the quality of its performance. But, again, Miller's distance from the writing community militated against such an impact, and his suggestion that the origins of deconstruction lay in Plato and Aristotle was only one
indication of the extent to which deconstruction was implicated in traditional
metaphysics. Miller's major departure from traditional metaphysics was the
degree of skepticism with which he approached the possibility of determining referentiality. In such areas as his emphasis on isolation from practical contexts during the onset of deliberations and his focus on the determination of truth, he could
not have been more traditional. Miller's deconstruction did not really lead very far
away from traditional metaphysics at all.

Miller's deconstruction, then, was little more help to writers in technical communication than the liberal or general education of Newman and Hutchins. Miller
actually raised questions about the claims of liberal or general education to enable
students to perform better on their future jobs. He identified two assumptions
underlying these claims—that reading the great authors was an important part of
a college education and that such reading would make people better lawyers, doc-
tors, scientists, bureaucrats, businessmen, or soldiers. Miller noted, however, that
the exact mode of the transfer from literary study to vocational activity had not
often been thought through clearly or made explicit. He suggested that perhaps
such "things don't stand much looking into" (1991, pp. 332–333). As has been
explored previously, Miller's surmise was correct. What he did not seem to realize, however, was that his own claims about helping writers through integration
with reading were equally questionable.

Interestingly, Miller (1991) compared deconstructionists to spiders making a
fruitless effort to escape a labyrinthine web they were themselves spinning (pp.
122–123). His association of deconstructionists with spiders was a bit surprising—not only given the traditional negative connotations that spiders carried,
but also because of the famous comparison of the spider and bee that Swift
used to disparage the moderns and praise the ancients in "The Battle of the
Books" (1958). Swift's image of a spider was a wonderful critique of a modern such as Descartes, who was accused of spinning too much of his philosophy from within himself without the benefit of possible correction by the world
around him. In like manner, Miller's use of the image for himself and other
deconstructionists, despite an effort to relate it to the mythological Ariadne,
constituted a wonderful bit of unconscious self-criticism. The deconstruction-

ists, too, were accused of being apart from life—off in a dark basement window corner—also spinning ideas without the benefit of possible correction by the world around them.

Miller's isolation prevented him from seeing that deconstruction alone could do little to solve any writing problems but those involved with analyzing literature deconstructively. It certainly would do little to address the writing problems that English majors heading for careers as technical communicators would encounter. It would not help students to recognize the limitations of the job definitions that would overly restrict them in work environments, nor would it equip them to challenge these definitions and become important collaborators throughout the product development process. It would not prompt students to acquire interdisciplinary education in such areas as computing and graphics. It would not empower students to overcome corporate or governmental insistence on the inappropriate use of such standards as mathematical measures and experimental proofs. It would not alert students to a concern for such potential problems as time, confidentiality, and the quest for profit at the expense of ethics. It would not direct students to the seeds of helpful methodologies in such writers as Isocrates, Cicero, and Quintilian. It would not expose students to contexts other than great works of literature in an effort to explore how different contexts call for different methodologies. And it would not, in any effort to devise a successful methodology for a particular context, encourage students to consider fully the critical importance of adequate scope as part of their logic of choice.

Of course, there was nothing wrong, in and of itself, with the university study of great literature and the development of critical sophistication in reading it. But English departments were guilty of an overemphasis. They focused almost exclusively on literature and personal reading and tended to ignore the theories of rhetoric that would further enable their students to improve their professional and public lives. By maintaining such an overemphasis, they were open to the charge of helping themselves at the cost of hurting other people. The decline in undergraduate literature enrollments and the inability of Ph.D. literature graduates to find jobs prompted a decrease in literature teaching, and the demand at all levels for increased writing instruction prompted an increase in teaching rhetorical approaches that would improve kinds of writing besides literary criticism. To persist in teaching literature in the face of such developments could enable English professors to continue to indulge themselves in the joys of literature, but only at the expense of pain to students without jobs or pain to others resulting from inept preparation for rhetorical tasks in professional and public arenas. Miller perceived this ethical problem clearly. He claimed that literature professors had to have a guilty and furtive air unless they addressed writing problems.

Miller's solution to this ethical problem was deconstruction. But such solutions only betrayed the isolation of literature professors and their ignorance about their responsibilities to the public and professional lives of their students and people in the larger society. These professors did not know the extent of the rhetorical tasks that occupied the future professional lives of undergraduate students who became hardware and software developers, nor did they know the extent to which they would fail and its impact on other humans; consequently, they did not know what they should be teaching in undergraduate service courses or how they should be collaborating with engineering and computer science professors to improve the situation. They had no idea how many of their undergraduate English majors became technical communicators, the range and depth of the problems they faced, the extent to which these problems led to failure, and the ways in which technical communicators and the users of their work were hurt; consequently, they were unaware that they should be developing new disciplinary and interdisciplinary curricula, establishing cooperative and continuing education programs, developing research in a broad range of new areas, helping make library facilities available to non-university workers, and striving at the federal level to eliminate inappropriate evaluation standards. They were unaware of the demand in computer corporations for Ph.D.'s to conduct research in technical communication and only dimly aware of the growing need for Ph.D.'s to teach technical communication in universities. They not only were ignorant of needs in technical communication, but also, partially as a result of this ignorance, created contexts in English departments that both militated against technical communication and shaped it too narrowly.

10

The Narrowness of Composition and Technical Communication

The forces that narrowed the scope of approaches to the university, the humanities, and literary criticism in the 19th and 20th centuries—in addition to militating against technical communication—also contributed to that odd creation that has been called, variously, "English composition," "freshman composition," and "freshman English." This creation, which I shall call "first-year composition," represented the triumph of a number of the ideas that I have associated with Plato, Aristotle, Christian philosophers, and the apologists for science. It was disdainfully linked with rhetoric by many in English departments in the 20th century. For instance, as indicated earlier, I. A. Richards (1936) viewed rhetoric as the dreariest and least profitable part of the waste that the unfortunate traveled through in freshman English.

The placement of rhetoric in the initial year of university studies was extremely significant—a remarkable contrast to its placement by Cicero's Crassus and Quintilian in classical antiquity. First-year composition was hardly the crown of education, a subject engaged when all other studies were complete, a subject that included the vastness of all knowledge within its purview. On the contrary, it was the initiation rite of university education, a subject engaged before all other studies, a subject undertaken before students had begun to delve deeply in knowledge. As such, it represented the triumph of the beliefs of Augustine and Sprat that rhetoric was an area of work for younger people; it represented the triumph of the disparagement of rhetoric that we find in Plato and Aristotle.

In *The Anatomy of College English*, Thomas W. Wilcox (1973) included a profile of first-year composition that accorded well with my own experience. According to Wilcox, first-year composition was required at most universities: "Of all four-year colleges and universities in the nation, 93.2 percent require freshmen to take at least one term of English," while "77.8 percent require them to take two" (p. 69). Through various testing procedures, some students were exempted from the first-year composition requirement, and, in the early 1970s, a number of English departments were moving toward the elimination of such a requirement; but, when *Anatomy* was published, first-year composition was still "the largest single component of the American college and university curriculum" (p. 63).

Since first-year composition was intended for almost all students, the course tended to be restricted to those matters that would help all students. Teachers attempted to engage students with those matters that all of the forms of discourse had in common. Like Aristotle, they attempted to approach discourse in general terms. Since general approaches to discourse yielded more of value about style than organization or invention, they followed Cicero, Quintilian, and Ramus in emphasizing the former—with mechanics (spelling, punctuation, and so on) as an added emphasis. Robert. J. Connors (1985), in "Mechanical Correctness As a Focus in Composition Instruction," accurately captured the importance of the tradition of stylistic and mechanical correctness in composition: "Throughout most of its history as a college subject, English composition has meant one thing to most people: the simple-minded enforcement of standards of mechanical and grammatical correctness in writing" (p. 61). In first-year composition (despite the admitted value of work on style and mechanics), the decline of rhetoric assumed its ultimate form.

The goal of first-year composition was to prepare students to write not only in their university years, but also in their professional years beyond. First-year composition was crucial for both times because most students never again enrolled in a course that emphasized the creation of discourse. For students becoming either practitioners such as hardware or software developers or professionals such as technical communicators, then, first-year composition was likely to be their only exposure to a course with such an emphasis. Since first-year composition was intended to help students with their writing problems after graduation, some professors made the mistake of assuming that the course was largely shaped by industrial needs.

Richard Ohmann made this assumption in his 1976 *English in America*. Ohmann saw first-year composition as a response to the needs of business, industry, and government. According to him, industries needed managers who could determine needs, organize material, marshal evidence, solve problems, and communicate decisions. Government and other bureaucracies had a similar need for exposition, argument, and allied skills. Writing became a tool of production and management, and the goals of first-year composition were framed in response to the needs of the industrial state and its governing class (pp. 93–94). Ohmann mistakenly believed that first-year composition was "reasonably good" in preparing students for industry (p. 297).

In shaping their composition courses, however, composition specialists developed both rhetorical approaches that were imbued with the ideas of Plato, Aristotle, and Christian philosophers and experimentalist approaches that were imbued with the ideas of the apologists for science. As a result, the courses that they created were far too narrow to be effective in preparing their students for industrial environments. In addition, because composition was so influential in shaping technical communication, courses in this area also lacked scope in preparing students for later work. Some examples, largely from the 1970s and 1980s, can help suggest these deficiencies.

SOME EXAMPLES OF RHETORICAL AND EXPERIMENTAL APPROACHES TO COMPOSITION

Among the more prominent professors in composition directing attention to rhetoric were Christians following Hutchins's lead in looking to Aristotle and Plato for leadership. For instance, in 1959, Daniel Fogarty, S. J., dean of the School of Education at Saint Mary's University, wrote *Roots for a New Rhetoric*, an effort to provide a rhetorical theory to enable teachers to "make the choices and adaptations that suit the needs of their first-year courses, variously titled English I, composition, the writing of speeches, and communication" (p. 5). Fogarty's Catholicism inclined him to the same ultimate roots as Hutchins and Newman: "Most students of Aristotle would admit that he made the greatest contribution to rhetoric up to our time. The 'Rhetorica' not only sums up the best of all the elements developed prior to his time but, together with his own and Plato's ideas, forms the best synthesis of any before or since" (p. 12).

James L. Kinneavy is ideal, for a number of reasons, to suggest the extent to which Christian rhetoricians associated with first-year composition promoted general education and militated against technical communication. Among the reasons for Kinneavy's being ideal, his most important work—*A Theory of Discourse* (1971)—was designed to help teaching assistants who were "handling typical freshman composition courses" (p. ix). It also served as an example of at least one version of the Aristotelianism that so imbued rhetoric in the 1970s and 1980s, took a stand on locating technical communication within the world of discourse, and was highly respected.

In fact, James A. Berlin claimed—in his 1987 *Rhetoric and Reality*—that *A Theory of Discourse* remained "the best theoretical treatment of discourse theory" (p.

135). Furthermore, Anthony O'Keefe, in Moran and Journet's *Research in Technical Communication* (1985), made a similar claim for technical communication, arguing that Kinneavy's *Theory of Discourse* remained the essential book-length grounding in the issues and ideas from which a systematic framework in the theory of writing pedagogy could be built (p. 100). He also referred to an article by Elizabeth Harris (1979), which was useful in suggesting the applications of Kinneavy to technical communication.

In a festschrift edited by Rosalind J. Gabin (1995) and titled *Discourse Studies in Honor of James L. Kinneavy*, Valerie M. Balester, Phillip Sipiora, and Gabin provided relevant biographical information about Kinneavy. He was educated in seminaries and assumed the name Brother Cornelius Leo in 1937. In 1949, Kinneavy enrolled as a graduate student at Catholic University of America. In the late 1950s, he was granted a full dispensation from his holy orders but remained, in his words, "a cultural Catholic" (pp. ix,x). His *Theory of Discourse* was most influenced by the New Criticism and was an application of New Critical techniques of analysis to nonliterary discourse (p. xi). Numerous textbooks were based on *A Theory of Discourse* (p. xiii).

All too aware of the disparagement of composition by literary critics, Kinneavy intended to improve the stature of this area by showing that composition could "very legitimately carve out a respectable domain in the field of English" (1971, p. 2). His strategy was to place composition within "a coherent and unified view of the field of English" (p. ix). He was attempting no less than "a *general* science or art of communication" (emphasis added, p. 4). He himself reported his reliance on the literary methodology called the New Criticism: "By constructing norms parallel in a sense to the techniques of new criticism, the analysis of writing other than literary and the composition of such works also can be improved" (p. 2). The resulting *Theory of Discourse* had many affinities with the work of not only Crane, but also the philosopher on whom Crane relied so heavily—Aristotle. In fact, at key junctures in his work, Kinneavy expressly credited Aristotle for his views.

In both theory and practice, Kinneavy—like Crane, Hutchins, and Newman— was limited by textuality. Kinneavy's focus on texts was elaborated in his discussion of the aims of discourse. According to him, the aims of discourse were crucial: "Purpose in discourse is all important. The aim of a discourse determines everything else in the process of discourse" (p. 48). The aim of a discourse itself was determined not by inquiring about the intent of the author or the impact of the discourse on an audience, but by examining the text: "Rather than the encoder or decoder being the determinants of aim, it seems better to find the aim which is embodied in the text itself—given the qualifications of situation and culture mentioned above" (p. 49). Human invention and reception not revealed by texts belonged to the field of psychology rather than discourse study (p. 50). Such views suggested the extent to which the influence of the New Criticism focused Kinneavy's attention on reading, on an analysis of "what is" rather than a deliberative consideration of "what ought to be." They also suggested the extent to which he shied away from viewing reality unmediated by texts.

Kinneavy's practice was as textbound as his theory: "This book attempts to bring together, in a systematic framework, various approaches to the teaching of composition from classical and contemporary sources" (p. ix). Kinneavy began his synthesis with induction, Aristotle's starting point for acquiring knowledge. Kinneavy used his induction to formulate definitions of four discourse kinds. Expressive discourse emphasized the creator. Persuasive discourse emphasized the audience. Reference discourse emphasized reality. And literary discourse emphasized the product or text. Kinneavy's theory of discourse, then, comprised "an intelligible framework of different types of discourse with a treatment of the nature of each type, the underlying logic(s), the organizational structure of this type, and the stylistic characteristics of such discourse" (pp. 4–5). He gave credit to Aristotle for his four-part framework and suggested its influence: "Because of Aristotle's influence, this structure has dominated rhetorical theory for twenty-three centuries" (p. 18).

Kinneavy acknowledged the artificiality of supposing that actual discourse had but a single emphasis or aim (p. 60). He understood that his methodology took him to a high level of abstraction. His textuality directed him away from the uniqueness of present contexts to the history of general statements about past contexts. His focus on four isolated aims directed him away from the complexities of interacting aims. And his effort to discover what could be generalized about each of the isolated aims directed attention away from the differences that could attend a particular aim. Kinneavy, then, worked at several removes from the uniqueness of realistic and full contexts. His decontextualization was profound.

Yet Kinneavy considered his theory of discourse to be productive of further good. For instance, in his discussion of reference discourse, his claim about the applicability of his theory could have hardly been stronger: "It is hoped that a careful presentation of the theory will enable the student to analyze reference discourse and to produce some such discourse himself" (p. 75). He encouraged the student to move from general to particular, from theory to application, without the important admonition that a deliberative theory or methodology for a particular problem could not be determined without the fullest awareness and use of the concrete problem context in the process of formulating the theory or methodology.

Kinneavy considered technical writing to be a kind of reference discourse (Horner, 1990, p. 200). He described the goal of reference discourse as designating reality or truth (p. 39). Elizabeth Harris (1979), who has been credited with suggesting how to apply Kinneavy's *Theory of Discourse* to technical communication, followed Kinneavy in defining technical writing as reference discourse: "I would propose defining technical writing, to follow Kinneavy's model, as mainly *reference discourse*—discourse the primary purpose of which is to represent reality" (p. 627). With their narrow focus on the identification of truths, Kinneavy and

Harris ignored the large body of technical communication with other goals, among them, the improvement of the natural and technological world around us.

Perhaps Kinneavy's most serious limitation, however, was his reliance on scholarly texts to analyze technical communication. In 1971, when *A Theory of Discourse* was published, technical communication was a large, thriving, growing area for industry and government, a substantial area for teaching the standard course for the professions at the undergraduate level in universities, but an almost nonexistent area for scholarly publication. *The Journal of Technical Writing and Communication* only began publication in 1971, and *The Technical Writing Teacher* did not begin publication until 1973. As a result, Kinneavy could draw on few scholarly texts in technical communication and had almost nothing to say about the area. A major focus in technical communication at the time was style, and a major stylistic focus was jargon. As a result, one of Kinneavy's few references to technical writing called attention to the area's denunciation of unnecessary jargon (p. 176). Helping technical communicators required far more than the analysis of scholarly texts. It required the fullest possible immersion in the richness of corporate life and the attempt to discover the full range of needs confronting technical communicators. These needs—trivialized by a focus on such matters as unnecessary jargon—had some of their roots in the very decline of rhetoric and rise of philosophy that Kinneavy himself perpetuated.

Kinneavy was not the only composition specialist to adopt the theories of literary critics. Numerous composition specialists attempted to resolve the gap between composition specialists and literary critics by minimizing the differences between them. Among the more prominent, Winifred Bryan Horner edited a book entitled *Composition & Literature: Bridging the Gap* (1983a). In her introduction, Horner saw her book as a response to "the widening gulf between research and teaching in literature and research and teaching in composition" (p. 1). This gulf could be bridged by a recognition that "the 'teaching' of writing and the 'teaching' of literature are applications of theories that are closely connected, often inseparable, and always fundamental to the study of language" (p. 2). She argued that "composition theory and critical theory" were "philosophically connected" (p. 2). She limited rhetoric to precisely that tradition that I have highlighted as responsible for the decline of rhetoric and triumph of philosophy: "In its oldest tradition, rhetoric was concerned with discovering and communicating truth. Those arts and the teaching of those arts occupied some of the greatest minds in Western history—Plato, Aristotle, Augustine, and Francis Bacon" (p. 3). Unfortunately, Horner's statements were all too characteristic of approaches to rhetorical theory by composition theorists.

If the composition community developed rhetorical theories that were imbued with the ideas of Plato, Aristotle, and their theological successors, it also—in contrast to literary criticism—derived theoretical approaches from scientific experimentalism. The need for the experimental justification of action was felt as strongly among many researchers in first-year composition as it was in industry.

In 1912, for instance, in the third number of the first volume of *The English Journal*, the official organ of the National Council of Teachers of English, Sherwin Cody published "Scientific Principles in the Teaching of Composition."

Cody recommended our applying "modern scientific method to the study and teaching of the English language and literature" (p. 163). He indicated that this method involved formulating a hypothesis and testing it for results. According to Cody, this method enabled teachers of composition to achieve the proper results. What emerged from calls such as Cody's in the 20th century was what Stephen M. North, in his 1987 *Making of Knowledge in Composition: Portrait of an Emerging Field*, called "the oldest and, in terms of numbers of investigations, largest of Composition's Researcher communities" (p. 141). In surveying the century, North called experimental research "the dominant mode of formal educational research in this century over the past 75 years or so" (p. 141).

Education schools were a major source of researchers and teachers who tried to approach first-year composition using scientific methodologies, and among the forces promoting such approaches was John Dewey's strong call for the application of experimental method to education. When Hutchins published his *Higher Education in America*, his narrowness did not go unchallenged. In a 1937 article in *Social Frontier*, for instance, Dewey challenged Hutchins's belief "in the greatest possible aloofness of higher learning from contemporary social life" (1937/1987, p. 399). Dewey argued that escape from problematic social tendencies could require the study of social needs. He suggested that higher education could have a role to play in social reconstruction.

But Dewey, for all the appropriateness of his criticism of Hutchins and his belief that the university should become involved in contemporary social planning and implementation, was himself too much a philosopher and too involved in the science of his times to escape the siren call of truth. For instance, in a work such as *The Quest for Certainty* (1929), Dewey expressed his belief in industrialization as applied science, as "the direct fruit of the growth of the experimental method of knowing" (p. 79). He wanted more extensive "transfer of experimental method from the technical field of physical experience to the wider field of human life" (p. 273). He was concerned that there had been "so little use of the experimental method of forming our ideas and beliefs about the concerns of man in his characteristic social relations" (p. 271). Despite the great differences between Dewey's ideas of science and those of the early apologists for science, he limited his role for the university to the same goals as these apologists—discoveries of truths (p. 207). He differed from these apologists, among other ways, in looking for his truths in a different area: social affairs.

North's *Making of Knowledge in Composition* (1987) suggested the extent to which Dewey's call was heeded in composition. The very subject of North's book—"how knowledge is made in the field that has come to be called Composition" (p. 1)—placed him in the philosophical tradition. He ascribed the birth of modern composition to a series of events that included the appointment of a committee in 1962 by the National Council of Teachers of English

> to review what is known and what is not known about the teaching and learning of composition and the conditions under which it is taught for the purpose of preparing for publication a special *scientifically* based report on what is known in this area. (emphasis added, Braddock, Lloyd-Jones, & Schoer, 1963, p. 1)

The resulting report, published in 1963—*Research in Written Composition* by Braddock and colleagues—included 504 studies that were largely experimental. While the authors were severely critical of past experimental research, they nevertheless conveyed that only through the methodological rigor of the physical sciences would composition studies reach maturity. All of the five studies selected by the authors as superior models for future research were experimental approaches. That such a report gave impetus to experimental approaches was hardly surprising.

With the publication of *Research in Written Composition*, according to North, methodology assumed a prominent role in composition:

> It would be no great exaggeration to call *Research in Written Composition* the charter of modern Composition. With the image it fosters—of a sort of ur-discipline blindly groping its way out of the darkness toward the bright light of a "scientific" certainty—it sets the stage for what I have already characterized as the field's methodological land rush. (1987, p. 17)

A new era demanded "new kinds of knowledge produced by new kinds of inquiry" (p. 17).

Research in Written Composition was succeeded by a book by George Hillocks, Jr., titled *Research on Written Composition: New Directions for Teaching* (1986), which summarized and evaluated research between 1963 and 1982. Included in the research from this period that Hillocks surveyed were studies of the following: the writing process, techniques of invention, the assessment of composition, modes of instruction, and the effects of teaching grammar. Hillocks strongly backed experimental approaches and considered their support for sentence combining to be their greatest achievement. He quoted John Mellon as evidence: "I don't know of any component in our arsenal of literacy-teaching methods that is better supported empirically than sentence combining" (p. 143). Given such status, then, sentence combining can serve as an excellent example of the "general communication skills" that experimental researchers recommended.

The pedagogy of sentence combining was given impetus by a large body of research stemming from a 1965 report written by Kellogg Hunt titled *Grammatical Structures Written at Three Grade Levels*. Hunt was interested in description, in the quest for truths about differences in the writing of students in grades 4, 8, and 12. Instead of exploring the entire writing situation, Hunt focused attention on a small part of that situation—the syntax of students. He devised an instrument—

the T-unit, which was a main clause with its modifiers, such as subordinate clauses—to extend human capability and limit human error. He used this instrument to measure syntax, and his most significant finding was that average T-unit length and average clause length increased as grade levels increased. The focus on quantification translated all student texts to one homogeneous scheme by moving from the concrete to the universal or general by selecting and abstracting the mathematical from the diversity of the experienced artifact. The quantitative results represented an intelligible, simple, and uniform order achieved through reason.

Hillocks (1986) reported that sentence combining was one of the elements of the pedagogy resulting from this research. In sentence combining, students were "presented with sets of two or more sentences and asked to combine them into a single effective structure" (p. 141). Hillocks was so enthusiastic about sentence combining that he was tempted to agree with Charles Cooper that no other single teaching approach had "'ever consistently been shown to have a beneficial effect on syntactic maturity and writing quality'" (p. 151). However, one fact served to limit Hillocks's enthusiasm. He acknowledged that most sentence combining treatments assumed that an increase in length, in itself, was a valued goal and somehow related to quality (p. 148). It was to his credit that he was troubled by the leap from "a descriptive measure" to "an instructional goal" (p. 148). What Hillocks sensed was a very serious flaw in 20th-century thinking: the move from description to prescription without the understanding shared by Isocrates, Cicero, and Quintilian that different contexts demanded different approaches. It was unfortunate that Hillocks did not see that the whole thrust of his book and even its very title—*Research on Written Composition: New Directions for Teaching*—embodied the same flaw.

It was not that an observation of the empiricists—for instance, that growing maturity brought longer sentences—could not be right; rather, it was a question about why a commonplace—that the more complex thought of maturity often demanded sentences of greater length or, to state it another way, that children were hardly producing the sentences of a Gibbon or Burke or Faulkner—ever needed verification. It was not that the pedagogies that they recommended—for instance, sentence combining—were not fruitful; rather, it was a question about why such an old hat and proven pedagogy—recommended, for instance, by Fred Newton Scott and Joseph Villiers Denney in their 1897 *Composition-Rhetoric*—could be trumpeted forth with such fanfare or why the trumpeting was not balanced—as it was in the Scott and Denney text—by a pedagogy for promoting expertise in composing short sentences, which were also in demand in many situations in maturity. It was not that the empiricists could not produce insights of value; rather, it was a question about the disappearance of incredible amounts of time and money down the sinkhole of fruitless empiricism and the perpetuation of the incredible fraud that experimentalism could provide accountability for human choice and action.

What was truly droll in this situation was the position of the federal government. On the one hand, it was pouring large sums of scarce resources into composition research, and among the supposedly important results of this research was the discovery that T-unit length increased with maturity. An important goal of writing instruction based on the concept of stylistic maturity was to have students writing longer T-units at the end of their education than at the beginning. After students graduated from universities and were hired by industries as professionals, supposedly the highest level of maturity, they were informed by federal procurement agencies such as the Naval Air Systems Command that all of their writing had to be in line with readability formulas. The same complex of ideas that focused attention on length in composition research promoted attention to length in government and industry. But, alas, composition research called for longer T-units, while readability formulas mandated brevity. The calls for length and brevity may have been reconcilable; but they came from groups sublimely unaware of one another, so no effort at reconcilement was attempted. Such were the wonderful realities of modern compartmentalization.

On the face of it, one might have expected composition researchers to try to break through this compartmentalization and find out about technical communication. After all, technical communication contained context-rich examples of the very writing that composition specialists were attempting to teach. For most composition specialists, however, technical communication was as invisible to them as they were to literary critics. In part, the view of composition as a discipline or social structure within itself militated against movement outside. In part, the strong focus on first-year composition militated against consideration of advanced or graduate rhetoric—a limitation that also seriously compromised most of composition's histories of 19th-century rhetoric. In part, many teachers in composition had Ph.D.'s in literary criticism, advocated liberal or general education, and were as biased against vocationalism as literary critics. In part, since most of technical communication was based on experience, they considered it methodologically inferior and considered the path of knowledge as flowing from them to technical communication rather than the reverse. In part, composition was a more mature area than technical communication, and mature areas in universities tended to ignore less mature areas, even when they were writing about these areas.

The invisibility of technical communication to composition researchers was apparent in numerous publications. In Gary Tate's *Teaching Composition: 10 Bibliographic Essays* (1976), technical communication was ignored, even though Kinneavy and C. Robert Kline, Jr., included a chapter titled "Composition and Related Fields." When Robert M. Gorrell, Patricia Bizzell, and Bruce Herzberg wrote *The Bedford Bibliography for Teachers of Writing* (1984), they also ignored technical communication, and not until the fourth edition (in 1996) did Bizzell and Herzberg announce a new category called "Writing in the Workplace," which ignored all nonacademic publication and all publication before 1979. As a final example, James A. Berlin (1987), in *Rhetoric and Reality: Writing Instruction in American Colleges 1900–1985*, totally ignored technical communication in the body of his book and included only a few academic citations in his bibliography.

Yet all of these researchers were meeting and, in some cases, exchanging ideas with numerous technical communication researchers at the Conference of College Composition and Communication.

Even when technical communication was mentioned by composition researchers, the attitude was usually pejorative and condescending. In the 1983 edition of Horner's *The Present State of Scholarship in Historical and Contemporary Rhetoric*, Kinneavy wrote: "It must...be said that not much interesting work has gone on in the rhetoric of technical communication. No major theoretical work has yet influenced writers of texts or teachers in this area or practitioners" (p. 181). In the 1990 revised edition of the same book, Kinneavy emphasized the extent to which the area was derivative: "Books in this field are still limited to guides, manuals, and textbooks that traverse well-worn paths" (p. 201). With such attitudes, it was little wonder that most rhetoric and composition specialists paid as little attention to technical communication as literary critics paid to rhetoric and composition. Yet a book such as *Engineers As Writers: Growth of a Literature* (1953), by Walter Miller and Leo E. A. Saidla, was sufficient in itself to refute Kinneavy's claims.

If composition specialists tended to ignore my community, however, technical communication specialists did not ignore composition. Because so many teachers in technical communication came to the area from composition, ideas from composition had a strong influence on technical communication. This influence was particularly noticeable if pedagogies in the two areas were compared. Still, as the next section suggests, technical communication teachers were at least somewhat closer to industrial environments than their composition counterparts, and, as a result, tended to approach their courses with greater scope. Unfortunately, too few composition teachers were aware of this scope and used it to inform their courses.

PEDAGOGY IN COMPOSITION AND TECHNICAL COMMUNICATION

The narrowness of research in composition was mirrored by the narrowness of its pedagogy. A composition course should encourage students to use encompassing enough approaches so as not to ignore considerations that might compromise the quality of their performance, but first-year composition did not escape the trend in the 19th and 20th centuries toward ever-increasing specialization. At different times and at different places, first-year composition was defined differently, but, in line with the Platonic and Aristotelian emphasis on definition, first-year composition tended to be narrowed to such a degree that much was excluded that would have helped students heading for technical communication to improve their performance. The attention of these students was directed away from concerns that were important to them.

Composition teachers had the available resources to escape their narrowness. Practitioners and professionals in industry published a wealth of information based on experience, judgment, and practice about their procedures and problems. Two of the most useful of these resources were Stello Jordan's *Handbook of Technical Writing Practices* (1971) and Carlin Kindilien's *Technical Writing and Communication* (1963). Jordan's handbook contained 36 chapters and two ancillary sections written by 35 of the most respected and experienced practitioners and professionals in technical communication. These books together totaled over 1,541 pages. I have never encountered any reference to these or similar books in the publications of the composition community.

Because so many composition teachers also became technical communication teachers, pedagogy in technical communication—at least initially—tended to resemble pedagogy in composition. Through force of habit or simply through lack of knowing what else to do, teachers tended to use approaches in technical communication similar to those used in composition. Furthermore, since the writers of technical communication textbooks understood that teachers were coming to technical communication from composition, they tried to use similar approaches in the effort to make the transition easier. Over time, however, because teachers of technical communication had greater exposure to the experience of practitioners and professionals, they were inclined to broaden their courses and include much that composition teachers excluded. A comparison and contrast can prove helpful in suggesting similarities and differences in these two areas of pedagogy.

As Richard Fulkerson wrote in a 1990 article, the dominant textbook in first-year composition between 1960 and 1990 was James M. McCrimmon's *Writing with a Purpose*: "*Writing with a Purpose* has been the preeminent rhetoric in the United States for the last three decades at least" (p. 415). An analysis of one of its editions—say, the seventh, published in 1980—suggests the extent to which it not only failed to alert students heading for technical communication about many of the problems they would face, but also misled them in important ways. The contents of this edition of McCrimmon's textbook reflected a number of historical changes, among them, the separation of composition from an area such as speech.

Perhaps the most symbolic event in the separation of composition from speech was the secession of 17 speech teachers in 1914 from the National Council of Teachers of English (NCTE). These speech teachers formed the National Association of Academic Teachers of Public Speaking (NAATPS) and began issuing their official journal, *The Quarterly Journal of Public Speaking*, in April 1915. In 1916, in the fourth issue of that journal, Charles H. Woolbert published an article titled "The Organization of Departments of Speech Science in Universities" that set forth the argument for the establishment of speech departments separate from English. Among Woolbert's many arguments, English teachers were hostile or lukewarm toward speech, and speech teachers, who were in the minority, could not acquire the resources they needed to perform well. English focused on thought that was written, speech science on thought that was spoken.

At some universities in the 20th century, efforts were made in first-year composition to reverse this division. For instance, at the University of Iowa, where I taught first-year composition as well as technical communication as a teaching assistant, first-year composition was called a "communication" course and involved instruction not just in writing, but also in speaking, reading, and listening. The popularity of this kind of course became sufficiently widespread for the term to be included in the name of the major convention and journal for first-year composition teachers—The Conference on College Composition and Communication and *College Composition and Communication*. On the whole, however, the dominant emphasis in first-year composition across the country remained on writing.

The first word in the title of McCrimmon's text *Writing with a Purpose* was not insignificant, nor was the cover illustration of the 1980 edition: a fountain pen, which was symbolic of the narrowness of the text. Never mind the numbers of people who wrote with pencils, typewriters, or, by 1980, even computers. The focus on writing was so narrow that not only was the rhetoric of oral discourse excluded, but also the role of oral discourse in writing. Students heading for technical communication in industry received no hint at all of the extraordinary interdependence of oral and written discourse from the beginning to the end of the product development process in industry. McCrimmon used a few examples of oral discourse to illustrate points about writing, but he studiously avoided any mention of acquiring information for writing projects directly from people, that is, through such means as informal networks, interviews, surveys, or speeches. Writers acquired information from libraries, not people. Writers asked *themselves* questions about a project, not others. The writer, during the writing process at least, was a worker isolated from the rest of humanity—perhaps a truth for many of the creative writers of concern to literary critics, but hardly a truth for the writers in technical communication.

Perhaps the worst illusion created by texts like McCrimmon's, in the absence of any mention of the dependence of writers on others, was the suggestion that it was within the power of writers themselves to achieve quality in their performance. As suggested earlier, a whole host of decisions made before a project in technical communication was even begun might seriously compromise the quality of the project, among a very few examples, government contract requirements, the availability of educational programs, confidentiality rules, job definitions, scheduling, head count, equipment, and access to libraries. One of the most important goals of technical communicators in industry was to acquire the power to have a say in decisions that affected the quality of their performance, a goal requiring strong speech capabilities. Far more was required of the members of my community in industry to achieve quality than was required of McCrimmon's students.

McCrimmon's text was used in two varieties of writing courses. Wilcox, in his *Anatomy of College English* (1973), suggested that one variety emphasized literature. McCrimmon's *Writing with a Purpose* (1980) acknowledged the importance of this variety of first-year composition by including a major section on

"The Critical Essay," and it also acknowledged the tendency to focus on literature in the introductory remarks to the section: "since the favorite subject for critical essays in an English class is literature, this chapter will be limited to that subject" (p. 269). Courses in first-year composition that emphasized literature were as valuable as other courses in literature, but they also carried the same limitations regarding technical communication that I suggested in my discussions about Crane and Miller.

The second and more common of the two major varieties of first-year composition was described by Wilcox as emphasizing "composition or rhetoric as such, with relatively little concern for subject matter or what is expressed" (p. 80). The aim of teachers in such a course was to train their students to use formal devices that would "serve on many different occasions to express many different contents" (p. 81). Wilcox elaborated: "Courses in composition which are based on this set of assumptions...usually consist of readings in nonliterary expository prose, discussion of verbal patterns and rhetorical strategies, and a sequence of writing assignments" (p. 81). While McCrimmon's *Writing with a Purpose* contained a major section acknowledging the importance of courses emphasizing literature, the book as a whole tended to be oriented toward this more common variety of first-year composition. The readings in expository prose mentioned by Wilcox—for instance, standard essays such as George Orwell's "Shooting an Elephant," Wallace Stegner's "The Town Dump," and E. B. White's "Once More to the Lake"— were usually assembled in a text such as *The Norton Reader* (Eastman, 1977), which was assigned along with *Writing with a Purpose*.

Students in this variety of first-year composition would regularly read and discuss essays from their readers. Although there were exceptions, these essays tended to be the classics of the genre, in line with the emphasis on classics by Newman, Hutchins, Crane, and Miller. The authors of the essays were frequently the same authors studied in literature courses, among them Bacon, Donne, Milton, Swift, Addison, Johnson, Shelley, Emerson, Thoreau, Newman, Arnold, and Forster. As might be expected, discussions of these essays were often indistinguishable from the discussions in regular literature courses, so this variety of first-year composition was imbued with a literary orientation as well. As was the case in literature courses, the emphasis on classics directed attention away from failure, the formulation of ideas for performance that led to avoidance, and those areas of study that had no classics.

Essays in readers served as models for students to imitate in their own writing. In the course of a semester, many students were assigned to write a variable number of short, personal essays, usually about three or four typewritten pages in length, and a longer, final paper—a library research report—perhaps some 15 typewritten pages in length. Students usually had free rein in choosing the subjects for these essays; they were encouraged to choose topics that aroused their curiosity or interest (McCrimmon, 1980, p. 10). Students heading for technical communication received little or no sense of the ethical urgency of writing decisions, of the ways that these choices could hurt or help others. McCrimmon's *Writing with a Purpose* seemed to suggest that writing was like a leisurely, carefree stroll through a park, the direction dictated by the whims of casual interest. Students heading for technical communication would enter a world of failure, with human well-being and even, on occasion, human life in the balance. They seemed more like privates on the losing side of a war than strollers in a park.

In writing their short personal essays and library research report, students were always cautioned not to choose subjects that were too large for the number of pages assigned. For instance, McCrimmon mentioned a number of subjects that were "too broad for a student essay of three or four typewritten pages" (p. 10). He called for subject restriction: "The obvious solution to these problems is to *restrict* the general subject to something that can be treated in some detail with the space available—that is, to reduce the scope of the subject in order to treat it in more depth" (p. 11). Students in first-year composition heading for technical communication, then, were being taught to restrict the scope of their subjects arbitrarily, while their later jobs would give them little choice in their subjects and require the broadest possible scope so as not to ignore important factors.

In line with Kinneavy, part of the restriction in determining the scope of a paper was selection of a single purpose. Consider the last two words in the title of McCrimmon's text *Writing with a Purpose*. Kinneavy might well have recognized the artificiality of supposing that actual discourse had but a single purpose, but, in the decontextualized vacuum that was first-year composition, McCrimmon encouraged students to believe that they wrote with a single purpose in mind. Students heading for technical communication were not encouraged to realize that their jobs would focus on problems with a welter of conflicting goals, that they would need a powerful ethics to enable them to allocate priority, and that they would need a powerful rhetoric of adjustment to resolve conflicts that were not amenable to settlement by ethical priority.

As might be expected, McCrimmon and other textbook writers were able to find few general insights about invention in the work of rhetoricians such as Kinneavy. As has already been suggested, more could be said in general about an area such as style than about invention. What was noteworthy about McCrimmon's *Writing with a Purpose* was how very little it contained about invention. For instance, it contained nothing about the importance of writers keeping abreast of change and grasping the uniqueness of a problem context. It contained nothing about the challenges involved in these tasks, among them, the inadequacies of an abstract medium such as language in grasping particulars, the wealth of present and past reality essential to provide a basis for comparison and contrast in any effort to determine particulars, and the techniques of discovering paths of relatedness to materials that could be helpful in solving problems.

McCrimmon did not ignore actual writing contexts. For instance, he included an interview with a professional writer to promote insights about writing in such contexts, but the insight most striking to anyone familiar with these contexts was how little McCrimmon knew about them. To suggest just one example, McCrimmon was silent about visual communication. Given occasional articles promoting attention to the visual arts, among them, Joseph J. Comprone's "The Uses of Media in Teaching Composition" in Tate's *Teaching Composition* (1976), one might have expected a reasonable amount of attention to be devoted to visual rhetoric. But topics such as the uses of visualization in invention; the history of visual rhetoric; media options such as printed publications, online screen display, and film; illustration options such as graphs, charts, drawings, and photographs; layout and design; the visual rhetoric of verbal texts; and graphic reproduction processes such as letterpress or offset were never broached. Since visual rhetoric was ignored in most places in universities—engineering graphics and the history of art were among the notable exceptions—students heading for industries were notoriously wordbound.

McCrimmon's textbook, like most textbooks in first-year composition, was dominated by the tradition of correctness. For instance, one of the four major parts, comprising roughly one-fourth of the text, was a "Handbook of Grammar and Usage." Among the problems covered in the handbook were run-on sentences, sentence fragments, dangling modifiers, wrong meanings, awkward word order, subject-verb agreement, misuse of punctuation, and misspelling. Some sections of the "Handbook" were nothing more than references back to the second of McCrimmon's four major parts, titled "Writing and Rewriting." In this second part, one set of problems included faulty parallelism, unemphatic order, inconsistent diction, vague diction, trite diction, and ineffective imagery. Another set included the traditional fallacies in the reasoning process, among them, ignoring the burden of proof, argumentum ad hominem, begging the question, red herring, unjustifiable emotional appeal, hasty generalization, and the either-or fallacy. McCrimmon also included an appendix titled "A Checklist of Troublesome Usages."

The tradition of correctness was ideal for a course designed to prepare all students to write. Such a course had to include materials that were relevant to all students. A problem in subject-verb agreement was as gauche for a student intending to major in economics as it was for one heading for art history. A problem in punctuation had to be avoided as much in engineering as in anthropology. The standards for correctness came very close to being rules for all discourse in all situations, and such standards were ideal for a course intended to prepare students for all situations. Of course, there were all those confounded exceptions. For instance, sentence fragments could have been inappropriate in some reports, but they could have been perfectly appropriate in some novels.

McCrimmon's *Writing with a Purpose*, then, certainly reflected the Aristotelian recommendation that rhetoric focus on means rather than content or subject matter. It accorded well with those passages in Cicero where Crassus followed Aristotle in drawing a sharp distinction between discovery and presentation, between philosophical areas and their oratorical treatment. It accorded well with Quintilian's parallel statement that the orator used what experts in subject matter provided. And it accorded well with both the strong emphasis in Cicero and Quintilian on the areas of style and delivery and the narrow definition of rhetoric in Ramus that excluded all areas but these two. It was the kind of emphasis one would expect for young students beginning a university education and as yet unfamiliar with a particular subject. Developing an awareness of a subject area was the task of a student's major, and the courses constituting a major were mostly taken during the third and fourth years.

Although technical communication was often taught in the third and fourth years—largely so that students would be able to use the knowledge derived from their majors in their writing—its pedagogies often resembled those in composition. After all, the same academics—usually with backgrounds in literary criticism—were teaching both kinds of courses, and some of these academics recommended that technical communication derive its pedagogies from composition. Perhaps no article offered more unfortunate advice in this area than one of my own early works—"Against Substituting Technical Writing for Freshman English" (Whitburn, 1975):

> In freshman English the student receives practice in all of the various rhetorical skills. If the student then takes technical writing, he learns to apply these skills to specific kinds of communication....The basis for distinguishing between technical writing and freshman English, then, has...been...the kinds of communication involved. While freshman English concerns itself with general communications skills, technical writing involves an application of these skills to special kinds of communication. (p. 50)

My experience in industry ought to have taught me that an approach that moved solely from theory to application had to be replaced by an approach that used context in the development of the approach itself.

It was not surprising, then, that teachers of technical communication attempted to use the ideas that I have associated with Aristotle, Hutchins, Crane, and Kinneavy—combined in various ways under the banners of the liberal arts or humanities—as theoretical approaches to technical communication. Such a conjunction would certainly have struck Hutchins as ironical. Under the banner of liberal education, he lashed out against a concern in universities for the useful, the problems of society, and the changing particulars of vocationalism, yet here was a university area ostensibly concerned about all of these matters that was attempting to apply his ideas.

Given the strong emphasis on science in technical communication, a substantial number of teachers in my community devoted much of their effort to the criticism of classic scientific texts. Among these teachers were Masse and Kelley (1977), and the source of their classic scientific texts was noteworthy:

> This tradition of technical and scientific writing is...a great tradition. We show students the greatness of the tradition through Robert M. Hutchins and Mortimer J. Adler's edition of *The Great Books of the Western World*...that represents Hutchins and Adler's attempt, when they were both at the University of Chicago, to return twentieth-century education to the great books of the centuries as the source of all education worthy of the name. (p. 81)

Hutchins's theory of education might have been expected to send followers to his texts.

The liberal arts tradition also inclined a number of teachers to encourage the reading of literary texts in technical communication courses. Steven W. Lynn, in his talk at the 1982 Modern Language Association convention, encouraged the use of drama, novels, and poetry:

> My argument here would tend to suggest that technical writing courses and other writing courses, even writing about literature courses, may well have much more in common than is usually allowed....I know of a colleague at the University of Texas who has his students write memos and informational reports about the novels, plays, poems, and stories they read. This seems to me very intelligent.

Lynn's argument justified the use of the same materials in a technical communication course as in a literature course, reminiscent of the same approach used in some first-year composition courses. English professors educated in literary criticism could go right on teaching what they had always taught.

Among other aspects of pedagogy affected by the liberal arts tradition was a strong emphasis on genre, an echo of the similar emphasis in the work of literary critics such as Crane. A textbook such as Thomas E. Pearsall and Donald H. Cunningham's *How to Write for the World of Work* (1978) can suggest the extent to which pedagogy in technical communication could be dominated by a concern for genre. The textbook was generically divided into two parts: "Correspondence" and "Reports." The first section was generically divided into such subsections as "Inquiry and Response Letters," "Employment Letters and Interviews," "Customer Relations Letters," and "Persuasive Letters." The second section was generically divided into such subsections as "Bibliographies and Literature Reviews," "Mechanism Description," "Process Description," "Instructions," "Analytical Reports," and "Proposals." Instead of using the term "genre," Pearsall and Cunningham used the term "formula" (p. 2).

In some respects, however, the Pearsall and Cunningham approach to genre differed from that of a literary critic such as Crane. To suggest one of a number of examples, Crane inclined his readers away from a consideration of audience, while Pearsall and Cunningham strongly encouraged their readers to make audience analysis and adaptation a major consideration in the development of discourse. Their recommendation was unqualified: "get to know your audience and their needs and keep them in mind while you're planning and preparing your report" (p. 86). A consideration of audience could profoundly affect a kind of technical communication: "There may be times when they make the conditions for the report and establish specific requirements concerning the content, organization, format, and publication procedure or delivery" (p. 87). Pearsall and Cunningham's call for audience awareness suggested the need for at least some awareness of context during the creation of technical communication.

If the need for an awareness of some context in the creation of technical communication was too obvious to ignore, however, the genres of Pearsall and Cunningham had potential disadvantages. For instance, genres placed too great an emphasis on the structure of final texts and too little emphasis on the creation process, resulting in profound decontextualization. Pearsall and Cunningham did not avoid this decontextualization despite their calls for greater awareness of context, as a comparison of the content of their textbook with the issues raised earlier would verify. A reader would search in vain for such potential problems as inadequate attention to ethics; the pressures of capitalism; poor management of budgeting, scheduling, and headcount; failures in collaboration; the lack of power of new communities; excessive confidentiality; and appalling government and corporate accountability standards.

The liberal arts tradition in technical communication, then, had the potential for other than salutary effects. To the extent that attention was directed to the classic texts of science, to that extent attention was directed away from the performance crises of technical communication in industry, away from areas of experience unmediated by texts, away from the study of failure. To the extent that attention was directed to genres, to that extent attention was directed away from creation processes and the full contexts that prompted technical communication. With such centers of attention, academics in my community were often as remote from industry problems as literary critics. They had difficulty escaping the aura of the ivory tower.

Still, academics in technical communication were more likely to come into contact with practitioners and professionals, and this contact extended their range of concerns. While textbooks in technical communication continued to resemble textbooks in composition, they also began to differ in various ways. Consider, for example, the most widely used textbook in the 1970s and 1980s, *Reporting Technical Information*, by Kenneth W. Houp and Thomas E. Pearsall (1977). To a very great extent, this textbook did continue to resemble textbooks in composition. In "Technical Writing Textbooks: Current Alternatives in Teaching," Carolyn R. Miller (1984) cited this textbook as striving to "help the English teacher connect the teaching of technical writing to the more familiar teaching of general composition" (p. 35). A comparison of this textbook with McCrimmon's *Writing with a Purpose* (1980) supports Miller's claim.

Teachers of first-year composition would have encountered much in Houp and Pearsall's *Reporting Technical Information* (1977) that they experienced as familiar. For instance, students were expected to write a number of short papers followed by a longer library report as the final assignment in the course. A chapter was devoted to helping students find their way in the library. Other chapters presented such matters as gathering information, analyzing an audience, limiting the subject, and outlining a paper. One of the four major parts of the textbook was a handbook that emphasized correctness, and the emphasis on correctness was found in other parts of the textbook such as the chapter on technical writing style. These similarities to first-year composition textbooks may have been helpful in giving new teachers confidence that they could teach technical communication.

Still, the contexts of business, industry, and government were not without their impact on Houp and Pearsall and many of their colleagues in technical communication. For instance, although visual communication did not receive the attention it deserved, given the wide range of problems associated with visual communication in professional environments, it certainly was not often ignored, as it usually was by teachers of first-year composition. Even *Reporting Technical Information*, a text used to bridge first-year composition and technical communication, had a chapter titled "Graphical Elements" that explored tables, graphs, drawings, diagrams, and photographs.

The contexts of business, industry, and government also prompted teachers of technical communication to devote greater attention to oral discourse than was usually the case in first-year composition. While McCrimmon focused on writing and avoided not only the rhetoric of oral discourse, but also the role of oral discourse in writing, Houp and Pearsall were far more inclusive. In a chapter titled "Speech and Group Conferences," they explored not only talks delivered by single speakers, but also group discussions aimed at solving problems. In a chapter titled "Gathering Information," they also explored a wide range of techniques for obtaining information from people. McCrimmon's writer was an individual isolated from people except through the medium of print, while Houp and Pearsall's communicator inhabited a social world filled with oral exchanges.

Increasingly aware of the need to increase their scope, many academics in technical communication reported in publications about efforts to devise special pedagogies to expand student awareness of contextual considerations. Among these efforts were the development of case studies for use in the classroom, and among the best developers of these pedagogies, if not the best, were Barbara Couture and Jone Rymer Goldstein. In a 1985 article on writing cases, "Procedures for Developing a Technical Communication Case," Couture and Goldstein stressed the importance of devising cases "through which the student can experience the *full* communication process on the job" (emphasis added, p. 40). In their important textbook, *Cases for Technical and Professional Writing* (1985), they also emphasized the importance of using cases to give students experience in confronting the full scope of contextual concerns: "Cases in communication give students the unique opportunity to participate actively in the *whole* process of analyzing on-the-job problems in communication" (emphasis added, p. v). Couture and Goldstein later specified some of the contextual concerns found in their cases that were not found in traditional pedagogies—political pressures, company policies, and deadlines. The wealth of contextual concerns revealed in the pedagogical literature associated with cases was not only helpful in informing technical communication pedagogy, but could also have been useful in broadening the scope of composition.

If cases were helpful in suggesting a greater awareness of contextual concerns, however, they were far more limited than Couture and Goldstein suggested. To claim that cases could enable students to experience the full range of contextual concerns in work environments was misleading. In "Procedures for Developing a Technical Communication Case," Couture and Goldstein (1985) themselves stressed that a case, however much it was rooted in reality, was nonetheless a fiction. Indeed, Couture and Goldstein suggested a range of contextual concerns that they themselves believed should be omitted from cases—matters beyond the comprehension of students, sensitive proprietary information, and personas with sexual and ethnic identities and strong character traits (pp. 36, 38, 41).

Some technical communication professors tried to move beyond the limited realism of cases and encourage academics to develop projects in actual work environments. A number of teachers described communication projects that they developed for students at their universities. For example, in "A Mini-Internship in a Professional Writing Course" (1977), James P. Zappen described a range of projects that he found for his students at Western Michigan University:

> The academic records office needed help with form letters addressed to students on probation. The annual fund office was always looking for fund-raising appeals. The budget office needed a revised budget request form which could be sent to heads of academic departments, returned to the budget office, and forwarded to the state legislature. (p. 134)

Zappen described many of the "very real day-to-day problems of organizational life" that his students experienced (pp. 134–137).

Teachers of technical communication devised student internships or cooperative education programs to serve the same end. Work experience was considered so educationally important at Rensselaer that it became a requirement for obtaining the M.S. in Technical Communication. In "The Value of a Summer Internship in Technical Writing" (1975), one of Rensselaer's students—Donald Tessier—emphasized his growing awareness of the scope of the tasks confronting professionals. Tessier wrote:

> I began to realize that a full-time technical writer might well spend less time writing than he would planning and organizing other aspects of the total production process. The successful production of a finished product at NUSC [Naval Underwater Systems Center] seemed to require an understanding of and much interaction with the photography, graphic arts, and printing departments. (pp. 16–17).

Among the most valuable contributions of internships and cooperative education in technical communication, then, was their promotion of an expanded awareness of realities in corporate environments.

The increase in the scope of pedagogy in technical communication can serve as an example of similar increases in scope in research and service in this area. In the same way that professionals were driven by their context to increase the scope of their concerns in industries, so academics were driven by their contexts to increase the scope of their concerns in universities. Nobody should underestimate the pluck of those academic pioneers of technical communication who pursued these efforts in defiance of the ideologies of Hutchins and Crane and, all too often, at great cost to themselves. Instead of directing their attention to knowledge for its own sake, they responded to the call of the useful. Instead of focusing on truths and texts, they responded to the needs of humans. Instead of glorying in the freedom to cultivate their intellects by contemplating the universal and the permanent in some abstruse way, they responded to the ethical imperatives of a concrete and contemporary social problem. In English departments where "vocational" and "pedagogy" were dirty words, they considered the professional to be as important as the private and public, and they tried to devise the best pedagogies to enable both themselves and students to perform well in their professional lives.

In the years since the 1970s and 1980s, academics in technical communication have made remarkable strides in broadening the scope of technical communication. They have responded to an increasingly global economy by exploring the extraordinary range of ways that international communication must be adapted to various cultures; the special issue on international communication in the Summer 1998 *Technical Communication Quarterly* (Andrews) could serve as an example. With innovations in computing and other technologies, they have expanded the scope of their classroom audiences through distance learning and developed new pedagogies involving such areas of computer-mediated communication as e-mail, real-time chat, bulletin boards, lists, newsgroups, and conferencing systems; the special issue on distance learning and the World Wide Web in the Winter 1999 *Technical Communication Quarterly* (Brown & McMurrey) explored some of these developments. Innovations in computing have even expanded the range of media options that academics must consider; as the special issue on hypertext and hypermedia in the Winter 1995 *Technical Communication Quarterly* (Scott) suggested, academics must explore the presentation of information as a combination of text, pictures, animation, sound, and full-motion video.

If the scope of technical communication has expanded dramatically since the 1970s and 1980s, however, the ideas that I have associated with the philosophical tradition are still so powerful that performance is compromised not just in technical communication, but also in numerous areas of modern society. Narrow goals, social structures, and methodologies still militate against adequate scope in approaching problems. Only rhetorics like those proposed by Isocrates, Cicero, and Quintilian at their broadest have sufficient scope to improve our approaches. Such rhetorics have the potential to revolutionize society.

11

Conclusion

As we move into the 21st century, Western civilization continues to confront an extensive range of problems of narrowness related to those facing technical communication in the 1970s and 1980s. These problems of narrowness also have roots in the triumph of philosophy and decline of rhetoric beginning in classical antiquity and continuing throughout the 20th century. The triumph of philosophy manifests itself in the rise to dominance of ideas that I have associated with such centers of power as Plato, Aristotle, Christian philosophers, and the apologists for science. Although the ideas associated with each of these centers may vary through history and although the philosophies associated with these centers may differ in important ways from one another, the ideas that they share reinforce one another and militate against ideas that I have associated with a rhetorical tradition that includes Isocrates, Cicero, Quintilian, and some followers in the Renaissance.

Different centers of the philosophical tradition continue to be influential in different institutional contexts. For instance, industries continue to be predominantly affected by the scientific center of the philosophical tradition, while the humanities in universities continue to be profoundly affected by the Platonic, Aristotelian, and theological centers of the philosophical tradition. Yet, whether they like it or not, both industries and the humanities in universities confront matters similar to those associated with the Isocratean rhetorical tradition—current human problems, their changing particulars, the prominence of decision-making, the value placed on usefulness, and the necessity of using judgment. Observers still perceive a struggle between the sciences and the humanities in modern society, but this struggle is actually a minor skirmish between philosophical cousins with the real alternative to the two—the Isocratean rhetorical tradition—left in the shadows.

A search through history for sources of liberation from the narrowness of current approaches inevitably leads back to Isocrates, the champion of scope in Western civilization. Although Isocrates, in response to academic competition with Plato, himself narrows the scope of his approaches to social affairs and never develops a fully articulated rhetoric, his ideas—together with those of such successors as Cicero, Quintilian, and the Renaissance humanists—at least point in useful directions and can help liberate us from our narrowness. Isocrates and his successors can help move the resurrection of rhetoric beyond Aristotle and reverse the course of history that began going awry in the very cradle of civilization. Rhetoricians today must undertake the extraordinarily difficult task of moving beyond Isocrates and providing more substance to rhetorics adequate to modern deliberation.

Humans approaching problems must be careful not to use approaches where they are inappropriate. Unlike such rhetoricians as Isocrates and such philosophers as Plato in classical antiquity, however, moderns involved in action and identification must not disparage one another's approaches in and of themselves. They must acknowledge that approaches associated with both action and identification are crucial to effective performance. In engaging problems of any kind, humans must have at their disposal a complex of approaches so extensive that no approach that might prove useful is excluded. What is essential is an art of sufficient scope to guide us in all of our thoughts and all of our actions. This art will be sufficiently flexible to assume different forms in the engagement of different problems.

Whether this new art is called an art of performance, rhetoric, philosophy, logic, or something else is unimportant. Certainly, Isocrates uses the term "philosophy," but philosophy has taken such a different path since his day that drastic changes in that area of work would be essential for that term to become appropriate. I shall continue to use the term "rhetoric"—at least for the time being—simply because that is the tradition from which I stem, although rhetoric, too, needs to broaden itself for the term to become appropriate. A phrase such as "philosophy of rhetoric" should be recognized as an oxymoron—at least today—and rejected accordingly. If philosophy does not expand its scope, it may eventually become necessary for universities to establish a Doctorate of Performance or Rhetoric, reaffirming the role of rhetoric as the crown of education.

Among the more important ideas promoted by the new rhetoric must be the insistence that humans confronting problems in changing circumstances cannot simply apply approaches derived from the engagement of past problem situations, but must use the particulars of new problem situations to generate the approaches appropriate for those situations. The generation of these approaches must involve an oscillation between the particulars of new problem situations and as much of reality related to them—both present and past—as can be discovered. The fullest range of history must be carefully examined for problem situations that compare and contrast with the new problem situations. Such comparisons and contrasts must help identify the particulars of new problem situations and help suggest the new approaches that might be appropriate for engaging them.

Humans attempting to respond to problems in changing circumstances, then, must generate a different history for each different problem situation. Instead of generating a single history for their area of work, they generate multiple histories. Instead of attempting to achieve consensus with others about a single definition and then using that definition as a guide for inclusion, they use past and current awareness as an aid in determining the particulars of a situation and use these particulars as an aid in generating a history that itself serves as an aid in reassessing the particulars of the situation—a process that may involve many recursions before the approaches are appropriate to situations. Instead of scope being arbitrary, no particulars in a situation and its history that have a bearing on performance should remain unnoticed or ignored. The unique rhetorics generated by engagement of some problems must be compared to the unique rhetorics generated by engagement of other problems, and the resulting art of comparative rhetoric can help future generations attain the richness and flexibility of deliberation essential to enable humans to approach problems with the scope they require.

To avoid hurting others, humans approaching problems must deliberate with sufficient scope to enable ethical performance in governments, industries, and universities. Humans need sufficient scope to achieve an ethical balance between minimizing the afflictions and maximizing the pleasures in their own lives and helping other humans, present and future, do the same in their lives. To achieve such an end, no humans affected by a decision should be ignored in the deliberations preliminary to choice. Unfortunately, however, the world currently consists of an agglomeration of social structures within which humans usually set more limited goals. Isolation within these social structures is strengthened by the emphasis on definition and specialization promoted by Plato, Aristotle, and their followers in the history of Western civilization.

Far more attention must be devoted to analysis of the ways that definition and specialization compromise performance by limiting the scope of deliberation. Cicero's recognition of the confinements of definition and the dangers of their institutionalization in society must become an active force to broaden deliberation until it is adequate to the problems confronting it. Deliberation must be broadened to acknowledge the extent to which the adequacy of performance depends on a huge flow of information between and within governments, industries, universities, and their subunits—a flow impeded by the relative isolation of these defined communities from one another. New social structures must become part of a seamless system of interlocking and interconnected deliberation.

As an example of the problems caused by overly narrow deliberation resulting from the isolation of social structures, humans in federal, state, and local governments make decisions that can adversely affect humanity, present and future, throughout the world, but their systems of accountability incline them to place the welfare of constituents in their government areas before the welfare of constituents elsewhere. Humans in these governments must be prompted by new structures of accountability at the point of decision-making to insure a concern for the welfare of constituents outside their government areas; they must be held accountable to global structures of governance. Humans have become so dependent on one another for their welfare that specialized divisions of governance unchecked by accountability to other humans are no longer tolerable.

Forms of international governance such as the United Nations are essential to address such global problems as the threats of war, nuclear annihilation, pollution, overpopulation, unfair trading practices, resource depletion, and unethical multinational corporations, which, with their financial resources, increasingly manifest the power to control even federal governments of the size of the United States. Political theorists need to continue to work on versions of international governance that promote mutual understanding and accountability until these versions can gain the confidence of humanity. Given the need for an open, seamless human society, calls in the United States for reduced involvement in the United Nations, the failure of the United States to pay its taxes to the world body, and the Republican Party's advocacy of a shift of power away from international and national to state and local governments are irresponsible.

Above all else, governing bodies at every level need to work together to promote peace. They need to discourage hostile divisions that limit collaboration and encourage confidentiality and secrecy. They need to avoid arms races—supporting rapid innovations in science and technology—that outrun our ability to adjust our deliberative powers. They need to prevent powerful interest groups such as the military-industrial complex from using the potential of conflict to create a climate of fear as a rhetorical device to attract excessive resources. They need to preclude the attacks on self-criticism that inevitably follow the outbreak or increase of hostilities. Peace will enable a major shift of resources from defense and various kinds of science and technology to activities supporting ethical performance.

During roughly the last 60 years, one nation-state that has fostered an industrial policy emphasizing military hardware is the United States—the most powerful and therefore one of the most dangerous countries in the world. As a result of this policy, large numbers of people and social structures have become dependent on military expenditures—in governments, industries, and universities—and these groups are powerful lobbyists for additional, defense-related expenditures on science and technology. The United States must be careful that military expenditures are brought into line with the extent of external threats and, as seems far more possible now, more attention is devoted to both international collaborative planning to address global problems and domestic collaborative planning to improve such areas as education, the environment, and health. The United States may have demonstrated some greatness in helping humanity during World War II, but an equally important test of its civilization is its ability to mobilize to help humanity during peace.

Collaboration must replace competition as a national ideal. A politics of competition favors the mature over the emerging, the wealthy over the poor, and the militarily strong over the weak—a process that favors some social structures over others. Furthermore, it encourages humans to try to exploit humans in other social structures rather than collaborate with them to work toward the common good. The world has a good illustration of some of these deficiencies in the operation of the U.S. Congress, where senators and representatives consistently attempt to help their own constituents regardless of the national common good—at great cost to the legitimacy of Congress and the welfare of both the nation as a whole and, all too often, other nation-states. The constituents whom they help are largely the wealthy, who gain influence by supplying reelection funds. In this way, the United States has become a plutocracy—a far cry from the democracy it touts as an ideal. One result has been the increasing sense of powerlessness felt by American citizens.

Cultural behaviors that promote national narrowness rather than global scope should be criticized. The United States is open to criticism for its intermittently resurgent patriotism that manifested itself perhaps most egregiously during the Reagan Administration. Even such phenomena as pledges of allegiance and the playing of the national anthem at sports events are not without their impact. Stakeholders in other countries should note with some concern the extent to which self-focus manifests itself in the United States and elsewhere and should organize at the international level to insure that their interests are considered.

The need for revolution in industries is even greater than that in governments. Practitioners in industries far too often place the narrow goal of profit before the wider goal of ethical performance in their decisions, causing widespread damage to society and raising serious questions about the legitimacy of current industrial governance. Industrial leaders, without sufficient checks and balances from others in society, weaken or destroy their own corporations with devastating consequences for employees and communities, seriously degrade the environment and leave many of the expenses of clean-up to taxpayers, allow unsafe working conditions and create harmful or fraudulent products, use their power to attract an excessive share of society's resources (often by using campaign contributions to direct the attention of government toward their own narrow interests and away from the broader good of society), and, in the face of a promise early in the century to increase every family's leisure, now involve both husbands and wives in a new kind of economic bondage with very little leisure at all. Practitioners have far too much latitude to pursue profit at the expense of human welfare.

Some industrialists have already accepted the principle that profit must be governed by the need for ethical performance. But implementation must follow acceptance. The choices of industrial leaders have the potential to affect so many humans so quickly and so adversely that traditional after-the-fact reactions to institutional abuse such as bringing public pressures to bear, developing laws, or punishing offenders no longer suffice. A system of checks and balances needs to be implemented to promote a concern for human welfare at all key decision-making points. Such collaboration would not only serve as a check on abuse, but would also facilitate the transfer of needed education from one institution to the next. The ultimate goal might well be a seamless system of interconnections to prevent the exploitation of the many by the few and to promote the empowerment of all. In moving toward ethical performance, industrialists would lose the taint associated with the narrow goal of financial profit and make themselves more attractive as sources of governance and education, where their experience is desperately needed.

Until now, a politics of competition in industries has fostered secrecy and speed that reinforce separation and limit collaboration; secrecy militates against the free flow of information so essential in an increasingly interdependent world, and speed leaves employees with insufficient time either to colloborate or to approach their tasks with their full range of capabilities. Among the results, industries do not communicate frequently and openly with universities, and universities are unable to provide sufficiently helpful education, continuing education, and research for industries. And even within industries themselves, different units are often so isolated from one another that problems in communication are almost inevitable, and serious problems result.

Among the ways that the problem of divisions between units within industries can be addressed is to insure employees a reasonable measure of responsibility for choices that affect the quality of their performance. Employees must have the opportunity to "buy into" decisions that affect their art of choice. Accepting employment in industries must no longer carry the aura of becoming an instrument or abdicating responsibility. Industries must create an environment of participatory management tolerant of reasonable individual challenges to institutional tendencies. As in all institutions, the environment in industries must honor the free expression of ideas toward the end of ethical performance—especially the ideas of reasonable whistleblowers who expose industry choices as ethically irresponsible. Promoting tolerance of whistleblowers adds to the system of checks and balances to insure appropriate deliberations at all key decision-making points.

If industries allow their employees the opportunity to "buy into" decisions that affect their art of choice, they will find themselves transforming social structures based on the division of labor into collaborative and interlocking project teams not only within but beyond corporate boundaries. Such a system of decision-making in industries would necessitate the abandonment of secrecy—a step that has important advantages besides enabling checks on abuse. Among these advantages, industries would be better able to avoid product incompatibilities and language inconsistencies. Furthermore, they would be better able to assume their much-needed role in the international educational process. One of the most important initiatives in the 21st century would make the financial structures supporting education as strong as those supporting health, enabling lifelong education. By abandoning secrecy and taking advantage of these financial structures, industries would be able to establish their own educational programs for universities, governments, and other industries.

Industries must also acknowledge and accept that extensive collaboration will necessarily reduce the speed of development, which would also have important advantages. Industry, government, and university representatives would have more time to prevent the speed of innovation from outrunning their ability to consider whether decisions help or harm constituents. Employees would not confront schedules so short that they cause unnecessary stress and preclude their being able to use what they know to inform their performance. Employees would also have more time to enable them to acquire the education to change jobs either within or outside industries when desirable or necessary. Because a reduction in speed, the abandonment of secrecy, and other steps to insure ethical performance could be unfairly used against an industry by other noncomplying industries, negotiations need to take place at the international level to insure full participation and to establish an appropriate system of incentives and protections.

Universities also would not remain untouched by the revolution. Of course, universities have come a long way since the times when Hutchins's theories were highly influential. Most sectors of universities no longer exclude efforts to determine what to do to be useful in society, and professional schools and programs are thriving. But the theories of education in universities are lagging far behind their actions. It is not the interested response to ethical imperatives but the disinterested quest for new knowledge—the descendent of Aristotle's quest for truths motivated by curiosity—that still dominates so many goals statements in universities. Far too many university leaders still look to the pursuit of truth as their primary guide to action rather than having that goal balanced or governed by the pursuit of human welfare. Few university sectors have rediscovered the theoretical importance of rhetoric in approaching human affairs.

As a result, numerous sectors of universities are only now beginning to move away from the liberal education of leaders such as Hutchins, and they face the prospect of radical transformation. In responding to human welfare rather than the pursuit of truth as a primary guide to action, these sectors must shift major resource allocations from identification prompted by wonder to deliberation about choice prompted by human need. Instead of working in monastic seclusion, telling their texts and instruments in ivory towers, professors must become actively involved in professional and public affairs. Only through such involvement can they familiarize themselves with the problem contexts of civilization and acquire the power to participate in deliberations about choice. Only through such involvement can they determine their missions and the dramatic changes in education, research, and service essential to achieve them. No adequate civilization can tolerate an intelligentsia purchasing freedom from external interference at the expense of social impotence and educational ineptitude.

Some sectors of universities—English departments at the most prestigious universities come most readily to mind—are almost as much in the grip of the modern tradition of liberal education as they were in the 1970s and 1980s. Professors in these departments still direct their attention to classical texts and away from such practical areas of everyday living as industries, despite the fact that they supposedly have responsibility for the future writing capabilities of university graduates. These professors still reject efforts to respond to the rapidly changing particulars of professional problems and restrict hiring, curricular innovation, and resource allocation in such areas as technical communication.

Since these professors observe practitioners in industries often acting without sufficient regard for ethical performance, they might well be reluctant to respond to calls for help from industry, fearful that they might themselves become instruments of unethical industrial actions. But the relative failure of literature professors at the most prestigious universities to respond to technical communication problems in industry is itself ethically questionable. Since English departments are responsible for writing in universities, they are responsible for the ethical impact of their teaching in this area. But literature professors tend to ignore the professional lives of their students after graduation, unaware that many of these graduates become practitioners, professionals, and teachers of technical communication. They are unaware of the nature of industrial contexts and the problems in technical communication that these graduates face. And they are unaware, too, of the failures of these graduates and the resulting adverse impact on the larger society. Consequently, when urged by others to respond to such matters, they do not react with ethical urgency, have no idea what curricula they should be developing, falsely claim that their literature courses address all writing problems, and, when they do allow development in writing, actually worsen problems by supporting courses and programs that are shaped by narrow Aristotelian ideas. Such ethical irresponsibility seriously undermines the legitimacy of English departments.

Responding adequately to problems in professional and public contexts would necessitate thoroughgoing changes in university organization. Universities must afford government and industry representatives a role in decision-making that insures that universities assume their responsibilities in engaging important social problems. For instance, university humanists ought to be prompted to take cognizance of their name and reaffirm the necessity of buttressing civilization rather than remaining antithetical to it. A department such as English, which—at various times in its history—has ignored social needs in oral and written communication to such an extent that these areas have remained underdeveloped and professors interested in them have felt compelled to leave, must be exposed to a more effective system of checks and balances.

The reward system in universities must undergo perhaps the greatest transformation. This system should be based not on new knowledge, but rather on human need. Professors must never again be encouraged to minimize their attention to students so as to have more time for publication. Professors in emerging areas, who necessarily need to devote more attention to teaching and service, must never again be punished for devoting less attention to research. And educational administrators, afflicted as much as the rest of society with the fear of judgment and the desire to find mathematical criteria for evaluation, must never again be allowed to make numbers of publications the major criterion for reward—a system that militates against lengthy projects and quality and adds to the huge quantities of relatively useless publications flooding our society.

The ongoing fragmentation of universities into schools and departments so limits the responsibilities of these units that the scope of approaches of academics is often inadequate to the tasks that confront them. This division of the university into schools and departments, reinforced not only by Aristotelian specialization, but also by the limits of human capability and the needs of practical administration, must be replaced by a system that acknowledges that problems dictate their own scope—a scope that increasingly extends far beyond the precipitous definitions that shape modern university units. While some problems might call for narrower units resembling those in place, other problems— such as those confronting technical communication in the 1970s and 1980s— would require sufficient organizational flexibility to enable interdisciplinary collaboration among the widest diversity of units on campus. They would also require a receptivity to innovation that would insure that academics engaging new problems in society could work within current structures and would not be forced to create new narrow units in a pattern of increasing university fragmentation that militates against a need for synthesis. Interdisciplinary collaboration on campus and at conferences would promote the creation of a metalanguage for performance that would better enable academics and others to understand and profit from one another's discoveries and critiques. To the credit of many universities, calls for cross-disciplinary collaboration and the establishment of cross-disciplinary project teams have been increasing.

Changes in goals and social structures would enable universities to become more involved in lifelong education, including distance and transition education—that is, to become omnipresent in society rather than being confined to isolated sites. Such changes would also enable universities to achieve numerous economies that would further buttress financial strength. Changing the disproportionate emphasis on research, stemming from a focus on truth, should achieve countless economies by reducing the torrents of fruitless publications and presentations driven by the demands of promotion and tenure rather than human need. Eliminating all those needless excrescences in universities resulting from the overdominance of science in the 20th century, especially those areas attempting to apply scientific methodologies to problems that require other approaches, should help, as should reducing needless academic duplication in universities by reversing fragmentation and working toward synthesis. All of these developments should enable colleges and universities to focus less on fundraising and more on other aspects of performance.

Changes in goals and social structures must be accompanied by changes in methodologies. All of the major institutions in Western civilization—including governments, industries, and universities—could profit from a reconsideration of methodologies. With the historical narrowing of the scope of rhetoric through definitional exclusion and the decline that necessarily results from this process, rhetoric is perceived as so narrow by problem-solvers at the beginning of the 21st century that they fail to understand how helpful it can be in engaging their problems. Totally unaware of Isocratean rhetoric—or even the rhetorics of Cicero or Quintilian for that matter—they accept the dominant Aristotelian view of rhetoric and, not unexpectedly, fail to see how such a limited area could possibly be helpful to their broader needs. These problem-solvers are cut off by a narrow definition from important history that could help them.

With their failure to understand the importance of the Isocratean rhetorical tradition, they have no alternative ideas to liberate themselves from dominant philosophical ideas that militate against methodologies important to their needs. Without the stimulus of Isocrates and others who promote the importance of history in engaging human problems, problem-solvers devote far too little attention to history and, when they do engage it, are inclined by professionalism and disciplinarity to limit their explorations to events and texts exclusively associated with narrow disciplinary terms, failing to perceive how other history—for instance, that associated with rhetoric—could help them understand and address their problems.

Inclined by the philosophical tradition to take methodologies appropriate for fixing truths about relatively stable phenomena and misapply them in situations calling for choices in changing environments, problem-solvers too often use induction to derive insights from past experience and then use deduction to apply these insights to current problems, making the mistake of using preset methodological approaches rather than using the full particularity of problem situations to generate the unique methodologies appropriate to them. The philosophical emphasis on generality, on what is common to all places and times, inclines problem-solvers to search for rules or universals that hold for all situations, unaware of the inappropriateness of such a process when a prior context differs substantially from a current context.

In their quest for rules and universals, problem-solvers use experimental methodologies to justify choice, an example of an inappropriate leap from description to prescription, and far too often adopt mathematical methodologies where they are inappropriate. They are reinforced in this quest by their philosophical predisposition to acquire certainty about what is universal, unchanging, and permanent rather than use judgment to make decisions about what is particular, changing, and temporary.

We must seriously question whether democracy—at least as practiced in the United States—can meet the challenges of this revolution in governments, industries, and universities. Civilization has grown so complex that increasing the scope of deliberation in human affairs will require leaders of exceptional intelligence, education, and experience reaching decisions through dialogue beyond the capability of most humans. But conditions in the United States do not now sufficiently encourage the participation of its intellectual community, which possesses important intellectual and historical resources and is located largely in universities. On the one hand, some ideas associated with democracy—that the power of reason in all humans is adequate to have a voice in governance and that elaborate reasoning about abstruse questions beyond the grasp of the majority is probably unnecessary—have created a profound anti-intellectualism in America that militates against a receptivity to the broad involvement of the professoriate. On the other hand, to the extent that professors focus on the acquisition of knowledge and shun political performance, to that extent they hold themselves aloof and neglect to acquire the experience requisite for participation in governance.

Furthermore, the success of democracy is dependent on the powers of evaluation of the majority in any population—hardly the source of the standards of excellence through history. And the low state of public dialogue in America, reinforced by a media that must sell itself to general audiences, prevents deliberations from achieving levels of sophistication commensurate with their inherent complexities. What results is an emphasis on the superficial, sensational, and superstitious rather than the substantive—to the extent that humans of competence are alienated. Qualities such as fame assume precedence over more important qualities, and too often our leaders are war heroes, astronauts, athletes, and actors. Seeing the Reagan Administration's ability to use such smokescreens as patriotism, religion, and a friendly smile to attract wide public support while shifting wealth from the lower and middle classes to a controlling plutocracy hardly inspires confidence in the public's ability to look after its own welfare. The public has not been able to avoid thoroughgoing manipulation by an oligarchy of the wealthy and, as a result, has a system of governance called democracy in name only. What is needed is an improved system that is able to hear and respond appropriately to the needs of all humans, but remains uncompromised by the majority's intellectual, educational, and experiential limits.

The magnitude of the problems confronting rhetoricians should not be underestimated. For instance, while problem situations call for the fullest awareness of the relevant present, requiring immersion in public affairs, the same problem situations call for the fullest awareness of the relevant past, a demand that can drive rhetoricians into nearly monkish isolation, increasingly ignorant of a world that they are supposedly trying to help. While—to avoid the effects of change—problems call for almost instantaneous results, the scope of these problems is so vast that they can take well over a decade to explore; the study of a current problem turns into a historical analysis of the past with crucial evidence no longer available. When Cato grumbled that Isocrates's students wasted their whole lives on education and would have to use their knowledge to plead before Minos in the underworld, he presaged the plight of all those long-distance runners probing the complexity of human affairs.

Scholars such as Bolgar, who criticize Cicero for the impracticality of his quest for scope, no doubt have such problems as these in mind. But such scholars are themselves guilty of impracticality if they think that problems can be approached in bits and pieces that are tailor-made to human capabilities. Specialization is an anthropocentric lie that humans have been using for 24 centuries to delude themselves. Cicero, the most practical of men, understood that lie and accurately perceived the scope of the deliberations essential to engage his problems. Because Western civilization did not heed his call, except for a brief period during the Renaissance, the opportunities for developing a rhetoric with the scope essential for appropriate performance were lost.

As we move into the 21st century, the opportunity is again at hand. The time has come to make the effort to determine where an ideal Isocratean rhetoric—devoid of Isocratean limitations—would lead. Centuries of attention to the approaches associated with such a rhetoric, if humanity lasts that long, might prove as fruitful as those centuries of attention devoted to approaches associated with identification. Everyone setting out on such a quest must acknowledge the difficulties and accept the possibility that the quest is doomed to failure. Human needs may simply be incommensurate with human possibilities. But we must at least try. Cicero's call for the resurrection of rhetoric must once again resound throughout civilization.

References

Abrams, M. H. (1973). *Natural supernaturalism; Tradition and revolution in Romantic literature*. New York: Norton. (Original work published 1971)

Allbutt, T. C. (1925). *Notes on the composition of scientific papers*. London: Macmillan. (Original work published 1904)

Anderson, P. V. (1980). The need for better research in technical communication. *Journal of Technical Writing and Communication, 10,* 271–282.

Andrews, D. C. (Ed.). (1998). Special issue on international communication in the scientific and technical professions. *Technical Communication Quarterly, 7.*

Aristotle. (1941). *The basic works of Aristotle* (2nd pr., R. McKeon, Ed.). New York: Random House.

Aristotle. (1991). *On rhetoric* (G. A. Kennedy, Ed.). New York: Oxford University Press.

Armstrong, A. H. (1972). St. Augustine and Christian platonism. In R. A. Markus (Ed.), *Augustine: A collection of critical essays* (pp. 3–37). Garden City, NY: Anchor-Doubleday.

Atkins, J. W. H. (1952). *Literary criticism in antiquity: A sketch of its development* (Vols. 1-2). New York: Peter Smith. (Original work published 1934)

Augustine. (1930). *Select letters* (J. H. Baxter, Trans.). London: Heinemann.

Augustine. (1952). *The confessions. The city of God. On Christian doctrine*. In R. M. Hutchins (Ed.), *Great books of the Western world* (Vol. 18). Chicago: Encyclopedia Britannica.

Aydelotte, F. (1917). *English and engineering: A volume of essays for English classes in engineering schools*. New York: McGraw-Hill.

Baker, R. P. (1919). *Engineering education: Essays for English*. New York: Wiley.

Bashe, C. J., Johnson, L. R., Palmer, J. H., & Pugh, E. W. (1986). *IBM's early computers*. Cambridge, MA: MIT Press.

Bate, W. J. (1982). The crisis in English studies. *Harvard Magazine, 85,* 46–53.

Battenhouse, R. W. (Ed.). (1956). *A companion to the study of St. Augustine*. New York: Oxford University Press. (Original work published 1955)

Beauchamp, T. (1983). *Case studies in business, society, and ethics*. Englewood Cliffs, NJ: Prentice-Hall.

Beck, C. E., Levinson, M., & Wegner, K. (1993). Ethics for technical communication: A framework for the profession. *Technical Communication, 40,* 524–535.

Beckman, F. W., O'Brien, H. R., & Converse, B. (1927). *Technical writing of farm and home.* Ames, IA: Journalism Publishing.

Bell, D. (1973). *The coming of post-industrial society: A venture in social forecasting.* New York: Basic Books.

Benzon, W. L. (1981). The computer and technical communication. *Journal of Technical Writing and Communication, 11,* 103–114.

Berlin, J. A. (1987). *Rhetoric and reality: Writing instruction in American colleges, 1900–1985.* Carbondale, IL: Southern Illinois University Press.

Berners-Lee, T. (1999). Realising the full potential of the Web. *Technical Communication, 46,* 79–82.

Bethke, F. J. (1984). Advice to novice technical writers: A veteran speaks. *The Technical Writing Teacher, 11,* 157–159.

Bitzer, L. F. (1978). Rhetoric and public knowledge. In D. M. Burks (Ed.), *Rhetoric, philosophy, and literature: An exploration* (pp. 67–93). West Lafayette, IN: Purdue University Press.

Bitzer, L. F., & Black, E. (Eds.). (1971). *The prospect of rhetoric: Report of the National Development Project.* Englewood Cliffs, NJ: Prentice-Hall.

Bizzell, P., & Herzberg, B. (1990). *The rhetorical tradition: Readings from Classical times to the present.* Boston: Bedford Books of St. Martin's Press.

Bizzell, P., & Herzberg, B. (1996). *The Bedford bibliography for teachers of writing.* Boston: Bedford Books of St. Martin's Press.

Blair, H. (1783). *Lectures on rhetoric and belles lettres* (Vols. 1-2). London: Strahan, Cadell, and Creech.

Bloom, H., de Man, P., Derrida, J., Hartman, G., & Miller, J. H. (1979). *Deconstruction and criticism.* New York: Seabury.

Boies, J. L. (n.d.) *Buying for Armageddon: Business, society, and military spending since the Cuban missile crisis.* New Brunswick, NJ: Rutgers University Press.

Bolgar, R. R. (1958). *The classical heritage and its beneficiaries.* Cambridge, England: Cambridge University Press. (Original work published 1954)

Booth, W. (1981). The common aims that divide us; or, is there a "Profession 1981"? *Profession 81,* 13–17.

Boulding, E. (1988). *Building a global civic culture: Education for an independent world.* New York: Teacher's College Press.

Braddock, R., Lloyd-Jones, R., & Schoer, L. (1963). *Research in written composition.* Champaign, IL: National Council of Teachers of English.

Briggs, J. C. (1984). Philosophy and rhetoric. In M. G. Moran & R. F. Lunsford (Eds.), *Research in composition and rhetoric: A bibliographic sourcebook* (pp. 93–124). Westport, CT: Greenwood Press.

Bronson, J. G. (1987). Unfriendly eyes. *IEEE Transactions on Professional Communication, PC 30,* 173–178.

Brown, R. M., & McMurrey, D. A. (Eds.). (1999). Special issue on technical communication, distance learning, and the World Wide Web, *Technical Communication Quarterly, 8.*

Brummer, J. J. (1991). *Corporate responsibility and legitimacy: An interdisciplinary analysis.* New York: Greenwood Press.

Bryan, J. (1996). The need to know. *Intercom, 43,* 8, 343.

Burke, K. (1950). *A rhetoric of motives*. New York: Prentice-Hall.

Campagna, A. S. (1994). *The economy in the Reagan years: The economic consequences of the Reagan administrations*. Westport, CT: Greenwood Press.

Campbell, C. (1986, February 9). The tyranny of the Yale critics. *The New York Times Magazine*, 20–28, 43, 47–48.

Carliner, S. (1995). Finding a common ground: What STC is, and should be, doing to advance education in information design and development. *Technical Communication, 42*, 546–554.

Casey, B. E. (1981). The impact of the technical communicator on software requirements. *Journal of Technical Writing and Communication, 11*, 361–372.

Cassirer, E., Kristeller, P. O., & Randall, J. H., Jr. (Eds.). (1969). *The Renaissance philosophy of man*. Chicago: University of Chicago Press. (Original work published 1948)

Christensen, C. M., & Stordahl, K. E. (1955). The effect of organizational aids on comprehension and retention. *Journal of Educational Psychology, 46*, 65–74.

Cicero. (1949). De oratore. In E. W. Sutton (Trans.), *Cicero in twenty-eight volumes* (Vol. 3, pp. 1–479; Vol. 4, pp. 1–185). Cambridge, MA: Harvard University Press. (Original work published 1942)

Cicero. (1971). Brutus. In G. L. Henrickson (Trans.), *Cicero in twenty-eight volumes* (Vol. 5, pp. 18–293). London: Heinemann. (Original work published 1939)

Cicero. (1976). De inventione. In H. M. Hubbell (Trans.), *Cicero in twenty-eight volumes* (Vol. 2, pp. 1–346). Cambridge, MA: Harvard University Press. (Original work published 1949)

Clarke, M. L. (1953). *Rhetoric at Rome: A historical survey*. London: Cohen & West.

Cody, S. (1912). Scientific principles in the teaching of composition. *The English Journal, 1*, 161–172.

Coles, P., & Foster, J. J. (1975). Typographic cueing as an aid to learning from typewritten text. *Programmed Learning and Educational Technology, 12*, 102–108.

Committee for Economic Development. (1971). *Social responsibilities of business corporations*. New York: Committee for Economic Development.

Conley, T. M. (1990). *Rhetoric in the European tradition*. New York: Longman.

Connors, R. J. (1985). Mechanical correctness as a focus in composition instruction. *College Composition and Communication, 36*, 61–72.

Cooper, L. (1932). *The rhetoric of Aristotle*. New York: Appleton.

Cope, E. M. (1867). *An introduction to Aristotle's rhetoric*. London: Macmillan.

Corbett, E. P. J. (1965). *Classical rhetoric for the modern student*. New York: Oxford University Press.

Couture, B., & Goldstein, J. R. (1984). Procedures for developing a technical communication case. In R. J. Brockmann (Ed.), *The case method in technical communication: Theory and models* (pp. 33–46). Association of Teachers of Technical Writing.

Couture, B., & Goldstein, J. R. (1985). *Cases for technical and professional writing*. Boston: Little, Brown.

Crane, R. S. (1952). *Critics and criticism: Ancient and modern*. Chicago: University of Chicago Press.

Crane, R. S. (1953). *The languages of criticism and the structure of poetry*. Toronto: University of Toronto Press.

Crane, R. S. (1967). *The idea of the humanities and other essays critical and historical* (Vols. 1–2). Chicago: University of Chicago Press.

Crouse, J. H., & Idstein, P. (1972). Effects of encoding cues on prose learning. *Journal of Educational Psychology, 63,* 309–313.

D'Amico, M. F. (1971). Educating the technical communicator. *Journal of Technical Writing and Communication, 1,* 11–16.

Demilia, L. A. (1968). Visual fatigue and reading. *Journal of Education, 151,* 4–34.

Descartes, R. (1956). *Discourse on method* (2nd ed., L. J. Lafluer, Trans.). New York: Liberal Arts. (Original work published 1637)

Dewey, J. (1929). *The quest for certainty: A study of the relation of knowledge and action.* New York: Minton, Balch.

Dewey, J. (1987). President Hutchins' proposals to remake higher education. In J. A. Boydston, (Ed.), *The later works, 1925–1953* (Vol. 11, pp. 397–401). Carbondale, IL: Southern Illinois University Press. (Original work published 1937)

Doran, M. (1964). *Endeavors of art: A study of form in Elizabethan drama.* Madison, WI: University of Wisconsin Press. (Original work published 1954)

Drake, S. (1957). *Discoveries and opinions of Galileo.* Garden City, NY: Anchor-Doubleday.

Dykhuizen, G. (1973). *The life and mind of John Dewey.* Carbondale, IL: Southern Illinois University Press.

Earle, S. C. (1911). *The theory and practice of technical writing.* New York: Macmillan.

Eason, J. L., & Weseen, M. H. (1918). *English, science, and engineering: A collection of expository essays for students of science and engineering.* Garden City, NY: Doubleday, Page.

Eastman, A. M. (Ed.). (1977). *The Norton reader* (4th ed.). New York: Norton.

Eckman, M. (1979). An interdisciplinary program in technical communications: Problems encountered. *The Technical Writing Teacher, 3,* 87–91.

Edwards, P. (Ed.). (1972). *The encyclopedia of philosophy* (Vols. 1–8). New York: Macmillan and Free Press. (Original work published 1967)

Enos, R. L. (1993). *Greek rhetoric before Aristotle.* Prospect Heights, IL: Waveland Press.

Enos, R. L. (1995). *Roman rhetoric: Revolution and the Greek influence.* Prospect Heights, IL: Waveland Press.

Enos, T., & McNabb, R. (Eds.). (1997). *Making and unmaking the prospects for rhetoric: Selected papers from the 1996 Rhetoric Society of America Conference.* Mahwah, NJ: Lawrence Erlbaum.

Epstein, E. M., & Votaw, D. (1978). *Rationality, legitimacy, responsibility: Search for new directions in business and society.* Santa Monica, CA: Goodyear.

Eucken, C. (1983). *Isokrates: Seine Positionen in der Auseinandersetzung mit den zeitgenossischen Philosophen* [*Isocrates: His positions in the conflict with contemporary philosophers*]. Berlin: Walter de Gruyter.

Everett, M. (1989). *Breaking ranks.* Philadelphia: New Society.

Fletcher, F. W. (1986, April 23). The myth that's responsible for faculty malaise. *Chronicle of Higher Education,* p. 92.

Fogarty, D. (1959). *Roots for a new rhetoric.* New York: Teacher's College Press.

Fontenelle, B. de. (1970). A digression on the ancients and the moderns. In S. Elledge & D. Schier (Eds.), *The continental model: Selected French critical essays of the seventeenth century in English translation* (Rev. ed., pp. 358–370). Ithaca, NY: Cornell University Press. (Original work published 1688)

Frank, P. (1957). *Philosophy of science: The link between science and philosophy.* Englewood Cliffs, NJ: Prentice-Hall.

Fulkerson, R. (1990). Composition in the eighties: Axiological consensus and paradigmatic diversity. *College Composition and Communication, 41,* 409–429.

Gabin, R. J. (Ed.). (1995). *Discourse studies in honor of James L. Kinneavy.* Potomac, MD: Scripta Humanistica.

Gange, C., & Lipton, A. (1984). Word-free setup instructions: Stepping into the world of complex products. *Technical Communication, 31,* 17–19.

Gangewere, R. J. (1972). The vices of technical writing. *Technical Communication, 2,* 57–62.

Gay, P. (1966). *The Enlightenment: An interpretation.* New York: Random House.

Gerber, J. (1975). Dialogue. *ADE bulletin, 47,* 21–24.

Gerber, J. (1972). Public hostility to the academy: What can chairmen of Departments of English do. *English Bulletin, 32,* 17–21.

Gilbert, N. W. (1960). *Renaissance concepts of method.* New York: Columbia University Press.

Gilson, E. (1960). *The Christian philosophy of St. Augustine* (L. E. M. Lynch, Trans.). New York: Random House.

Glassman, M., & Pinelli, T. E. (1985). Scientific inquiry and technical communication: An introduction to the research process. *Technical Communication, 32,* 8–13.

Gorrell, R. M., Bizzell, P., & Herzberg, B. (1984). *The Bedford bibliography for teachers of writing.* Boston: Bedford Books of St. Martin's Press.

Grabo, N. S. (1979). Bifocals and the Bartleby syndrome [Special issue]. *ADE Bulletin,* 66–69.

Graff, G. (1989). *Professing literature: An institutional history.* Chicago: University of Chicago Press. (Original work published 1987)

Greenwald, J. (1984, June 18). How does this #%c@! thing work? *Time,* 64.

Grice, R. A. (1987). *Technical communication in the computer industry: An information-development process to track, measure, and ensure quality.* Unpublished doctoral dissertation, Rensselaer Polytechnic Institute.

Hall, A. R. (1954). *The scientific revolution 1500–1800: The formation of the modern scientific attitude.* London: Longmans, Green.

Harrington, J. L. (Ed.). (1905). *The principal professional papers of Dr. J. A. L. Waddell, civil engineer.* New York: Virgil H. Hewes.

Harrington, J. L. (1907). *The value of English to the technical man.* Kansas City, n.p.

Harris, E. (1979). Applications of Kinneavy's *Theory of discourse* to technical writing. *College English, 40,* 625–632.

Hayhoe, G. F. (1999). Technical communication: A trivial pursuit? *Technical Communication, 46,* 23–25.

Hazard, P. (1963). *The European mind (1680–1715).* New York: Meridian-New American.

Heilbroner, R. L. (1970). The future of capitalism. In R. Romano & M. Leiman (Eds.), *Views on capitalism* (pp. 273–300). Beverly Hills, CA: Glencoe Press.

Heines, J. M. (1984). *Screen design strategies for computer-assisted instruction.* Bedford, MA: Digital.

Hellstrom, W. (1979). Academic responsibility and the job market [Special issue]. *ADE Bulletin,* 95–99.

Hillocks, G., Jr. (1986). *Research on written composition: New directions for teaching.* Urbana, IL: ERIC and NCRE.

Hillyer, P. (1985). Going by the book. *Think, 51,* 34–37.

Hodgkinson, R., & Hughes, J. (1982). Developing wordless instructions: A case history. *IEEE Transactions on Professional Communication, PC-25,* 74–79.

Horner, W. B. (Ed.). (1983a). *Composition & literature: Bridging the gap.* Chicago: University of Chicago Press.

Horner, W. B. (Ed.). (1983b). *The present state of scholarship in historical and contemporary rhetoric.* Columbia, MO: University of Missouri Press.

Horner, W. B. (Ed.). (1990). *The present state of scholarship in historical and contemporary rhetoric* (Rev. ed.). Columbia, MO: University of Missouri Press.

Houp, K. W., & Pearsall, T. E. (1977). *Reporting technical information* (3rd ed.). Encino, CA: Glencoe Press.

Howell, W. S. (1956). *Logic and rhetoric in England, 1500–1700.* Princeton, NJ: Princeton University Press.

Hunt, K. (1965). *Grammatical structures written at three grade levels* (*NCTE Research Report No. 3*). Champaign, IL: National Council of Teachers of English.

Hutchins, R. M. (1936). *The higher learning in America.* New Haven, CT: Yale University Press.

IBM. (1984). *An IBM guide to choosing business software.* Wayne, PA: Banbury.

The idea and practice of general education: An account of the College of the University of Chicago. (1950). Chicago: University of Chicago Press.

Ijsseling, S. (1976). *Rhetoric and philosophy in conflict: An historical survey.* The Hague, Netherlands: Martinus Nijhoff.

Isocrates. (1954). *The works of Isocrates* (Vols. 1–3, G. Norlin, Trans. & Ed.). Cambridge, MA: Harvard University Press. (Original work published 1928)

Jaeger, W. (1939–1944). *Paideia: The ideals of Greek culture* (Vols. 1–3, G. Highet, Trans.). New York: Oxford University Press.

Jebb, R. C. (1909). *The rhetoric of Aristotle* (J. E. Sandys, Ed.). Cambridge, England: Cambridge University Press.

Johnson, W. R. (1976). Isocrates flowering: The rhetoric of Augustine. *Rhetoric and Philosophy, 9,* 217–231.

Jones, E. L., & Durham, P. (1961). *Readings in science and engineering.* New York: Holt, Rinehart and Winston.

Jones, R. F. (1951). *The seventeenth century: Studies in the history of English thought and literature from Bacon to Pope.* Stanford, CA: Stanford University Press.

Jones, W. P. (1978). *Writing scientific papers and reports.* Dubuque, IA: Brown. (Original work published 1946)

Jones, W. P., & Johnson, Q. (1963). *Essays on thinking and writing in science, engineering, and business.* Dubuque, IA: Brown.

Jordan, S. (Ed.). (1971). *Handbook of technical writing practices* (Vols. 1-2). New York: Wiley-Interscience.

Kant, I. (1968). *Critique of judgment* (J. H. Bernard, Trans.). New York: Hafner. (Original work published 1790)

Kelley, P. M., & Masse, R. E. (1977). A definition of technical writing. *The Technical Writing Teacher, 4,* 94–97.

Kennedy, G. (1963). T*he art of persuasion in Greece.* London: Routledge and Kegan Paul.

Kennedy, G. (1972). *The art of rhetoric in the Roman world.* Princeton, NJ: Princeton University Press.

Kestner, J. (1981). *Government intervention in productivity and the work environment.* Tulsa, OK: University of Tulsa, Office of Business Research.

Kimball, B. A. (1986). *Orators & philosophers: A history of the idea of liberal education.* New York: Teacher's College Press.

Kindilien, C. T. (1963). *Technical writing and communications.* Waterford, CT: Prentice-Hall.

Kinneavy, J. L. (1971). *A theory of discourse.* Englewood Cliffs, NJ: Prentice-Hall.

Kirby, R. S. (1913). *The elements of specification writing· A text-book for students in civil engineering.* New York: Wiley.

Klare, G. R. (1963). *The measurement of readability.* Ames, IA: Iowa State University Press.

Kristeller, P. O. (1961) *Renaissance thought: The Classic, Scholastic, and Humanist strains* (Rev. ed.). New York: Harper & Row. (Original work published 1955)

Lakoff, G. & Johnson, M. (1980). *Metaphors we live by.* Chicago: University of Chicago Press

Latourette, K. S. (1937–1945). *A history of the expansion of Christianity* (Vols. 1–7). New York: Harper.

Leitch, V. B. (1983). *Deconstructive criticism: An advanced introduction.* New York: Columbia University Press.

Lewis, M. (1995, November 18). Whatever happened to the leisure class. *New York Times,* Sec. 6, p. 66.

Locke, J. (1700). *An essay concerning humane understanding* (4th ed.). London: Awnsham and John Churchill. (Original work published 1690)

Lovejoy, A. O. (1948). *Essays in the history of ideas.* Baltimore, MD: Johns Hopkins University Press.

Lovejoy, A. O. (1960). *The great chain of being: A study of the history of an idea.* New York: Harper & Row. (Original work published 1936)

Lynch, R. E., & Swanzey, T. B. (Eds.). (1981). *The example of science: An anthology for college composition.* Englewood Cliffs, NJ: Prentice-Hall.

Lynn, S. W. (1982, December 29). *The use of literary techniques in technical writing: Four questions converging.* Paper presented at the MLA convention, Los Angeles, CA.

Macdonald-Ross, M., & Smith, E. (1977). *Graphics in text: A bibliography.* Milton Keynes, England: Open University, Institute of Educational Technology.

Mandel, S. (1959). The challenge to writers in industry. In S. Mandel (Ed.), *Writing in industry* (pp. 15–30). Brooklyn, NY: Polytechnic Press.

Markusen, A., & Yudken, J. (1992). *Dismantling the cold war economy.* New York: Basic Books.

Marrou, H. I. (1956). *A history of education in antiquity.* New York: Sheed and Ward.

Marrou, H. I. (1960). *St. Augustine and his influence through the ages.* New York: Harper. (Original work published 1957)

Masse, R. E., & Kelley, P. M. (1977). Teaching the tradition of technical and scientific writing. In T. M. Sawyer (Ed.), *Technical and professional communication* (pp. 79–87). Ann Arbor, MI: Professional Communication Press.

McCrimmon, J. M. (1980). *Writing with a purpose* (7th ed.). Boston: Houghton Mifflin.

McLaughlin, G. H. (1966). Comparing styles of presenting technical information. *Ergonomics, 9,* 257–259.

Mead, J. (1998). Measuring the value added by technical documentation: A review of research and practice. *Technical Communication, 45,* 353–379.

Miller, C. R. (1984). Technical writing textbooks: Current alternatives in teaching. *Technical Communication, 31,* 35–38.

Miller, J. H. (1979). The function of rhetorical study at the present time [Special issue]. *ADE Bulletin,* 10–18.

Miller, J. H. (1991). *Theory now and then.* Durham, NC: Duke University Press.

Miller, W. J., & Saidla, L. E. A. (1953). *Engineers as writers: Growth of a literature.* New York: Van Nostrand.

Mische, G., & Mische, P. (1977). *Toward a human world order: Beyond the national security straitjacket.* New York: Paulist Press.

Mitchell, J. H. (1976). It's a craft course: Indoctrinate, don't educate. *The Technical Writing Teacher, 4,* 2–6.

Moore, P. (1997). Rhetorical vs. instrumental approaches to teaching technical communication. *Technical Communication, 44,* 163–173.

Murphy, J. J. (1981). *Rhetoric in the Middle Ages: A history of rhetorical theory from St. Augustine to the Renaissance.* Berkeley, CA: University of California Press. (Original work published 1974)

Naval Air Systems Command. (1976). *Technical manual preparation guide for technical writers, editors, and illustrators.* n.p.: NAVAIR.

Newman, J. H. (1959). *The idea of a university.* Garden City, NY: Doubleday. (Original work published 1852)

North, S. (1987). *The making of knowledge in composition: Portrait of an emerging discipline.* Upper Montclair, NJ: Boynton/Cook.

Ohmann, R. (1976). *English in America: A radical view of the profession.* New York: Oxford University Press.

O'Keefe, A. (1985). Teaching technical writing. In M. G. Moran & D. Journet (Eds.), *Research in technical communication: A bibliographical sourcebook* (pp. 85–113). Westport, CT: Greenwood Press.

Olsen, M. E. (1984). Terminology in the computer industry: Wading through the slough of despond. In *IBM technical report number 07.793: Writing in response to a changing environment* (pp. 95–108). Rochester, MN: Information Development, System Products Division.

O'Neil, D. J. (1999). *Writing to the World Wide Web and the relevance to classical rhetoric.* Unpublished manuscript.

Paradis, J. (1983). Bacon, Linnaeus, and Lavoisier: Early language reform in the sciences. In P. Anderson, R. J. Brockmann, & C. R. Miller (Eds.), *New essays in technical and scientific communication: Research, theory, practice* (pp. 200–224). Farmingdale, NY: Baywood.

Parker, W. R. (1967). Where do English departments come from? *College English, 28,* 339–351.

Paterson, D. G., & Tinker, M. A. (1940). *How to make type readable.* New York: Harpers.

Pattee, G. K. (1909). *Practical argumentation.* New York: Century.

Pearsall, T. E. (1982). Building a technical communication program. *ADE Bulletin, 71,* 15–17.

Pearsall, T. E., & Cunningham, D. H. (1978). *How to write for the world of work.* New York: Holt, Rinehart, and Winston.

Peterson, M. S. (1961). *Scientific thinking and scientific writing.* New York: Reinhold.

Pinelli, T. E. (1985). Introduction. *Technical Communication, 32,* 6–7.

Plato. (1973). *The collected dialogues* (E. Hamilton & H. Cairns, Eds.). Princeton, NJ: Princeton University Press. (Original work published 1961)

Plato. (1953). *Plato with an English translation* (Vol. 5) (W. R. M. Lamb, Ed.). London: Heinemann. (Original work published 1925)

Plato. (1985). *Phaedrus and the seventh and eighth letters* (W. Hamilton, Trans.). Harmondsworth, England: Penguin. (Original work published 1973)

Porat, M. (1976). *The information economy* (Vols. 1-2). Unpublished doctoral dissertation, Stanford University.

Poulakos, T. (1997). *Speaking for the polis: Isocrates' rhetorical education.* Columbia, SC: University of South Carolina.

Poulton, E. C. (1960). A note on printing to make comprehension easier. *Ergonomics, 3,* 245–248.

Pugh, E. W. (1995). *Building IBM: Shaping an industry and its technology.* Cambridge, MA: MIT Press.

Quintilian. (1980). *The institutio oratoria of Quintilian* (Vols. 1–4) (H. E. Butler, Trans.). Cambridge, MA: Harvard University Press. (Original work published 1920)

Ransom, J. C. (1938). *The world's body.* New York: Scribner's.

Rathbone, R. R. (1958). Growth of the technical writing profession. *Society of Technical Writers and Editors Review, 5,* 5–16.

Richards, I. A. (1936). *The philosophy of rhetoric.* New York: Oxford University Press.

Rickard, T. A. (1908). *A guide to technical writing.* San Francisco: Mining and Scientific.

Rickard, T. A. (1920). *Technical writing.* New York: Wiley.

Rivers, W. E. (1985). The current status of business and technical writing courses in English departments. *ADE Bulletin, 82,* 50–54.

Rubin, J. H. (1995, December 5). U.S. closing books on S & L crisis. *Times Union,* p. B11.

Schaefer, M. (1980). Introduction. *Technical Communication, 27,* 4.

Scott, A. M. (Ed.). (1995). Special issue on hypertext and hypermedia. *Technical Communication Quarterly, 4.*

Scott, F. N., & Denney, J. V. (1897). *Composition-rhetoric.* Boston: Allyn and Bacon.

Seigel, J. E. (1968). *Rhetoric and philosophy in Renaissance humanism: The union of eloquence and wisdom, Petrarch to Valla.* Princeton, NJ: Princeton University Press.

Shedd, W. G. T. (1878). *Literary essays.* New York: Scribner's.

Singer, C. (1925). Historical relations of religion and science. In J. Needham (Ed.), *Science religion and reality* (pp. 83–148). New York: Macmillan.

Smith, F. R. (1985). Editorial: The importance of research in technical communication. *Technical Communication, 32,* 4–5.

Solmsen, F. (1974). The Aristotelian tradition in ancient rhetoric. In K. V. Erickson (Ed.), *Aristotle: The Classical heritage of rhetoric* (pp. 378–409). Metuchen, NJ: Scarecrow.

Sonnenschein, H. (1999, April 7). *State of the university address* [Online]. Available: http://www.uchicago.edu/docs/education/state-univ99.html

Sopensky, E. (1994). The skill and art of collaboration. *Technical Communication, 41,* 709–713.

Sprat, T. (1667/1958). *History of the Royal Society* (J. I. Cope & H. W. Jones, Eds.). St. Louis, MO: Washington University Press. (Original work published 1667)

STC Board adopts new guidelines for communicators. (1995). *Mohawk Monitor, 18,* 5.

Steiner, G. A., & Steiner, J. F. (1988). *Business, government, and society: A managerial perspective* (5th ed.). New York: Random. (Original work published 1971)

Sullivan, J. W. N. (1933). *The limitations of science.* New York: Viking.

Swift, J. (1958). *A tale of a tub to which is added the battle of the books and the mechanical operation of the spirit* (2nd ed., A. D. Guthkelch & L. D. N. Smith, Eds.). Oxford: Claredon Press. (Original work published in 1704)

Sypherd, W. O. (1916). *A bibliography on "English for engineers."* Chicago: Scott, Foresman.

Sypherd, W. O. (1913). *A handbook of English for engineers.* Chicago: Scott, Foresman.

Tate, G. (1976). *Teaching composition: 10 bibliographic essays.* Fort Worth, TX: Texas Christian University Press.

Tessier, D. (1975). The value of a summer internship in technical writing. *The Technical Writing Teacher, 2,* 16–18.

Theremin, F. (1860). *Eloquence a virtue; or, outlines of a systematic rhetoric* (2nd ed., W. G. T. Shedd, Trans.). Andover, MA: Draper. (Original work published 1850)

Thonssen, L., & Baird, A. C. (1965). Cicero and Quintilian on rhetoric. In J. Schwartz & J. A. Rycenga (Eds.), *The province of rhetoric* (pp. 137–157). New York: Ronald.

Turnbull, A. D. (1981). Technical writing in the computer industry: Job opportunities for Ph.D.'s. *ADE bulletin, 67,* 26–30.

Valla, L. (1977). *De voluptate* (A. K. Hieatt & M. Lorch, Trans.). New York: Abaris.

Vickers, B. (1990). *In defence of rhetoric.* Oxford: Clarendon. (Original work published 1988)

Vives: On education. A translation of the De Tradendis Disciplinis *of Juan Luis Vives* (F. Watson, Trans.). (1913). Cambridge, England: Cambridge University Press.

Waddell, J. A. L., & Harrington, J. L. (1911). *Addresses to engineering students.* Kansas City, MO: Waddell and Harrington.

Wagner, R. H. (1965). The rhetorical theory of Isocrates. In L. Crocker & P. A. Carmack (Eds.), *Readings in rhetoric* (pp. 169–183). Springfield, IL: Thomas.

Wambeam, C. A., & Kramer, R. (1996). Design teams and the Web: A collaborative model for the workplace. *Technical Communication, 43,* 349–356.

Ward, J. (1759). *A system of oratory* (Vols. 1-2). London: John Ward.

Waterman, A. T. (1955). The future of report literature. In B. M. Fry & J. J. Kortendick (Eds.), *The production and use of technical reports* (pp. 3–8). Washington, DC: Catholic University of America.

Weiss, E. H. (1986). Getting DP professionals to document. *Technical Communication, 33,* 10–12.

Whitburn, M. D. (1975). Against substituting technical writing for freshman English. *Journal of Technical Writing and Communication, 5,* 47–51.

Wilcox, T. W. (1973). *The anatomy of college English.* San Francisco: Jossey-Bass.

Willey, B. (1953). *The seventeenth century background: Studies in the thought of the age in relation to poetry and religion.* New York: Anchor-Doubleday. (Original work published 1935)

Wimsatt, W. K., Jr., & Brooks, C. (1957). *Literary criticism: A short history.* New York: Knopf.

Winterowd, W. R. (1977). Getting it together in the English department. *ADE bulletin, 55,* 28–31.

Wirls, D. (1992). *Buildup: The politics of defense in the Reagan era.* Ithaca, NY: Cornell University Press.

Woolbert, C. H. (1916). The organization of departments of speech science in universities. *The Quarterly Journal of Public Speaking, 2,* 64–77.

Wotton, W. (1697). *Reflections upon ancient and modern learning* (2nd ed.). London: Peter Buck. (Original work published 1694)

Young, A., Gorman, M., & Gorman, M. (1984). The 1983–84 Writing and Literature Survey: Courses and programs. *ADE Bulletin, 79,* 48–55.

Zappen, J. P. (1977). A mini-internship in a professional writing course. In T. M. Sawyer (Ed.), *Technical and professional communication* (pp. 129–137). Ann Arbor, MI: Professional Communication Press.

Author Index

Subject Index